Caribbean Contextual Theology

Caribbean Contextual Theology

An Introduction

Carlton Turner

scm press

© Carlton Turner 2024

Published in 2024 by SCM Press

Editorial office
3rd Floor, Invicta House,
110 Golden Lane,
London EC1Y 0TG, UK

www.scmpress.co.uk

SCM Press is an imprint of Hymns Ancient & Modern Ltd
(a registered charity)

Ancient
&Modern

Hymns Ancient & Modern® is a registered trademark of
Hymns Ancient & Modern Ltd
13A Hellesdon Park Road, Norwich,
Norfolk NR6 5DR, UK

Scripture quotations, unless otherwise indicated, are from
New Revised Standard Version Bible: Anglicized Edition,
copyright © 1989, 1995 National Council of the Churches of
Christ in the United States of America. Used by permission.
All rights reserved worldwide.

British Library Cataloguing in Publication data
A catalogue record for this book is available
from the British Library

ISBN 978-0-33-406337-7

Typeset by Regent Typesetting
Printed and bound by
CPI Group (UK) Ltd

Contents

List of Abbreviations

ATR	African Traditional Religious Heritages
CAAD	Caribbean and African American Dialogue
CCC	Caribbean Conference of Churches
CCJCA	Caribbean Committee on Joint Christian Action
CCTR	Caribbean Commission for Theological Renewal
COP26	26th United Nations Climate Change Conference
MJR	Movement for Justice and Reconciliation
OCHA	United Nations Office for the Coordination of Humanitarian Affairs
SPG	Society for the Propagation of the Gospel
USPG	United Society Partners in the Gospel
UWI	University of the West Indies
WCC	World Council of Churches

Acknowledgements

This book would not have been possible without the many scholars who paved the way before the writing of it. There are too many to mention, but Caribbean theologians and their unique perspective have shaped my world. You, all of you, have been pushing boundaries, contesting Babylon, invoking spirit and daring to imagine a new world. I humbly write in honour of you!

Codrington College, Barbados, and the University of the West Indies (UWI) have been gifts to me in this project. I'm an alumnus of both! Theological training in Barbados was the place where I began to agonize about the lack of Caribbean theological reflection in formal theological studies in the region. Through divine timing, I was asked to develop and teach a course on Caribbean Theology at Codrington College, which is affiliated with UWI, at the same time as I was asked to write this monograph for SCM Press. In fact, it had always been my desire to write this textbook. But what a joy it was to test out these ideas with theological students of the Caribbean, some preparing for ordained ministry and others wanting to deepen their theological insights to bring about change and transformation in their society. My gratitude extends to the Revd Dr Michael Clarke and the students of the University of the West Indies' THEO3320 Module: Kristen Lynch, Rondeno Rolle, Howard Bethel, Michelle Leacock and Michelle Johnson. Your energy and imagining have helped the writing of this book more than you know.

I must express gratitude to the Queen's Foundation and the ongoing critical environment that allows me to feel, to think, to imagine and to simply 'be', theologically. Among my wonderful colleagues I need to acknowledge the place of Dr Dulcie

Dixon McKenzie in this work. Dulcie consistently challenges me to look at my blind spots and biases, and at how I'm so thoroughly shaped by my Anglican world and presuppositions. She invites me to open up my vision and check my exclusions.

Finally, I'm grateful to my native land and cultural heritage. I am a Bahamian. The contents of this book are not simply intellectual ramblings. They arise from people who know peril and death a little too much. They also arise from a people who know what it is to survive, to live and to love ... who know what it means to inhabit a joy that is bigger and deeper than pain.

Part 1

> Where are your monuments, your battles, martyrs?
> Where is your tribal memory? Sirs,
> in that grey vault. The sea. The sea
> has locked them up. The sea is History.
>
> *Derek Walcott, 'The Sea is History'*[1]

---

1 Derek Walcott, 'The Sea is History', in Derek Walcott and Glyn Maxwell, *The Poetry of Derek Walcott 1948–2013*, London: Faber & Faber, 2014.

I

Introduction:
Between Oh Lord and
Thank God!

'Between Oh Lord and Thank God!' Bahamian people, like Caribbean people generally, have some strange and often para-doxical ways of answering questions. Having been raised on a rural island in the Bahamas, sometimes older people, when asked, 'How are you doing?', would answer, 'Between Oh Lord and Thank God!' I find myself often answering in this way and chuckling to myself. I chuckle because while it seems nonsens-ical and paradoxical, it is so true of the Caribbean experience. On the one hand, we are a people of profound faith in the Christian revelation of God in Jesus Christ, present through the presence and power of the Holy Spirit. This is part of our iden-tity. On the other hand, we are a people often in survival, if not facing erasure, politically, economically, culturally, ecologically and existentially.

In this book I want to articulate a deep paradox of Caribbean life and what it means to live within it.[1] The dilemma present in idioms such as 'between a rock and a hard place' or 'between the devil and the deep blue sea' seem ways of framing Caribbean existence, just like 'Between Oh Lord and Thank God!' Michael Jagessar notes that the precarious nature of the sea, its depth, its strength, its uncertainty, is an adequate metaphor for what it is like to be Caribbean.[2] There is the fragile security of the land, but there is also the vast mystery of the seas in which the set of islands sit. The seas have brought much bloodshed, trauma and instability. So too has the land. Through this popular idiom,

Jagessar also invokes Derek Walcott's idea that the Caribbean Sea provides its own alternative history.[3] It is a history of in-betweenness, of transition, instability, of the unknown. While, for the European, the land represents the concretizing and memorializing of history, the Caribbean story remains untold, unfished; it is a deep dive into the unknown, and often the unfathomable and ineffable. This is the Caribbean experience in many ways. It is hard to put into words. You must live it to know it. Nonetheless, it is out of this experience, this liminal space, that this book attempts to do its theological reflection. Theology is done differently, and God and God's actions in the world are perceived differently by people within the grips of a hurricane that is simultaneously ecological, economic, political and historical. Priorities differ. Assumptions are different. Life is perceived differently. Perhaps in this introductory text we can discern a unique approach to theology, arising from a unique context.

A Caribbean Theology?

As an introductory text in Caribbean Contextual Theology, I must also begin by foregrounding the inherent difficulty in this task. Let's begin with a few underlying assumptions germane to the exercise of theology generally, and contextual theology particularly, especially as they relate to the region.

First, contexts are incredibly complex. The descriptor 'Caribbean', as will be examined further in Chapter 2, is difficult to pin down. Monolithic definitions are ultimately unhelpful, if not dangerous, to the lands and peoples of the region and the diaspora.

Second, context matters immensely. There is no theology that exists in a vacuum, nor is any hermeneutical exercise acontextual or normative. When using the term 'theology', or 'classical theology', what is not often declared are the cultural, political and historical processes that have shaped such theologies. This has been the charge against Western theological traditions that have often had devastating effects upon people and cultures of the majority world or the Global South, including the region called the Caribbean.

Third, not solely the themes or content of theology but the actual methodology or processes of theological reflection are shaped by context, culture and language, whether acknowledged or not. For example, I would argue that African Caribbean religious and cultural traditions, with drumming or rhythmic traditions as their focus, such as Carnival or Junkanoo traditions, Rastafari, Spiritual Baptists and Revivalism, are central to what it means to do theology grounded within a Caribbean context.

Finally, there is the question of telos. What is theology for? Contextual theologies answer this immediately! Theology is about bringing about positive transformation in the world, and not simply for the sake of knowing more! Contextual theologies are concerned about the concrete development of the world, and the everyday lives of people, especially those on the margins. There is no better example of this than the region that is the focus of this introductory text.

Difficulties in conceptualizing or theorizing the region lie in the fact that it is so historically, politically, culturally and ecclesiastically complicated that no singular narrative or reading will suffice. While it might be a small region, perhaps not foremost in the minds of many within the world, it has been the geographical location in which some of the most important moments in world history, particularly modern and contemporary history, have taken place. Perhaps the best way forward is not to attempt to provide a definitive narrative or history of the region, since this is not possible in this work, but to provide historical snapshots or vistas into a region that has been shaped, often brutally, by theological narratives. It has also been a region that has continued to ask profound theological questions since, from inception, it has existed on the utter brink of life and death.

Snapshots of a Unique History

Columbus's Landfall in 1492

Columbus's landfall in the New World in 1492 wasn't simply the meeting of a hitherto unknown people, it was an example of Christian missionary practices at the time. It was a demonstration of fifteenth-century Western European attitudes to the 'other', particularly theological assumptions about the place of the indigenous other within God's economy. There were also some significant assumptions about the primacy of European self-understanding, religiosity, culture and imagination. Columbus's journal gives a very good illustration of this.

> As I saw that they were very friendly to us, and perceived that they could be much more easily converted to our holy faith by gentle means than by force, I presented them with some red caps, and strings of beads to wear upon the neck, and many other trifles of small value, wherewith they were much delighted, and became wonderfully attached to us. Afterwards they came swimming to the boats, bringing parrots, balls of cotton thread, javelins, and many other things which they exchanged for articles we gave them, such as glass beads, and hawk's bells; which trade was carried on with the utmost good will. But they seemed on the whole to me, to be a very poor people ... It appears to me, that the people are ingenious, and would be good servants and I am of opinion that they would very readily become Christians, as they appear to have no religion. They very quickly learn such words as are spoken to them. If it please our Lord, I intend at my return to carry home six of them to your Highnesses, that they may learn our language. I saw no beasts in the island, nor any sort of animals except parrots. These are the words of the Admiral (Thursday 11 October 1492).[4]

Europe's introduction to the New World in 1492 began a chain of traumatic events that saw the decimation of the indigenous populations. Continental Europe – the Spanish, French, Portuguese and Dutch – dominated the first few centuries after the arrival of Columbus, eventually shifting their oppressive mercantilist attention from indigenous pre-Columbian slave labour to African slave labour. The English arrived in the seventeenth century, taking hold of the brutal but lucrative institution of slavery for expanding its presence and economic prowess into the New World.[5] We can discern several traumatic processes here. First, their very establishment within the region was brutal and violent, especially for the African enslaved. The very presentation of the Christian faith into this new and untouched setting was pathologically structured towards violence – since sword (or branding iron) and cross were inextricably linked.

British Landfall on St Kitts in 1624

The entrance of the English into the African Caribbean in 1624 under the leadership of Captain Thomas Warner on the Island of St Kitts was an act of colonization with a royal mandate to settle the land. This initial attempt proved unsuccessful due to conflicts with the native inhabitants, the Caribs. A year later, again under the leadership of Captain Warner and with a mandate from Charles I of England to propagate the Christian faith, the clergyman John Featly joined, and a colony was established. Sequentially, other islands were captured, including Jamaica and Barbados, Great Britain's key colonies in the New World. According to Francis Osborne and Geoffrey Johnston, this second mission to conquer island colonies included clergymen and chaplains with the specific mandate to propagate the Christian faith.[6] Islands were, of course, organized into parishes, which reflected the political and ecclesiastical shaping of English society. This meant that the final process of trauma was slaves adapting to a society totally alien to their homeland, ingesting the culture, language, thought patterns and religion of their new home, plantation society. The legacies of the British Empire's involvement in the West Indian colonies, and particularly the role of the Church of England in plantation slavery and genocide, is something being debated in contemporary

British life. For example, the unique history of the Codrington plantations in Barbados and the role of the Society for the Propagation of the Gospel (SPG) in running them from about 1712 to 1838 is a case in point.[7]

Orlando Patterson gives a sociological account of plantation society within the Jamaican context and comes to an important insight that should always be borne in mind; that such societies were 'non-societies'.[8] What Patterson means is that they were not constructed for the flourishing of their inhabitants. These patterns include aspects of flourishing such as building family life and sustaining kinships, participating in the political processes, engaging in commerce and owning land or property. Patterson is clear: plantation society existed solely to produce economic profit. These were factories, not societies. A similar observation is given by Ian Strachan, who argues that the plantation never dissolved but re-emerged in the form of tourism where the myth of paradise still serves the ancient quest of Missionary Christianity and its settling of the New World. That quest was, and has always been, profit, which has always signified disastrous consequences for the indigenous populations and their ways of life.[9]

The Haitian Revolution in 1804

Haiti has the distinction of being the first Black republic in the modern world, gaining independence from France in 1804, after an almost 15-year revolution and revolt, eventually defeating Napoleon Bonaparte under the successive leadership of Toussaint Louverture and Jean-Jacques Dessalines (later Emperor Jacques I). Today, Haiti has the reputation of being the poorest country in the Western hemisphere, but its historic defeat of France remains a symbol of hope and possibility throughout the region. It is often suggested that later slave rebellions across the region looked to the Haitian Revolution for inspiration. In fact, the Haitian Revolution is the inspiration for the famous anti-colonial historical text, *The Black Jacobins: Toussaint L'Ouverture and the San Domingo Revolution*, by the

Trinidadian historian C. L. R. James.[10] The story of the nation, though, is inseparable from its identification with Vodou. In many ways, and perhaps because of the historic defeat of the Europeans through the African Traditional Religion of Vodou, as legend states, contemporary global perceptions consider it to be evil and demonic.

Apprenticeship/Emancipation in 1834/1838

To many, the abolition of the slave trade (1807) and emancipation (1838) have been dates on the historical calendar that demonstrate Great Britain's moral resolve to dispense with the inhumane treatment of African persons traded from West and Central Africa to work plantations in the Caribbean. For Caribbean people, this naive view of history is insulting. Eric Williams' *Capitalism and Slavery* has long argued that enslavement as a colonial commercial enterprise failed not because of moralistic and ethical impulses but purely because Caribbean plantations were, by then, deemed unprofitable.[11] In fact, not only did the Church of England engage in and defend the enslavement of African persons and the perpetuation of slavery as an enterprise, it greatly resisted attempts at arguing for abolition and emancipation on theological grounds.

When thinking about the ideas that undergird this wide-scale involvement in and justification for the enslavement of Black people within the British Empire, the documentary *After the Flood: The Church, Slavery and Reconciliation* (2022) is important.[12] Commissioned by the UK charity Movement for Justice and Reconciliation (MJR), it is based on the research idea by Professor Robert Beckford, executive produced by Claire Lasko, and produced and directed by Sheila Marshall FRSA. Alton Bell, Chairman of MJR, said, 'We commissioned *After the Flood* to raise awareness, among the Christian communities, of the legacies of the Transatlantic Slave Trade and 18th-century industrial exploitation. We want to achieve reconciliation, but we can't have reconciliation without repairing the damages from the past.'[13] They cover a range of things but focus on the racist idea that the Curse of Ham in Genesis 9, after the flood had subsided, was God's damnation of 'the Black Race' to lives of enslavement. This gross, racist misreading of the Bible led to legal, theological, cultural, economic and existential oppression of Black people within Britain's empire. They also explore the cruelties of the Codrington plantations in Barbados and the involvement of the then SPG. They further challenge popular conceptions of the abolitionist movement. While there was a transatlantic movement for abolition, it did not go far enough. It did not deal with the deep ideas and beliefs within British society – both Church and state – that permitted such atrocities. Beckford states:

> The focus on abolition is an obfuscation of the horror of the slave trade and a willingness to collude with the sub-humanization of black people. What it means ultimately is there is no recognition of how the church's theological ideas made slavery possible.[14]

Marcus Garvey in 1920

The defeat of the Italians by the Abyssinians in 1896 fed the prophetic visions of Jamaica's freedom fighters, George Liesle, Alexander Bedward, Nanny of the Maroons, James Lowe, James Webb, and especially Jamaica's national hero Marcus Mosiah Garvey. Garvey's vision of radical, African and liberation consciousness led to him founding the Universal Negro Improvement Association (UNIA) in 1914. Garvey's fame grew across the Atlantic, and his particular power base in the United States became a target for the US government. By the time Selassie had risen to power, Garvey had been deported back to Jamaica. Garvey's following commendation of Selassie proved instrumental in the formation of the Rastafari: 'Ethiopia is hidden for many centuries, but gradually she is rising to take a lead place in the world and it is for us of the Negro race to assist in every way to hold up the hand of Emperor Ras Tafari.'[15] Rasta communities formed throughout the region through

Jamaica's connections. These included the United States, Panama and Costa Rica, beside the expanse of islands within the English-speaking and wider Caribbean. In 1966, Haile Selassie visited Jamaica, sparking the largest crowd in Jamaica's history and gaining extensive press coverage. This deep attention to ethnicity, identity and consciousness, often outside of the institutions of power such as the government and the Church, has continued to be a strong trend in the region.

The Grenada Invasion in 1983

Following the internal political tensions on the island of Grenada, exacerbated in September 1983 with the deaths of the then prime minister Maurice Bishop, his partner Jacqueline Creft, two other Cabinet ministers and two union leaders, the Reagan administration launched a military invasion of the island, a move that was internationally criticized as an abuse of power. A significant factor in these events was the adoption of a communist form of government on the island from 1979, which, after the Cuban embargo, simply could not be afforded by Reagan's administration engaged in the Cold War.[16] Added to this can be the short-lived West Indies Federation that began in 1958 but collapsed in 1962. Hilary Beckles argues that the implosion of the former colonies of Great Britain in the region was through a 'back-office diplomatic design formally to support but financially to subvert the federation by starving it of capital and fiscal development support'.[17] These events only highlight the continued political dependency and insecurity of the region despite the long list of independence exercises. The political might of the United States of America and its vassal-like relationship with nations of the Caribbean has been something Caribbean theologians have criticized from inception.[18]

Earthquake in Haiti in 2010

The date 12 January 2010 was a significant moment in Caribbean history with the striking of the 7.0 magnitude earthquake in Haiti, 15 miles west of Port-au-Prince. An estimated 3 million people were affected by the catastrophe, with an estimated 100,000–160,000 people killed. Aid appeals eventually proved problematic as the goals of international agencies and the real needs of Haitians did not quite align. What was also highlighted was the continued political and economic vulnerability of the nation, which had been indebted and impoverished for more than two centuries. However, Haiti is but one example. The Caribbean remains one of the most vulnerable places on earth, with fierce hurricanes, such as Irma, which devastated 90 per cent of Barbuda in 2017; the eruption of the volcano in Montserrat in 1997; the flooding and landslides in Dominica in 2017; or the might of hurricane Dorian over the Bahamas in 2019.

A Barbadian Republic in 2021

Mia Mottley's COP26 (United Nations Climate Change Conference) speech on climate justice settlement in Glasgow, 2022, captured the global imagination.[19] Mottley spoke as the first female prime minister of Barbados. She spoke as the first Caribbean leader to represent a country that had become a republic, removing the former colonial power, the British monarchy, as head of state. The only time this had been accomplished in the region was after the Haitian Revolution, which came at a great price to the Haitian nation and people. In the contemporary Caribbean, Mottley and Barbados set the tone for other nations seeking the realization of earlier visions of sovereignty and self-determination.

The contemporary Caribbean continues with ongoing geopolitical conversations regarding the relationship between the region and the rest of the world, especially Europe and North America, both of whom have significantly shaped, and also been resourced by, the region. One significant conversation is that of reparations. Two eminent historians of the Caribbean, Professors Hilary Beckles and Verene Shepherd, have been at the forefront of the reparations movement when considering the legacies of slavery and colonialism within the British Empire. Beckles' book, *Britain's Black Debt*, argues that Britain's moral bankruptcy is compounded by its failure to answer the call for reparations given that British slaveowners were paid 20 million pounds in compensation for surrendering their slaves in 1838.[20] This amounts to almost 2.4 billion pounds sterling in today's currency according to the CPI Inflation Calculator.[21]

Beckles states:

> The case for reparations should be made against the British state and a select group of its national institutions, such as merchant houses, banks, insurance companies and the Church of England. These institutions exist today. Their slave-derived wealth is not in question. From slavery to the present day, these institutions continue to accumulate wealth. The state is the recognized institution that legally and financially implemented and sustained the crimes against humanity, from which it was enriched and in other ways benefited directly and indirectly. Collaborating financial and social institutions operated the slave regimes and paid corporate taxes to the state on their slave wealth in an economy regulated by the government.[22]

But Beckles continues: 'The role for the British state was not confined to the regulation and fiscal management of slavery. The state was also engaged directly in the slave system as an important investor and owner. Slaves were owned and employed by the state.'[23]

Perennial Issues

In their assessment of Caribbean realities in the compilation *Caribbean Theology: Preparing for the Challenges Ahead*, Noel Titus and Barry Chevannes suggest the following as persistent

Caribbean realities: economic and political dependency; divisiveness across islands, language groups, cultural groups and Christian denominations; brain-drain and diasporan issues; natural disaster and environmental concerns.[24] Titus suggests that historical, geographical and cultural factors intertwine to produce an ambivalent and complex region. It is one in which religion and education, as shaping forces, continue to be colonially informed, with difficulties in foregrounding indigenous approaches. It is also one in which economic vulnerability undergirds much of life.[25] Chevannes, on the other hand, presents a sociological picture that also frames Caribbean realities, looking at religion, along with family life and mating patterns. The region has been shaped by Africa, with the exception of parts of the region such as Trinidad and Tobago and Guyana that have had a minority African population. Large questions remain about the underlying values that have persisted within Caribbean plantation societies, and how these have often been misunderstood within Western value systems.[26]

While these issues are perennial, there still exists a vibrant theological conversation within the region, in different forms and in different domains, not necessarily within the churches. Such realities highlighted above have not been without the attendant and robust theological conversations to address them. In a way, the task of this book is to present both: the political, historical, economic, cultural and religious realities of the region; but also the various forms of theological reflections that have emerged to address such realties by continually asking fundamental questions of the exercise of theology itself. However, more must be said about the methodological approach of this book.

A Contextual Theology

Part of the methodological conversation must be about the term 'Contextual Theology'. Within theological circles it is often debated that the descriptor 'contextual' is not needed, and if it is used it should not be seen as an alternative to a systematic theological approach.[27] What 'contextual' intends to do is to guard against the constant danger of the exercise of theology eclipsing local and contextual realities. Like most non-Western contexts, the basic charge against Western approaches to theology has been that the goal of systematizing theological conversation, or the insistence on the exercise of theology as a 'method' steeped in post-Enlightenment European rationalism, has not served Caribbean people well. The coming of Missionary Christianity into the region assumed that those who were non-Western and 'other' were without civility, and certainly unable to enrich any kind of theological discourse. This book aims to show that Caribbean theologians have consistently been challenging theological approaches that have neglected the Caribbean experience. They have done this by questioning and challenging theologies of empire and colonialism, and articulating alternative ways of interrogating Scripture, history and doctrine, and by attempting to reconstruct emancipatory theologies effective for the region and beyond. Within their theological imagination, 'context', or attention to it, has been crucial. Theology or God-talk in the region, instead of being a method that leads to precision and divine truth in any narrow sense, has always needed to be an exploration of the people's ways of life. Approaches to theology grounded in the histories, cultures, languages and contexts of the region have been imperative to combat Western and European theologies of domination ubiquitous in its colonial beginnings. In short, an insistence on 'context' continues to be a precondition for doing theology in the region for the purpose of limiting colonial and imperial oppression. Theology itself, if not qualified, has led to lethal consequences for the people of the African Caribbean.

With regard to the discipline of theology, by 'contextual' I am referring to a particular approach to theological reflection that challenges the exercise of theology in some key areas. First, Contextual Theology is guided by the assertion that all theology is contextual and arises from concrete human experiences. In their two-volume offering *Theological Reflection*, Elaine Graham, Heather Walton and Frances Ward insist that a transition towards a more realized notion of 'local theology' took place at Vatican II, where 'The council recognized the autonomy of the Church in each culture to articulate the gospel without the mediation of Western thought forms.' By this there was a renewed understanding of church, where mission churches, in Latin America and the Caribbean for example, were seen as equal partners. There was also a renewed understanding of 'method' in theology, where the inherent contextual and situated nature of theology was affirmed.[28]

Second, Contextual Theology insists that experience, culture and perspective are important. While classic texts such as Alister McGrath's *Christian Theology: An Introduction* remind us of the formative factors or sources of Christian theology, Scripture, Reason, Tradition and Experience, the latter has often been neglected in more classical approaches to theology.[29] Contextual and practical theologians such as Stephen Bevans and Robert Schreiter have long argued for an insistence on contextual and local approaches to theological reflection to counter a long tradition of exclusivist, classist and marginalizing tendencies within the discipline of theology.[30]

Third, 'truth' is iterative. This is a critical point within contextual and practical theologies that seek to preserve the mystery of God and the open-endedness of the Christian life and imagination. John Swinton and Harriet Mowat insist on a biblically grounded understanding of truth that is not confined to positivist, scientific presuppositions.[31] Truth that has ultimacy cannot be confined to philosophical or scientific methods. In a biblical and Christian imagination, ultimate truth does exist, but human beings will always have a partial view of it. This is St Paul's exclamation that 'we see in a mirror, dimly', but in time we will see 'face to face'.[32] We do not know all that we can know about a situation, and as contextual theologians we are theologically reflecting to make things clearer, to shed more light and wisdom about who God is, how God acts and, ultimately, how God wants us as human creatures to live in the world.

Finally, and in line with Practical Theologies more broadly, Contextual Theology insists on the transformation of contexts. As noted above, the goal of theology is not simply to know more but to transform life. Don Browning and David Tracy, who understand Practical Theology to be a process, a way of doing theology in which there is no distinction between theory and practice, bring theology and the social sciences into critical conversation with realities of everyday life. Therefore, while for David Tracy, Practical Theology is 'the mutually critical correlation of the interpreted theory and praxis of the Christian fact and the interpreted theory and praxis of the contemporary situation', for Browning, influenced by both Tracy and Hans-Georg Gadamer, Practical Theology is 'critical reflection on the church's dialogue with Christian sources and other communities of experience and interpretation with the aim of guiding its action toward social and individual transformation'.[33] Gadamer's influence on Browning is substantial. While Browning's process of theological reflection adapted from Tracy has the four theological stages of Descriptive Theology, Historical Theology, Systematic Theology and Strategic Practical Theology, a process that both brings the discipline of theology into dialogue with other academic disciplines, and also brings theory into dialogue with practice, Gadamer provides Browning's theology with method for making a largely intangible field such as philosophy a practical discipline – first by outlining the fact that practice is the foundation of and starting point for philosophical enquiry. Swinton and Mowat, too, insist on this cyclical process or method of theological inquiry in which theologians engage in a hermeneutical process holding together the situations of life, the Christian story and other disciplines that help further complexify the context under question. However, what it must also do is hold a hermeneutic of suspicion against present interpretations of the Christian tradition.[34] In short, theologies of any kind must be processes of self-awareness and self-criticism, careful of their grand narratives and absolutist claims.

Perhaps the biggest lesson that the Caribbean has learned, or continues to learn, is that talk of God originating outside the region has, to a great extent, not served the peoples of the region well. There is a need for a Caribbean Contextual Theology, or continued attempts at such, that does the following. First, it takes the history and experience of the region and its people seriously. Second, it is critical of the narratives of Christianity that came into the region and continue to operate. Third, it takes the cultural complexity of the region seriously as a fundamental source and starting point for theological reflection. Fourth, it is concerned with freedom, justice and equality for the people of the Caribbean, politically, economically, socially, ecclesiastically and in every sphere of Caribbean life. Finally, as a unique region at the centre of the development of the modern world, it challenges and contributes to every area of Christian theology in robust ways.

Outline and Approach of the Book

This book seeks to demonstrate that the unique history and situatedness of the region has consistently required critical and contextually rooted theological conversations to ensure the very survival of the region and its peoples. Caribbean Theology, in all its variety, continues to challenge the wider Christian theological tradition in fundamental questions about God; faith and culture; human and cosmological destiny; society and politics; Christian practice; and concepts of church.

In this work I must, however, declare my own positionality and biases. I come from the Anglican Church tradition, trained and ordained in the Caribbean. While I am aware of the complex religious and denominational nature of the region, I speak from a limited perspective. The intention is that the context of this book resonates with other experiences to a significant, if not almost identical, degree. I am also bound by the fact that my work has been shaped by the Anglophone African Caribbean perspective. I want to acknowledge other perspectives in the region – Francophone, Hispanic/Latin American, Lusophone and Dutch-speaking. While I try to include such voices, cultures and identities, this is largely an Anglophone, Anglican, African Caribbean perspective. Again, I must assert here that no one experience can encapsulate the region, and much of what happens in these other parts of the region resonate with the whole. There is much that we can learn from each other. Also, some referencing is done to my own work, both in books and articles, as I have been a student of African Caribbean theological reflections for some years and have had to wrestle with some of these issues in book chapters, articles and academic presentations. In such cases I will speak more personally, seeing this textbook as but a collation and continuation of my work throughout the years.

A further clarification must be made. This is not 'a' theology of the Caribbean. I make no such claim and cannot speak for the region, only as a particular experience within it. I also have the experience of writing this book while living and teaching outside of the region. Even though I maintain a strong connection to the Caribbean and particularly the Anglican Church in the Province of the West Indies (CPWI), I still bring a diasporic viewpoint. With that said, this book, as I envision it, can be read in several ways. First, this is a resource for persons seeking to engage the Christian theological tradition, but from a Caribbean perspective. I attempt to generously bring together voices and perspectives from Caribbean theologians themselves, across the decades and across the various nations. Second, this is a collation of the theological ideas and approaches from across the region. I try, as far as possible, to point others to pan-Caribbean conversations that have been taking place since the 1970s. Third, this is an attempt to point to areas of the Caribbean experience that can broaden, inform and challenge contemporary theological ideas undergirding the practice of the Christian faith in our contemporary world. It is my belief that the ideas that have shaped the modern world were first tested out in the Caribbean, and the region's critical and revolutionary responses are of theological importance for imagining a new world. Finally, this book is a generous invitation to a conversation that seeks to be honest about what it means to be a Caribbean person in the world, negotiating a faith that, trans-historically and trans-regionally, has always had to be critically evaluated, simply for the sake of survival. The Church in the Caribbean is strong, and has remained so despite colonialism, genocide, neocolonialism and persistent natural disaster, to list but a few examples. But why is this so? The answers to this question are complex, and not as easy to articulate as one might think. It is hoped that the chapters of this book might begin to tease out the underlying critical issues and sub-issues that can inform the intended conversation.

The book is organized into two main parts. Chapters 1 to 3 set the foundation for conceptualizing the region or theorizing how theology might be exercised within such a complex space. Chapter 2, 'Situating God in the African Caribbean', explores the African Caribbean context in all its complexity, arguing that it has been shaped by theological motives, from Columbus's landfall to the Haitian Revolution. The concept of God is deeply embedded in the very complex historical, political, cultural and theological emergence of the region. Chapter 3, 'From "Troubling of the Waters" to "Overcoming Self-Negation"', tries to make sense of the formal theological conversations in the region. It attempts to organize the various theological approaches and emphases in the region over time, noting that they overlap in many ways and consistently respond to the same reality of fragility.

Part 2, which includes Chapters 4 to 8, further explores specific themes relevant to and arising from the region that might have relevance for contemporary theological conversations. Chapter 4 centres its reflection on the colonial construction of the African Caribbean and the nature of role of the Church within it. The nature of the region requires concepts of mission and church to be continuously unfolding in order to disentangle from the deep reaches of colonial and imperial Christianity. Chapter 5 shifts its focus to African Traditional Religious Heritages (ATRs) in the Caribbean, and how they have functioned to survive Missionary Christianity. It ultimately explores the possibility of a Caribbean Christ amid a plural and complex religious region. Chapter 6 explores the potent decolonial and anti-colonial hermeneutical traditions that were birthed in the region and are at the disposal of any attempt at a Caribbean Contextual Theology. In this chapter the revolutionary nature of the Spirit is proposed, a pneumatology that vibrates within and beyond formal theological spaces. Chapter 7 is a little longer than the others. It surveys the works of Caribbean women theologians who have, more than others, explored complex issues around gender, sexuality and the body within general and theological discourse in the region. This chapter then looks at the construction of 'sin' and 'salvation' in the African Caribbean context, and the wisdom it might offer to Christian theology in general. Chapter 8 argues that a Contextual Theology of the Caribbean is liturgically and melodically orientated and has space to bring together reflections on the ecological, environmental, political and spiritual vulnerability of the region. It then explores the ecological lament inherent in Caribbean theological discourse that can never be ignored.

Chapter 9, the conclusion, provides a summary of the various chapters, themes and arguments of the book, but also provides a postscript, a plea that is dear to my heart and theological imagination. It is this: the discipline of theology, no matter the context, must be mindful of its primary intentions and preoccupations. It can be argued that much of classical and Western theological preoccupation, as it has been exercised in non-Western contexts, has been concerned with being right, precise or 'true'. Being very aware of machinations and influence of colonialism and imperialism on Caribbean life, Caribbean theological discourse asks what theology and praxis would look like if the primary preoccupation was about being 'whole'.

Notes

1 'Between the devil and the deep blue sea' is a well-known idiom denoting a dilemma of some sort. Either decision is problematic. One is 'damned' if they do or 'damned' if they do not.

2 Michael Jagessar, 'Chanting Down the Shitstem: Resistance with Anansi and Rastafari Optics', in *Religion and Power: Theology in the Age of Empire*, ed. Jione Havea, London: Lexington/Fortress Academic, 2019.

3 Derek Walcott's seminal poem, 'The Sea is History', in Derek Walcott and Glyn Maxwell, *The Poetry of Derek Walcott 1948–2013*, London: Faber & Faber, 2014.

4 See Christopher Columbus, *The Journal of Christopher Columbus (During His First Voyage, 1492–93) and Documents Relating the Voyages of John Cabot and Gaspar Corte Real*, ed. and trans. Clements R.

Markham, Cambridge: Cambridge University Press, 2010, Cambridge Library Collection, Hakluyt First Series.

5 For further information on the histories of the pre-Columbian peoples of the Caribbean and Latin-American, see Hilary McDonald Beckles and Verene A. Shepherd, *Liberties Lost: Caribbean Indigenous Societies and Slave Systems*, Cambridge: Cambridge University Press, 2004.

6 Francis J. Osborne and Geoffrey Johnston, *Coast Lands and Islands: First Thoughts on Caribbean Church History*, Jamaica: UTCWI, 1972, p. 27.

7 SPG is now the USPG, United Society Partners in the Gospel. I am currently a Trustee of the USPG and have been involved in much of the conversation around USPG truth-telling and reparations. It is clear from the historical records that the SPG was a missionary arm of the Church of England and key bishops and cathedrals in Britain were directly connected to the Codrington plantations.

8 Orlando Patterson, *The Sociology of Slavery: An Analysis of the Origins, Development and Structure of Negro Slave Society in Jamaica*, Studies in Society, London: MacGibbon & Kee, 1967.

9 Ian G. Strachan, *Paradise and Plantation: Tourism and Culture in the Anglophone Caribbean*, New World Studies, Charlottesville, VA: University of Virginia Press, 2002, https://www.loc.gov/catdir/toc/fy036/2002010190.html (accessed 7.7.23).

10 C. L. R. James, *The Black Jacobins: Toussaint L'Ouverture and the San Domingo Revolution*, 2nd edn, New York: Vintage Books, 1963.

11 Eric Williams, *Capitalism and Slavery*, Chapel Hill, NC: University of North Carolina Press, 1961.

12 Sheila Marshall, *After the Flood: The Church, Slavery and Reconciliation*, documentary, Movement for Justice and Reconciliation, 2022.

13 Marshall, 'After the Flood', news release, 5 May 2022, https://www.thersa.org/fellowship/news/after-the-flood-the-church-slavery-reconciliation-film-screening (accessed 7.7.23).

14 'Exhibition shows Church of England's links to slave trade', Movement for Justice and Reconciliation, 2023, https://www.mjr-uk.com/news/exhibition-shows-church-of-englands-links-to-slave-trade (accessed 3.5.23).

15 Nathaniel Samuel Murrell, *Afro-Caribbean Religions: An Introduction to their Historical, Cultural, and Sacred Traditions*, Philadelphia, PA: Temple University Press, 2010, p. 289.

16 For further information, see John Walton Cotman, 'Coming in from the Cold: Grenada and Cuba since 1983', *The Round Table: The Commonwealth Journal of International Affairs* 102, no. 2, 2013.

17 Hilary Beckles, *How Britain Underdeveloped the Caribbean: A Reparation Response to Europe's Legacy of Plunder and Poverty*, Jamaica: The University of the West Indies Press, 2021.

18 See reflections on this in Adolfo Ham, 'Caribbean Theology: The Challenge of the Twenty-First Century', in *Caribbean Theology: Preparing for the Challenges Ahead*, ed. Howard Gregory, Barbados: Canoe Press, 1995.

19 For a video of the speech, see https://www.youtube.com/watch?v=PN6THYZ4ngM (accessed 10.7.23).

20 Hilary Beckles, *Britain's Black Debt: Reparations for Caribbean Slavery and Native Genocide*, Jamaica: University of the West Indies Press, 2013. For a deeper understanding of the history of genocide and systems of slavery as it pertains the New World and the Caribbean, see Beckles and Shepherd, *Liberties Lost*.

21 https://www.in2013dollars.com/uk/inflation/1833?amount=20000000 (accessed 13.7.23).

22 Beckles, *Britain's Black Debt*, p. 163.

23 Beckles, *Britain's Black Debt*, p. 163.

24 Gregory (ed.), *Caribbean Theology*.

25 Noel Titus, 'Our Caribbean Reality', in *Caribbean Theology*, ed. Gregory.

26 Barry Chevannes, 'Our Caribbean Reality', in *Caribbean Theology*, ed. Gregory.

27 See for example Elaine L. Graham, Heather Walton and Frances Ward, *Theological Reflection: Methods*, London: SCM Press, 2005; Stephen B. Bevans, *Models of Contextual Theology*, rev. and expanded edn, Maryknoll, NY: Orbis Books, 2002.

28 See Graham, Walton and Ward, *Theological Reflection: Methods*. See also Elaine L. Graham, Heather Walton and Frances Ward, *Theological Reflection: Sources*, London: SCM Press, 2007.

29 Alister E. McGrath, *Christian Theology: An Introduction*, 5th edn, Oxford: Wiley-Blackwell, 2011.

30 See Bevans, *Models*. Robert J. Schreiter, *Constructing Local Theologies*, Maryknoll, NY: Orbis Books, 1985. Robert J. Schreiter, *The New Catholicity: Theology Between the Global and the Local*, Faith and Cultures Series, Maryknoll, NY: Orbis Books, 1997.

31 John Swinton and Harriet Mowat, *Practical Theology and Qualitative Research*, London: SCM Press, 2006.

32 Paul's biblical verse, 1 Corinthians 13.12.

33 Don S. Browning, *A Fundamental Practical Theology: Descriptive and Strategic Proposals*, Minneapolis, MN: Fortress Press, 1991, p. 49. David Tracy, 'The Foundations of Practical Theology', in *Practical Theology: The Emerging Field in Theology, Church, and World*, ed. Don. S. Browning, San Francisco, CA: Harper & Row, 1983, p. 36.

34 Swinton and Mowat, *Practical Theology and Qualitative Research*.

2

Situating God in the African Caribbean

While our last chapter introduced broad strokes of history that reveal some theological tensions at the heart of the experience of the region, it is important now to look more deeply into the region of which we speak. The Caribbean is a complex region; while being mostly of African cultural and religious foundations, it is also constituted of most world religions, cultures and ethnicities, and has been home to some of the world's most ancient civilizations. Hence, 'God-talk' or theology there can never be straightforward or simplistic.

Naming and Branding: Definitions Matter

The Caribbean can be conceived in different ways and there is considerable debate within the region about this. Geographically, the term 'Caribbean' might refer to countries contained strictly within the Caribbean Sea. In such a case, places like the Bahamas cannot be considered. If we think geologically in terms of the Caribbean basin, then the region would include parts of South and Central America. There is also the diasporic factor. It is arguable that the movements of people from the Caribbean to other parts of the world, particularly metropolitan centres in Europe and North America, have only served to expand the region through kinships and cultural, economic and even political networks. It can also be seen socio-historically as countries or nation states that have a shared legacy of European colonialism, slavery and neocolonialism. Since there is no agreed-upon consensus, and any attempt would naturally be ideological, I define Caribbean in this socio-historical sense. The same processes that have taken place in Barbados, Jamaica, Belize, Guyana, Trinidad and others in the Anglophone Caribbean have also taken place in similar ways in the Dutch, Lusophone, Latinx/Hispanic and Francophone countries of the region. There is the shared history of colonialism, slavery and utter dependence on European and/or North American power.

But definitions do matter here. Throughout the book I switch between the terms African Caribbean and Caribbean, largely meaning the same thing, but mostly being clear about the significant shaping of the region by plantation slavery and the predominance of West and Central African religious and cultural heritages and cosmologies. When I use the term African Caribbean, I do several things. First, I want to preserve this transatlantic connection between the Caribbean region, Missionary Christianity and the African continent. Any consideration of the Caribbean must wrestle with how these three things intersect. Second, I wish to contest the common terminology, 'West Indies'. The West Indies, as in the Church in the Province of the West Indies (CPWI), might be more popularly used by those remembering the framing of the region as part of the British Empire. I imagine that contemporary anti-colonial persons like me reject this naming and framing by a former colonial power. Beyond Great Britain, we reject the original branding of the region as 'West Indian' by Columbus, who, while attempting to reach the East Indies by sailing westward, encountered the region by accident. There is place within contemporary Caribbean life to name ourselves.

But, with this said, even the term 'Caribbean' requires further discussion. The very name pays homage to the Carib people, pre-Columbian dwellers of the region. When the Europeans came, they identified three groups in the Caribbean and labelled them Arawaks, Caribs and Maya, although these groups had their own name. Hilary Beckles and Verene Shepherd alert us to the fact that the pre-Columbian peoples encountered were the *Ciboney* or the *Guanahacabibe*, whom the Europeans called 'Wild and as fleet as deer'. There were also the *Taino*, who were called Arawak by the Europeans. Finally, there were the *Kalinago*, who were called Caribs.[1] 'Carib' within Columbus's imagination was the wild savage, the uncivilized and the godless. Nonetheless, the name has remained. I suspect that this is due in great measure to the fact that the pre-Columbian peoples of the region were the first to experience genocide and annihilation by the coming of the Europeans. Similarly, the prefix 'African' is necessary, since they too have experienced genocide and annihilation.

Ultimately, what is being discussed is a region in which the concept of God has never been a solely European undertaking. Charles Jason Gordon, now Roman Catholic Archbishop of Port of Spain, Trinidad, argues for 'civilization' instead of 'culture' as a conceptual framework for thinking theologically in the region. While 'culture' is always evolving and dynamic, grounding a theology in Caribbean culture ultimately proves problematic. Gordon states: 'Essentializing any aspect of the vast realm of culture does not lead to epistemological clarity or adequacy. It ultimately leads to more confusion.'[2] He suggests: 'The shift to civilization and geographical space allows the grounding of knowledge in what does not change – the geography – while allowing critical analysis of what does change – the patterns of relating, the attributes and customs of the people.'[3] For Gordon, this is a much broader, longer and deeper theological reflection on all that has taken place within the region.

However, another Caribbean theologian, Michael St A. Miller, offers another approach to situating God-talk in the region. He too is preoccupied with how one does theology in the Caribbean context. The region is comprised of radically different religious and cultural traditions and experiences, as well as conceptions of God. He states:

> While the nature of God's relationship to the Caribbean culture sphere will continue to be debated, the fundamental conviction regarding God's purposeful presence continues in the contemporary era. This is associated with an underlying psychology which reflects the historical relations between

colonized and colonizer, enslaved and enslaver, African, Asian and European, those who inherited the benefits of the historic relations and those who felt cheated by it.[4]

The task of theology within the region, as with every context, is to 'engage in dynamic interaction within and between frameworks of thought and belief that open the possibility of progressively wholesome visions of reality'.[5] Miller offers an approach he names 'dialectical contextualism'. The approach to theology in the Caribbean must consider all the various identities, experiences and theologies, whether implicit or overt. He states:

> Inter-contextual interactions, which often-times begin with conflicting understandings of reality, can produce interesting interplays that constitute new frameworks of thought and belief, which in turn challenge the very contexts from which they were spawned, even as they become critical-creative components in other interactions.[6]

It is my contention that attention to this complex and often conflictual nature of Caribbean life holds promise for rich and creative conversations in every academic sphere, especially theology.

Beyond Simplistic Binary

In almost in every way the Caribbean defies easy conceptualization. It is a region that is multi-faith, multi-cultural, multi-ethnic and multi-lingual. For example, most speakers, by number, are Spanish speaking, then French, then English, then Dutch. However, the English-speaking Caribbean carries a particular weight because of the dominance of the former British Empire and the international value of the English language. But we cannot easily separate the region. There are other significant players in the region that merit constant attention. Haiti is its own republic with a remarkable history, particularly its

independence from France in 1804. Cuba has a similarly fas-
cinating history, with its fraught relationship with the United
States of America. Puerto Rico is an American extra-territory.

The complexity of the region deepens. Noel Titus makes
this contribution to the collection *Caribbean Theology* as he
outlines the deep complexity of the region, historically, demo-
graphically and linguistically:

> The region which we know as the Caribbean covers a large
> area and involves two groups of territories. On the one hand,
> there are several continental countries of the Central and
> South American littoral of the sea. On the other hand, there
> are large numbers of islands, forming what Franklin Knight
> describes as an inclined backbone from Florida to the north-
> ern coastline of South America. These islands vary consider-
> ably in size and topography. From the geographical point of
> view, the Caribbean suggests separation – scattering rather
> than gathering.[7]

Titus continues:

> It is not only geography that serves to separate our peoples.
> Differences in our history form both a separating and a
> unifying influence. Historical differences form a separating
> influence, in that many territories have emerged from separate
> and competing European powers. These included – at differ-
> ent times and for longer or shorter periods – Spain, France,
> Holland, England and Denmark. Historical influences form a
> unifying influence in a rather unique way.[8]

He then proceeds with the following insights worth remembering:

> Our history has done something else to us. Because of vary-
> ing backgrounds and European associations, we have tended
> to be pulled outward towards others in our loyalties rather
> than inward towards each other. The countervailing attitude,
> which seeks to encourage strength in togetherness, is far from

being firmly rooted in our consciousness. We see at present European nations, which had fought each other for centuries with the sugar islands as prizes, resolving to unite for their mutual self-preservation while the Caribbean territories seem unable to come together for their mutual survival.[9]

Titus further notes that religion and education, the shaping forces for continuing generations, remain colonially informed, with difficulties in foregrounding indigenous approaches. Also, economics is a stark reality of structural adjustment programmes, continued indebtedness and an inability or unwillingness to unite and support each other intra-regionally.

The Caribbean is also a place of paradox. While it has produced spectacular athletes such as Usain Bolt of Jamaica, the Golden Girls of the Bahamas, diabetes, health conditions and ill-health abound. While it is a vacation destination and paradise, it is beset by violence and societal turmoil, and social, political, economic inequity abound. Ian Strachan and several other Caribbean intellectuals have argued that paradise is simply the plantation reworked. The system is just as rigid, brutal and inhumane, especially for those who are left to maintain the plantation/paradise.[10] Carlos F. Cardoza-Orlandi speaks of this paradox of the region and, inevitably, the paradox of Caribbean Christian Identity. He notes that it is hard to arrive at a definition of Caribbean identity, and one can only get to such a sense indirectly, precisely because of the sometimes extreme tensions that the region contains.[11] This complexity and paradox are inevitably theological issues.

The Enduring Legacy of Slavery and Colonialism

With the decimation of the pre-Columbian people, mainly West and Central Africans were brought as beasts of burden under a brutal and strict social order, eventually becoming the predominant culture and ethnicity of the contemporary African Caribbean. They were seen as non-human and were not allowed to form social institutions such as families or independent religious bodies. Orlando Patterson's description of the plantation as a total institution is precise.[12] Slaves were forced to adopt a new language, take on a new religion and adopt a different world view. Much of the language, world views and religious and cultural practices were hidden, even in plain sight. For example, African concepts of time, which are not linear and are concerned with events and not simply the exactness of dates, continued to operate within and beyond largely European linear ones.[13] Africans were baptized as Christian but kept their pneumatologically expressive religious mannerisms within the confines of ordered Christian worship. At its foundation, African ontology has a belief in God who creates and sustains all life, the spirits who have influence in human affairs, the living dead (ancestors) who influence life and community action, and human beings who can have access to God or the spirits through gifted mediums, priests, people with special giftings, for good or for ill. Their street festivals mixed African, European and Amerindian, and formed totally new and spectacular religious and cultural productions.

The assertion that the region never existed for itself is not an exaggeration. It was never meant to survive or thrive. Peoples, cultures, languages were set apart through a very rigid system, yet something new was born, and is still being born. After the slave trade became unviable, Great Britain brought Chinese and Indian labourers to resource its many plantations. This period of indentureship after the abolition of the slave trade in 1807 and eventual emancipation in 1838 led to a further creolized and hybrid region. Nonetheless, this change did not resolve the issues of political dependency and lack of economic autonomy. The shaping of the region by colonial expansion remains a significant challenge economically and politically, but also theologically. Kortright Davis has remained important in helping us to conceptualize the enduring challenges of the region mainly due to its colonial shaping and its continued vulnerability to external forces. In his *Emancipation Still Comin'* he names six enduring crises for the region.[14] These are, first, persistent and structured poverty. The region was never created to sustain itself. Second, there is migration. This includes those coming into the region taking advantage of it, as well as those from within the region being forced to find better livelihoods elsewhere. Third, there is cultural alienation. Indigenous and non-Western religious and cultural traditions were always seen as something to be extirpated. Fourth, there is dependence. Plantation society only evolved into other forms of dependency, despite 'independence' exercises. Perhaps the biggest example of this is North American neocolonialism. Davis also reminds us of internal systems of patronage and dependency, especially within the political arena. Fifth, there is fragmentation. The region is geographically fragmented. One way that this continues to operate is inherent barriers between nation states speaking different languages owing to their former European colonial heritage. Also, the attempt at a West Indian Federation failed precisely because of the continued influence of former colonial powers. Finally, there are narcotics. At the time of writing his text, this was the case, especially since the Caribbean was a strategic midway point between South and Central America and the United States. However, since then the key issue, and no doubt arising from the drug wars of the 1980s and 90s, is increased gun violence and homicide. Another crisis that must be named that has become more salient since this period is health. Incidence of diabetes and different forms of cancer continues to be alarmingly high within the region. All of these remain interconnected, thus making it one of the most vulnerable places on the planet.

African Caribbean Spirituality

Perhaps at this point we should define what is meant by African Caribbean Spirituality. We know what is meant by the African Caribbean but let us define spirituality. The *Dictionary of Third World Theology* provides a rich and comprehensive definition:

> our connectedness to God, to our human roots, to the rest of nature, to one another and to ourselves. It is the experience of the Holy Spirit moving us and our communities to be

life-giving, and life-affirming. Throughout the Third World, spirituality is celebrated in songs, rituals, and symbols that show the energizing Spirit animating the community to move together in response to God.[15]

Dianne Stewart and others point out the different legacies of God that we find in the African Caribbean. Naturally there was no one concept of God or spirituality. There was and is colonial or Missionary Christianity with its Christendom baggage, and within contemporary conceptions of Christianity in the region there were and are all the other expressions or spiritualties, whether African or Asian. Stewart argues that this dichotomy exists and has been one that has pitted Christianity in the region against all other non-European cosmologies and theologies.[16] What we find is a legacy between 'God' (the European representation of Christianity) and the 'gods' (of African or Amerindian cosmology and theology). Before exploring Stewart's assertion in more detail, consider the the Verdun Proclamation, an international consultation meeting in Barbados in 1992 to discuss the long history of racism in the Americas. The proclamation made the following statement:

The existence of many religious beliefs and practices does not mean the acceptance of all of them. Those which are accepted are the ones the Europeans have approved. Afrocentric religious beliefs are still considered evil and even where there is religious tolerance there is still a great deal of suspicion. Except for students of anthropology, sociology, and history, little effort has been made to understand the religious beliefs and practices with an African base. The officials of the Christian churches do not recognize a need for dialogue with these religious beliefs, even when there is conflict between what the churches teach and what people believe. The fact that the Christian churches, which by and large are led by clergy who are the descendants of Africans, do not see any value in carrying on dialogue with the religious beliefs and practices found among African peoples goes to show the extent to which prejudice against Africans has been instilled within the peoples of the Caribbean. It also confirms how very Eurocentric the churches are in their thinking.[17]

Having engaged with John Mbiti's research into African philosophy and spirituality, Dianne Stewart offers six essential features of a distinctly African Caribbean Spirituality when considering Myal Spirituality in Jamaica, which finds its manifestation in Obeah, Jonconnu, Revivalism, Native Baptists, Kumina and Rastafari. First, there is an inherent 'communotheistic' (as opposed to a monotheistic or polytheistic) understanding of the divine, which includes venerated deities and invisible beings. It is hard for African Caribbean people to live out a theology where God and God's relation to the world is dynamic, varied and communitarian. Like Mbiti, there is the belief in the Divinities (energies or personifications of God, personalities that do God's biddings, like angels), the Spirits (while less than Divinities, these can be called upon but are dangerous), and the Living Dead (ancestors, guardians of the family and the traditions). However, it must always be emphasized that in the African cosmology, there is only one God, for example, *Grand Maitre* or *Bondye* in Vodou or *Olodumare* or *Olorun* in Candomblé and Santería.[18] Second, there is ancestral veneration. I am old enough to remember eating utensils or foods being left on graves. Funerary or remembrance traditions across the region, such as 'Nine Night' or 'Settin' Up', reveal the inherent belief that the worlds of the living and of the dead are porous. Rigid separations cannot be made. Third, there is possession trance and mediumship. When revival broke out in Jamaica in 1860–61, Stewart maintains that Myal Spirituality – divinations, prophecy, healing and visions, as well as possession, already inherent in Revival Zionism – was being expressed through the wave of Christianity. In short, African Caribbean Spirituality was given freedom of expression. Fourth, there are food offerings and animal sacrifice. These are present across the region in African Derived Religious Traditions such as Santería/ Palo Alto (Cuba), Vodou (Haiti), Obeah (Jamaica/Bahamas/ Barbados and the rest of the English-speaking Caribbean), and Orisha (Trinidad/Brazil/Cuba). Fifth, there is divination and herbalism. Many African Caribbean people have insisted on 'bush medicine' or natural herbs as preferable to modern scientific approaches. In fact, during the colonial period the use of herbs was highly honoured. One must understand that the Rastafarian doesn't only want to smoke marijuana, he/she believes in the healing power of herbs. Furthermore, Kumina is a healing tradition that prioritizes the healing power of women. Finally, there is an entrenched belief in neutral mystical power. Historians have erroneously made a distinction between Obeah (bad) and Myal (Good) as if they were separate things, like 'black' and 'white' magic in Western understandings. When considering African cosmology, John Mbiti and others speak of neutral mystical power. The power of Obeah or Myal is used for bringing either healing or harm depending on the situation. It is given for the wholeness and survival of the community.

Rebellion!

Legacies of God in the African Caribbean aren't confined to theological ideas and concepts. Peoples of the region have resisted the historical weight of colonial oppression in multiple ways. Across the region, almost every island has had slave revolts and uprisings, some of them key to the overall dismantling of slavery. The exhibition put on by the Windrush Foundation, 'Making Freedom: Riots, Rebellion, and Revolution', is a good place to explore the various slave rebellions and uprisings.[19]

Klaas/Court Plot, Antigua, 1736

Plantation owners on Antigua discovered a plan by enslaved people to steal gunpowder and blow up the island's gentry at a ball. As punishment, over the next six months 88 enslaved people were put to death, most of them by being burned alive. The leader of the plot, Prince Klaas or 'Court', was born in Ghana.

Tacky's Revolt, Jamaica, 1760

This was the largest uprising of enslaved people in a British colony in the eighteenth century. Tacky, of Fanti origin, was the prominent figure, who was royalty in his homeland before enslavement. Inspired by the first Maroon Wars of the 1730s, Tacky initiated a series of other uprisings on the island.

The Berbice Uprising , Guyana, 1763

Cuffee/Kofi led a major slave revolt of more than 3,800 slaves against the colonial regime. They militarily defeated their enslavers and placed a revolutionary government in power for almost a year.

Fédon's Revolt, Grenada, 1796

Fédon's revolt in Grenada was defeated by British troops. Inspired by the Haitian rebellion, the goal was to create an independent Black republic.

Bussa's Rebellion, Barbados, 1816

Led by African-born Bussa, enslaved people rose up in Barbados and burned a quarter of the island's sugar crop before the rebellion was suppressed.

Demarara Rebellion, Guyana, 1823

Under the leadership of Jack Gladstone, son of African-born Quamina, rebellion broke out due to lack of action by colonial authorities towards improving the conditions of the slaves. Out of an estimated 74,000 enslaved Africans in the colony about 10,000 took part in the rebellion. Interestingly, it was after this rebellion that two new bishoprics were created in the colonies in 1824, Jamaica and Barbados.

Sam Sharpe Rebellion, Jamaica, 1831–32

During a massive rebellion in Jamaica, more than 20,000 rebels seized control of the north-west corner of the island, setting planters' houses on fire. It took the British Army and militia a month to restore order. Some 200 enslaved African people and 14 white people died in the fighting. At least 340 enslaved people who had rebelled were hanged or shot afterwards.

Were these just struggles for survival? Or, rather, were these calculated and embodied theological responses to colonial oppression? When considering that the rebellion in Jamaica in 1831 was spearheaded by a Baptist deacon, Sam Sharpe, and that the Haitian Revolution began as an African traditional religious observance, the claim can easily be justified that these were deeply theological responses to the pervasive Afrophobic colonial violence.

Revolutionary Intellectual Traditions

The region also has a revolutionary intellectual tradition that cannot be separated from the long history of slave rebellions and critique of colonial power and Missionary Christianity. Other parts of the region have produced, in the nineteenth and twentieth centuries, powerful literary and political voices all consistently challenging the core tenets of European expansion, capitalism, colonialism, racism and xenophobia. Examples of these thinkers are José Martí, Gabriel Garcia Márquez, Aimé Césaire, Frantz Fanon, Éduoard Glissant and Michel-Rolph Trouillot, to name but a few.[20]

In the African Caribbean there have been key intellectuals and activists who have shaped anti-colonial thinking in the region. There is not enough scope to engage them fully, but their body of work remains quintessential in constructing robust Caribbean theologies aimed at decolonial practices. My contention here is that the region has produced extraordinary intellectuals and activists who have been shaped by the African Caribbean experience, and whose intellectual efforts have shaped modern and contemporary thought significantly. One such notable person would be Walter Rodney. Rodney advocated 'self-emancipation', 'self-organization' and 'self-mobilization' as alternative ways of living against capitalistic governance. In Chapter 1 of the *History of Guyanese Working Peoples*, Rodney makes it very clear that the environment, life and politics cannot be separated. Therefore, paramount within the Caribbean context would be the following: the organization of working people to end division; the belief in self-emancipation; and transition beyond capitalism.[21] His *How Europe Underdeveloped Africa* remains a classic political analysis, inspiring generations of thinkers.[22] Frantz Fanon is another compelling thinker often underutilized in the region. In an article on postcolonialism and theology, I have explored Fanon's works and insights as profitable for examining the psychological dimensions not only of coloniality but also colonial Christianity as it continues to be manifested in contemporary life.[23] Colonization is a violent process that perpetuates violence through its institutions. In his most famous writings, *Black Skin, White Masks* and *Wretched of the Earth*, Fanon both assesses the nature of coloniality and critiques the European intellectual ideas that were inherently racist and xenophobic.[24] One can read C. L. R. James's works as ways of doing history from the standpoint of the oppressed. James's belief was that history ought to be told, and truth ought to be understood, from the vantage point of the underclass within the colonial construct. In *The Black Jacobins*, he recounts the story of the Haitian Revolution from the perspective of the victors – the formerly colonized Haitian peoples under the leadership of Toussaint L'Ouverture.[25] In *Beyond a Boundary*, he argues that the Caribbean person has a way of taking something, such as cricket, and re-creating it into something distinctive, something new and lively, which transcends old conceptions of that thing.[26] He speaks of Caribbean uniqueness and giftedness and the need to celebrate these facts. At the heart of his work is a drive for a unification that transcends boundaries of all kinds – social, historical, cultural and political. Finally, the work of Sylvia Wynter cannot be ignored. Sylvia Wynter's canon of work, shaped by the African Caribbean context, explores and challenges prevailing ideas about race, colonialism and, ultimately, what it means to be human. She refuses to be confined, and her work integrates both prose and poetry, intentionally, exploring philosophy, the natural sciences, as well as literary theory, along with social, political and cultural analysis.[27] Beyond these revolutionary intellectuals mentioned here, others remain powerful interlocutors for robust theological reflection within the African Caribbean: for example, Eric Williams, Marcus Garvey, Derek Walcott, V. S. Naipaul, Stuart Hall, Carolyn Cooper, George Lamming, Hilary Beckles and Verene Shepherd.

These intellectuals are unconventional in both their content and their methodology. They reject standardization, and critique (or rather defy) conventional forms. It is a hope that within an interdisciplinary framework these scholars will inform contemporary theological thinking in the region through their deep and insightful engagement with the colonial condition. Very little of this has taken place. Exceptions to this include Gordon Rohlehr in *Troubling of the Waters*, who talks about doing theology using Derek Walcott and C. L. R. James.[28] Similarly, Noel Erskine engages Garvey directly in his book *From Garvey to Marley: A Rastafari Theology*.[29]

The Diasporan Question

The insecurity of the region has, throughout the decades, seen a vast migration of African Caribbean persons to other parts of the world. This African Caribbean diasporan reality has a theological significance, since the wider cultural networking of Caribbean people has been important for both the region and the many metropolitan cities that Caribbean people have migrated to. Two theologians have wrestled with the diasporan nature of any Caribbean theological reflection, reminding us that 'diasporan' is a reality for the region. The work of Delroy Reid-Salmon discusses what he refers to as *diasporan theology*. In his *Home Away from Home: The Caribbean Diasporan*

Church in the Black Atlantic Tradition, Reid-Salmon insists on diaspora as constitutive of the Black and Caribbean theological traditions.[30] Diaspora as an identifier also constitutes African Caribbean ecclesiologies. In short, as someone raised in Jamaica but doing theology and ministry in the United States, he locates his theology within the diasporan experience.

Michael St A. Miller as noted above, talks about *dialectical contextualism*. In his article 'He Said I Was Out of Pocket: On Being a Caribbean Contextual Theologian in a Non-Caribbean Context', he wrestles with the credibility of doing Caribbean Theology out of context, in a foreign land, and the ways in which that would strengthen African Caribbean theological reflection.[31] Miller critiques Reid-Salmon directly, asserting that his insistence on the 'Caribamerican' experience essentializes African Caribbean identity while ignoring all the complex experiences within it; for example, the South Asian or the Amerindian influences. Miller's approach to theology, which he explains as explicitly embracing a mitigated epistemological relativism, helps him to negotiate the 'in-between', and to address contextuality in both the USA and the Caribbean with keen insights from both. He is self-identified as a 'dialectical contextualist'. A similar approach is advanced in the work of Michael Jagessar, who employs the Anancy trickster figure in African Caribbean folklore as a way of doing theology from an African Caribbean, and inevitably an African Caribbean diasporan, perspective. He states:

> Anancy is the great survivor who wears innumerable masks that represent the behaviour and state of affairs of human beings. Anancy's negotiating of multiple identities and her in-between-ness underscores the multi-layered dimensions of human life. Whatever the mask, Anancy embodies the manifoldness of what *is*.[32]

Ultimately, these scholars who do their respective theologies between their Caribbean native lands and their homes and academic posts in the United States and the United Kingdom are critical for any theological exercise in the region. The region isn't

simply complex within; it is also dynamically engaged in metropolitan centres across the globe. Many scholars and theological
voices of the region have influenced the academy and the Church
internationally. The Caribbean has been the birthing place for
their deeply powerful and insightful reflections. I am one of these
persons, living and working in the UK, teaching contextual theology, training priests and advancing research that affects both
the Caribbean and the UK (and beyond). This is something that
can and should be owned and affirmed by the region.

Exploring the African Caribbean context in all its complexity
has been the aim of this chapter. An argument can be made that
much of the intellectual insights of the region remains underutilized in formal theological research. The region remains a
fertile ground for advancing research of all kinds, but theology,
or Caribbean Contextual Theology, has yet fully to take advantage of this. The region has been shaped by theological motives,
from Columbus's landfall to the Haitian Revolution. The concept of God is deeply embedded in the very complex historical,
political, cultural and theological emergence of the region. This
grounding is necessary before looking at formal Caribbean
theological movements over the decades, the aim of the next
chapter.

Notes

1 Hilary Beckles and Verene A. Shepherd, *Liberties Lost: The Indi-
genous Caribbean and Slave Systems*, Cambridge: Cambridge University
Press, 2004. For further exploration of the pre-Columbian peoples and
theories around the original settling of the New World, see Ivan van
Sertima, *They Came Before Columbus: The African Presence in Ancient
America*, New York: Random House, 1976.

2 Charles Jason Gordon, 'Theology, Hermeneutics and Liberation: Grounding Theology in a Caribbean Context', PhD, University of
London, 2003, p. 21.

3 Gordon, 'Theology, Hermeneutics and Liberation, p. 21.

4 Michael A. Miller, *Reshaping the Contextual Vision in Caribbean
Theology: Theoretical Foundations for Theology which is Contextual,
Pluralistic, and Dialectical*, Lanham, MD and Plymouth: University
Press of America, 2007, p. 13. See also Michael St A. Miller, 'He Said I

Was Out of Pocket: On Being a Caribbean Contextual Theologian in a Non-Caribbean Context', *Black Theology: An International Journal* 9, no. 2, 2011.

5 Miller, *Reshaping the Contextual Vision*, p. 19.

6 Miller, *Reshaping the Contextual Vision*, p. 217.

7 Titus, 'Our Caribbean Reality', in *Caribbean Theology: Preparing for the Challenges Ahead*, ed. Howard Gregory, Barbados: Canoe Press, 1995, p. 58.

8 Titus, 'Our Caribbean Reality', p. 58.

9 Titus, 'Our Caribbean Reality', p. 59.

10 Ian G. Strachan, *Paradise and Plantation: Tourism and Culture in the Anglophone Caribbean*, New World Studies, Charlottesville, VA: University of Virginia Press, 2002.

11 See Carlos F. Cardoza-Orlandi, 'Rediscovering Caribbean Christian Identity: Biography and Missiology at the Shore (Between Dry Land and the Sea)', *Voices from the Third World* 27, no. 1, 2004.

12 Orlando Patterson, *The Sociology of Slavery: An Analysis of the Origins, Development and Structure of Negro Slave Society in Jamaica*, Studies in Society, London: MacGibbon & Kee, 1967.

13 For more on this, see John S. Mbiti, *African Religions and Philosophy*, 2nd edn, Oxford: Heinemann Educational Publishers, 1969.

14 Kortright Davis, *Emancipation Still Comin': Explorations in Caribbean Emancipatory Theology*, Maryknoll, NY: Orbis Books, 1990, ch. 3.

15 Virginia Fabella and R. S. Sugirtharajah (eds), *Dictionary of Third World Theologies*, Maryknoll, NY: Orbis Books, 2000, p. 189.

16 Dianne M. Stewart, *Three Eyes for the Journey: African Dimensions of the Jamaican Religious Experience*, Oxford: Oxford University Press, 2004.

17 Oscar L. Bolioli (ed.), 'Reclaiming Identity: The Verdun Proclamation', in *The Caribbean: Culture of Resistance, Spirit of Hope*, New York: Friendship Press, 1993, p. 57.

18 Joseph Murphy, *Working the Spirit: Ceremonies of the African Diaspora*, Boston, MA: Beacon Press, 1994.

19 For a deeper discussion of the following rebellions across the Caribbean, look up the Windrush Foundation Exhibition, 'Making Freedom: Riots, Rebellions, and Revolution', https://makingfreedom.co.uk/making-freedom (accessed 14.7.23).

20 See this catalogue of Key Caribbean intellectuals from Centre for Latin-American and Caribbean Studies at the University of London: https://ilcs.sas.ac.uk/research-centres/centre-latin-american-caribbean-studies/clacs-research/research-resources-0-5?mibextid=Zxz2cZ&fbc lid=IwAR0azTmX25Y-G9UaBwCgWgLuYnggW-C-9dF6Ptug1fJ2ph Q-Bc8TGmxvB6o#george-lamming (accessed 14.7.23).

21 See Walter Rodney, *A History of the Guyanese Working People: 1881–1905*, Baltimore, MD: The Johns Hopkins University Press, 1981.

22 Walter Rodney, *How Europe Underdeveloped Africa*, London: Bogle-L'Ouverture Publications, 1972.

23 Carlton Turner, 'Deepening the Postcolonial Theological Gaze: Frantz Fanon and the Psychopathology of Colonial Christianity', *Modern Believing* 62, no. 4, Autumn 2021.

24 Frantz Fanon, *The Wretched of the Earth*, Harmondsworth: Penguin, 1967; Frantz Fanon, *Black Skin, White Masks*, New York: Grove Press, 1967.

25 C. L. R. James, *The Black Jacobins: Toussaint L'Ouverture and the San Domingo Revolution*, 2nd edn, New York: Vintage Books, 1963.

26 C. L. R. James, *Beyond a Boundary*, Durham, NC: Duke University Press, 1993.

27 Katherine McKittrick (ed.), *Sylvia Wynter: On Being Human as Praxis*, Durham, NC: Duke University Press, 2015. See also Sylvia Wynter, *The Hills of Hebron*, London: Jonathan Cape, 1962.

28 Gordon Rohlehr, 'Man's Spiritual Search in the Caribbean Through Literature', in *Troubling of the Waters*, ed. Idris Hamid, San Fernando, Trinidad: W. I. Rahaman Printery Limited, 1973.

29 Noel L. Erskine, *From Garvey to Marley: Rastafari Theology*, Gainesville, FL: University of Florida Press, 2005.

30 Delroy Reid-Salmon, *Home Away from Home: The Caribbean Diasporan Church in the Black Atlantic Tradition*, London: Equinox, 2008.

31 Miller, 'He Said I Was Out of Pocket'.

32 Michael Jagessar, 'Spinning Theology: Trickster, Texts and Theology', in *Postcolonial Black British Theology: New Textures and Themes*, ed. Michael Jagessar and Anthony Reddie, Peterborough: Epworth Press, 2007, p. 129; emphasis original.

3

From 'Troubling of the Waters' to 'Overcoming Self-Negation'

Setting the Context

It is important to set the scene before trying to make sense of the literary output of the region in any formal sense. We have established that the region was shaped by the historical realities of European colonial expansion, plantation slavery and continued political, economic and cultural oppression in forms such as indentureship and continued dependency on political economies outside the region. Christianity, and therefore the Church, has been deeply shaped by these experiences, and Caribbean Theology inevitably emerges from this milieu. The title of this chapter contains the title of what can be considered the seminal compilation of Caribbean theological reflections (1973) and the title of my first book, as one of the more recent contributions to Caribbean Contextual Theology (2020).[1] Before examining the scholarship in between these two publications, it is important to state that many regional and transnational political and theological movements have been antecedents to any formal sense of Caribbean Theology. It is helpful to name a few of these.

The Haitian Revolution

This is naturally a starting point for political but also theological questions in the region. The unprecedented triumph over Napoleon in France's prized colony, and Haiti's declaration of independence of Europe, became the impetus for anti-colonial reactions across the region. Little Haiti became the first Black republic in the world. This was simultaneously a political, cultural and theological revolt and cast a long shadow over any theological conversations in the region for centuries to come.

Emancipation

The entire process of full emancipation of slaves in the British West Indies, from slave revolts across the colonies to the abolition of the slave trade (1807), to the Act of Emancipation (1833), to Emancipation celebrations in the colonies (1838), signalled the end of an overt form of empire and its consequences for liberated Africans and their descendants. The word 'overt' is used intentionally since it can be easily argued, and has been by many in the region, that imperial oppression continued over the colonies in different ways after emancipation. Other and even more pernicious forms of abusive control persisted. But emancipation signalled the need for a theological conversation on the morality of the institution of enslavement, but also, and perhaps more importantly, theological questions regarding the African person and their place within the European theological imagination.

Labour and Industrial Strikes across the Region

The 1930s and early 1940s across the British colonies witnessed nationwide industrial protests. The racist and classist political structures of these plantation societies inevitably led to a minority, usually White, business class, exercising abusive power and control over a majority, usually Black, worker class. Trade Unions were set up and civil and industrial unrest, with the majority agitating for their rights to a better life, led to huge political changes. It is within this period that political, educational and even ecclesiastical leadership became increasingly Black.

The Second World War and Migration

The Second World War, like the First, left European nations in need of rebuilding. Within the British West Indies, with the advent of the war soldiers were recruited from across the colonies, the Caribbean being a natural place for such recruitment. After the war, scouts returned to the region seeking persons, particularly young men, to work in England and rebuild the country. The SS *Empire Windrush* took the first of these new migrants to Britain in 1948. This began the first of a wave of new migrants to Britain, eventually making Europe their home and facing continual racism and xenophobia, especially within the churches. In a similar vein, the post-war period saw the migration of many Caribbean people to Europe and North America seeking a better life for themselves and their families.

The Civil Rights Movement in the USA

The American Civil Rights Movement in the 1960s gained international attention. By this time, life under Jim Crow laws in the USA had become unbearable for black persons. The iconic Martin Luther King Jr, and others, inspired a theological look at racism and the response to it. The development of Black Theology in the United States, particularly in the work of James H. Cone, furthered this theological attention to race and racism as sins deeply entrenched in American society.[2]

The Cuban Embargo

Also looming large over any theological imagination in the region is the clash of political ideas and outlooks in Cuba in the 1950s and 60s. Cuba's relationship with the United States became increasingly strained, with the eventual proclamation of a trade embargo between the USA and Cuba in 1962. In 1959 the Cuban revolution led to the formation of a one-party state and eventually the entrenching of power for the Cuban

Communist Party under Fidel Castro in 1965. Again, as with Haiti in 1804, revolution was in the air.

The Black Power Movement

The 1960s Civil Rights movement did not end racism in the United States. The 1970s saw the emergence of the Black Panther and Black Power movements. While the latter paid attention to the concepts of, for example, Malcolm X, the former advocated for the use of arms and violence to secure racial pride, autonomy and self-determination. This movement found resonance in the Caribbean, where the ideas of Marcus Garvey, Aimé Césaire, Frantz Fanon and Walter Rodney, for example, provided inspiration and intellectual foundations. The region has always had revolutionary intellectual thinking concurrent with but also pre-dating race relations in the United States.

Latin American Liberation Theologies

While movements for justice and reconciliation dominated North America, Central and South America would provide another example for Caribbean nations: liberation movements in Latin America and the development of Liberation Theology. Attention to the poor and marginalized as objects of cultural, political and theological exploitation, particularly by super-structures such as the Church and the government, inspired similar movements across the world. Theology was understood and exercised differently, from a different vantage point, and God was seen as liberator, not oppressor as had been the case previously. It is important to note here that the Caribbean has always had ways of doing theology, contesting colonial and imperial oppression. It is also important to state, as earlier, that while Latin American liberation is a regional example with many aligned interests and perspectives, it is nevertheless a very different context. Too often the Caribbean is subsumed into the wider geopolitical, cultural and historical boundaries of North or South America, without attention to the distinctive history and concerns of the region. Key texts by Kortright Davis, Lewin Williams and Noel Erskine all spend time disambiguating Caribbean Theology from Liberation Theology.[3]

Independence Exercises

The 1960s also saw the beginning of independence exercises across the region, beginning with Jamaica and Trinidad and Tobago in 1962. While not all former colonies have become independent, the 1960s began a change in formal relationship with what was the British Empire. Formal independence exercises meant a change in political and legal relationship, from colony to part of the Commonwealth, but many debates have persisted over the level of economic independence. Recently, Hilary Beckles, paying homage to Walter Rodney, teases out the continued and persisting asymmetrical relationship between Britain and its former colonies. He explores (as is the title of his book) *How Britain Underdeveloped the Caribbean: A Reparation Response to Europe's Legacy of Plunder and Poverty*.[4]

General Trends

It becomes clear that Caribbean Theology has a rich reservoir of historical events to feed robust and contextually relevant theological reflection. Too much has taken place within the region. General conceptual strands when considering theology in the region include the following:

- reactions and revolutions within empire;
- transnational political clashes between capitalism and communism;
- migration and dislocation and the formation of diasporas;
- African identify, the trauma of racism and xenophobia;
- nation-building and regional development;
- the development of a robust theology to address all these concerns.

Kortright Davis reminds us that the 1960s was also a time when missionaries began retreating from the region and churches and their leadership started to become increasingly Black.[5] African slaves and their descendants always, and to varying degrees, interpreted and transformed Christianity into a force for spiritual sustenance and social survival. The 1970s, then, would begin a formal period of Caribbean theological reflection.

1970s ... an Energizing

The political unrest of the 1960s and the emergence of the Black Power movement in the Caribbean in the 1970s, along with questions around self-determination and indigenous expressions, needed a theological emergence. The Caribbean Conference of Churches (CCC) was established in Kingston, Jamaica. It was the successor to the first ecumenical agency, the Caribbean Committee on Joint Christian Action (CCJCA), which was further strengthened in the 1971 ecumenical consultation in Chaguaramas, Trinidad. While the CCC's aims are to 'promote ecumenism and social change in obedience to Jesus Christ and in solidarity with the poor', the seeds of a formal Caribbean Theology began to be formed.[6] At the CCC's inception in 1973 it comprised 16 major Christian denominations, representing the four major language groups in the region. Certainly, by the 1990s the CCC had been the largest pan-Caribbean effort addressing crises within the region. Its goal and activities were to:

- promote a spirit of self-reliance;
- provide catalysts for regional development efforts;
- contribute to the material well-being of the poorer classes;
- promote wider participation in the social and political process.

Out of the period of the 1970s key compilations featuring the sharpest theological minds in the region at the time sought to address the goals cited above. First, edited by Idris Hamid, *Troubling of the Waters* (1973) brought together prominent Caribbean intellectuals to look at the issues surrounding authentic theological reflection in the region.[7] Many of the issues surrounding colonialism were examined, and the need for grass-roots means of theological engagement was pointed out. In the collection, some, like William Watty, Ashley Smith and Earl Augustus, looked at the theme of decolonization and the efficacy and significance of the Black Power movement.[8] This compilation also featured the writings of Knolly Clarke, Gordon Rohlehr, Joseph Owens, Horace Russell and Robert Moore.[9]

The main concern of *Out of the Depths* (1977), also edited by Idris Hamid, was missiology within the Caribbean context. Astonishingly, no significant attempts were made to investigate fully how African religiocultural retentions would be able to assist the missiological concerns of the Church in the Caribbean.[10] Contributors mainly addressed the pervasive issue of colonialism within the region and the need to decolonize. These sets of reflections featured the writings of Kortright Davis, Terry Julien, Geoffrey B. Williams and Patrick A. B. Anthony.[11]

In this decade, perhaps the work of Idris Hamid himself looms largest. In 1971 Hamid was one of the contributors to the Caribbean Ecumenical Consultation for Development. His paper, 'In Search of New Perspectives', critiqued the theological methodology current in the region, asserting that the Eurocentric perspective needed to be broken.[12] Furthermore, he engaged with the writings of Earl Lovelace as an interlocutor for critiquing dualist, essentialist, hierarchical and colonial theological methodology. His contribution to *With Eyes Wide Open* would emphasize the key theme of Caribbean Theology.[13] It is also important to name the significance of Ashley Smith (*Real Roots and Potted Plants: Reflections on the Caribbean Church*) and William Watty (*From Shore to Shore: Soundings in a Caribbean Theology*), both of whom have been guiding theological conversations throughout the region since the 1970s.[14] The contributions of Smith and Watty to Caribbean Theology cannot be overstated. A recent publication has been devoted to Smith, framing him as a Caribbean prophet and public theologian.[15] Another publication from the 1970s worth mentioning here is Edmund Davis's *Real Roots and Blossoms*.[16]

1980s ... the Lost Decade

Unfortunately, the energy of the 1970s was not sustained in the 1980s. Caribbean theologians came to describe this as the lost decade. In discussing this lapse, Gerald Boodoo states:

> Increased economic viability and the multiplicity of projects only served to fill the void of our Caribbean theological reflection with things and lots of busy-ness. Yet, now in the nineties, all this theological busy-ness has left us no further along the road than the seventies.[17]

What Boodoo is pointing to is the perennial issue of funding. Development projects took precedence over theological initiatives and publications. Eventually, it became clear that theological advancement in the region was largely depending on outside investment.

1990s ... a Resurgence?

In the 1990s African religiocultural retentions came to the forefront of Caribbean theological reflection through a number of important consultations and conferences. In 1992 the Caribbean/African American Dialogue (CAAD) met in Barbados and produced the Verdun Proclamation, which clearly highlighted, among other things, indigenous clergy disparaging their ancestral heritages. In 1993 the Consultation on Theological Education in the Caribbean was held in Jamaica and published under the title *Caribbean Theology: Preparing for the Challenges Ahead.*[18] Issues such as identity, integration and new ways of doing and teaching theology within the Caribbean were explored. In 1994 the CCC held the ecumenical consultation on popular religiosity in Suriname, which was published as *At the Crossroads: African Caribbean Religion and Christianity.*[19] This consultation sought to increase awareness of the religious and cultural diversity of the region and the need for the Church to dialogue with this reality.

The 1990s also saw the publication of key Caribbean Theology textbooks. Kortright Davis's *Emancipation Still Comin'* (1990) argued for a contextual theology considering Caribbean-specific realities under the banner of emancipation.[20] Lewin Williams' *Caribbean Theology* (1994) sought to give conceptual foundations for a robust theology that could compete internationally.[21] Noel Erskine's *Decolonizing Theology* (1998) engaged fully with the theme of decolonization as a framework and goal for Caribbean theological reflection.[22]

Contemporary Texts and Foci

For the past 20 or so years there have been disparate publications and research. Inevitably, scholars have had to further their own academic interests. Attention has moved away from reflections on development to more interior conversations on culture and identity. Contemporary reflections tend to prioritize motifs such as decolonization, identity, culture and African Traditional Religious Heritages. Some more contemporary voices over this 20–25-year period include Barry Chevannes, George Mulrain, Michael Jagessar, Anna Kasafi Perkins, Dianne Stewart, Stephen Jennings, Charles Jason Gordon, Kirkley Sands and me, Carlton Turner. The work of these scholars will be explored to varying degrees in the subsequent chapters of this book.

With regard to PhD research projects, it is important to note that Caribbean scholars have completed further research across the broad spectrum of theological disciplines. Many of these theses have been conducted in British universities and are significant contributions to Caribbean intellectual life. Examples of these include Charles Jason Gordon,[23] Donald Chambers,[24] Karen Durant,[25] John Rogers,[26] Mikie Roberts,[27] Marjorie Lewis,[28] Winelle Kirton-Roberts,[29] Oral Thomas,[30] Novelle Josiah,[31] and my own work on Junkanoo and the Church in the Bahamian context.[32] By no means is this an exhaustive list. And many others can be added to this canon of work. What is evident is that these scholars approach the theological task from different perspectives. In their writing and research, we find

Biblical Studies, Contextual Theology, Systematic Theology, Political or Public Theology, Practical Theology, Historical Theology, and Ethics.

Important Observations and Absences

There are some important gaps to note. The following areas must be addressed if Caribbean Theology is to be viable for decades to come. First, there need to be more contributions by women of the Caribbean. Chapter 7 is devoted to the contributions of women in the Caribbean who have been consistently challenging colonial and patriarchal narratives in African Caribbean life. Second, there is a blatant absence of Pentecostal research and theological articulation. Much of the attention within Caribbean theological conversations has come from Anglicans, Baptists, Methodists, Roman Catholics and United Reformed (URC) traditions. Pentecostalism in the region, and its connection to African Caribbean traditional and religious cultural heritages, remains a rich and underexplored area for Caribbean theological reflection. Third, there is too much of a history of separatism. Academic theology in the Caribbean context that was initiated by the CCC struggles in its present manifestation to engage effectively the different islands, let alone the different denominations. However, an ongoing and vibrant conference does exist and is worth attention: The Conference on Theology in the Caribbean Today.[33] Fourth, there is the ongoing reality of brain-drain. Many capable and gifted theologians have had to migrate to Western metropolitan centres to sharpen their skills. Finally, there is an ongoing lack of investment in research and publication. Many theologians must find scholarships or resource their own postgraduate training research.

Various Approaches

An important point to make is that Caribbean theologians are by no means a monolithic group. Distinct personalities, from different decades since the mid-twentieth century, have been responding to concrete realities using the tools afforded them. This has meant that theology in the region has always advanced contextually, and while the historical theological output hasn't been too abundant, there is a rich diversity of perspectives. Ultimately, I argue for interdisciplinary perspectives in Caribbean Theology, but for now it would be helpful to offer some broad approaches existing in the region. This broad framing is simply that, a loose frame in order to bring clarity to the existing works. It is inevitable that these approaches overlap tremendously.

Contextual Theologies

While Caribbean theologians are doing Contextual Theology by definition, below are examples of theologians who ground their reflections in the concrete human situation and then proceed to speak to universal concerns. Two examples to begin with are Barry Chevannes and Joseph Owens and their work on the Rastafari of Jamaica. As an early contributor to *Troubling of the Waters*, Joseph Owens highlights the persecution of Rastafarians in the Jamaican context and its similarity to the persecutions of the early Christians in ancient Rome. Along with their powerful countercultural presence and their critique of religion and the Church, Owens also highlights their success at rehabilitating the self-image of the black person, while preaching an 'all-embracing universalism'.[34] His book, *Dread: The Rastafarians of Jamaica*, remains a classic text on Rastafari. Barry Chevannes, a noted Jamaican sociologist and anthropologist, has contributed to Caribbean theological thought by integrating theology and the social sciences. He argues for a theology embedded within African Caribbean culture, since Caribbean reality is principally 'shaped by Africa'.[35] He further suggests that two things are required for the Church to become indigenous: 'a liturgy which is culturally meaningful; and a theology which begins to reflect at least some of the spiritual values which are deeply embedded in our culture'.[36] With Chevannes in sight, we must also highlight the cultural and anthropological work of Nathaniel Murell's *Afro-Caribbean Religions* and particularly his edited work with William Spencer and Adrian McFarlane, *Chanting Down Babylon: A Rastafari Reader*.[37]

Noel Erskine should also be in this bracket with his books *Decolonizing Theology* and *From Garvey to Marley*.[38] However, we will consider him below. Dianne Stewart, also Jamaican, remains an important and distinctive voice within any indigenous theological approach in the region. Considering herself a 'theographer', she explains that there are two antithetical theological grammars at work within African Jamaican religious life: Missionary Christianity and Myalism.[39] This becomes clear in her *Three Eyes for the Journey*.[40] In this work Stewart posits the rationale for her research, looking to Myal and Kumina as means of bringing about anthropological wholeness, combating the pervasive anthropological poverty, anti-Africanness and Afrophobia perpetuated by Missionary Christianity. She also challenges the work of Noel Erskine and Lewin Williams for not dealing extensively with African religiocultural retentions and bringing a Christian bias to their work, one which overlooks the direct culpability of the Church in the African Caribbean in its anti-African practices. She accuses Williams of being too superficial in his treatment of folk religion as he fails to deal extensively with the 'protracted, pernicious censoring and vilification of African culture and religion across the Caribbean'.[41] Regarding theological approach, she argues for a 'transdisciplinary' approach as necessary for Africana religious studies.[42]

In the Bahamian context, Kirkley Sands and I have paid attention to the African indigenous spirituality within Bahamian national, cultural and theological life. Looking at the Junkanoo festival in the Bahamas and his wider work on Bahamian Slave Spirituality, Sands frames the festival as 'deeply rooted in Bahamian slave spirituality, traditional West African religiosity, and impacted by English Christianity'.[43] He also highlights its innate relationship with the Church in Bahamian society and sees the theological implications of Junkanoo as being its incarnational means of mediating the biblical revelation of Jesus Christ. My work theorizes the relationship between Junkanoo (and other African Traditional Religious Heritages) and the Christian Church in the Bahamas as a self-negating one. There is an entrenched dynamic wherein African religious and cultural productions are vilified, even though embracing them would mean a revitalization, even reformation, of Christianity in the region.

Political Theologies

The political dimension of theology has come to the forefront in theologies that consider the impact of empire and the wars that ensue as a result of imperial expansion. Political theology has been a rising discourse in academia and noted scholars have been and continue to be helpful, for example Jione Havea, *Religion and Power: Theology in the Age of Empire*; Mark G. Brett, *Political Trauma and Healing: Biblical Ethics for a Postcolonial World*; Walter Brueggemann, *The Prophetic Imagination*; and John Hull, *Towards the Prophetic Church*.[44] However, from inception, Caribbean Theologies were birthed in political discourse, being aware of the complicated allegiances and dependent relationships with global superpowers such as Europe and North America. *Troubling of the Waters* sets the tone, with key thinkers such as Idris Hamid engaging in what could only be described as a regional political theology. William Watty's contribution to both *Troubling of the Waters* and *Out of the Depths*, and his publication *From Shore to Shore: Soundings in a Caribbean Theology*, foreground the political situatedness of the region. Finally, Kortright Davis's best-known work, *Emancipation Still Comin'*, wrestles politically with the complex land- and seascapes of the region and argues for a central metaphor or point of reflection that best galvanizes the Caribbean experience, that of 'emancipation'.

This rise of decolonial and postcolonial theologies stands alongside Caribbean theologians who have used such lenses in their reflections explicitly. Examples of these are the works of Robert Hood, *Must God Remain Greek?*; Noel Erskine, *Decolonizing Theology*; Oral Thomas, *Biblical Resistance in a Caribbean Context*; and Michael Jagessar, 'Spinning Theology: Trickster, Texts and Theology'.[45]

Biblical Studies

Caribbean theologians have always taken the Bible seriously, paying attention to questions around hermeneutics. For example, two theologians who attend to how the Bible is interpreted are George Mulrain and Oral Thomas. For Mulrain, Caribbean hermeneutical techniques involve use of the historico-critical method to understand the original context of the Bible; the interpretative lens of the reader and his/her community context; the interaction between the text of Scripture and the lived experiences of Caribbean peoples – 'slavery, oppression, colonialism, suffering, victimization, marginalization, anonymity'; the awareness of the multi-faith reality of Caribbean life; a commitment to liberation; and an insistence on hope.[46] Thomas's *Biblical Resistance Hermeneutics in a Caribbean Context* notes that Sam Sharpe, Paul Bogle and Marcus Garvey, as examples, represent biblical interpretative strategy for the 'concrete socio-economic transformation of oppressive social systems and practices'.[47] Others have carried out doctoral research in biblical studies but there is scope for further research in this area. For now, there is John Roger's PhD thesis on the book of Deuteronomy and his concept of 'Siege Mentality', and Karen Durant's PhD on the Psalms and their implications for ethics in light of the principle of the 'Imitation of God'.[48]

Intercultural Theologies

While culture or enculturation are inevitably part of any conversation in the region, and these are inherently part of any kind of Contextual Theology, there is a need to highlight the importance of intercultural work that is necessary within the region. The formative text for this kind of engagement is the compilation *At the Crossroads: African Caribbean Religion and Christianity*, edited by Burton Sankeralli.[49] This consultation on interfaith dialogue in the region in 1993 directly explored the divergence of spiritualities and even religions in the region, including Islam and Hinduism, while Noel Erskine's *Decolonizing Theology*, as well as Kortright Davis's *Emancipation Still Comin'*, both spend time exploring African Traditional Religious Heritages in the region. Perhaps the two best examples of this emphasis on interculturality are Dianne Stewart in her study of Myalism within the Jamaican Context, *Three Eyes for the Journey*, and George Mulrain in his study of Haitian Vodou in *Theology in Folk Culture*, as well as his work on Caribbean Calypso.[50]

Liturgical Theologies

With a lively and vibrant singing and cultural tradition, there is also scope for further liturgical work within the region. Part of inheriting missionary church traditions has always been the requirement for indigenous regional styles and liturgies. Early on, Knolly Clarke expressed the need for an indigenous liturgy that connected to inner life, native language and daily experiences of Caribbean people. Being Trinidadian, he proposed the use of a Calypso Mass for that setting and the use of steel bands to replace inherited Mass settings and pipe organs.[51] Mikie Roberts' PhD remains foundational as a work looking particularly at liturgy within the Caribbean context. Considering hymnody and identity, he argues that congregational singing is fundamental to the formation of identity, looking particularly at Caribbean contexts and the sole ecumenical hymnal in the Caribbean, *Sing a New Song*. He advances an attractive concept, 'hymnic performativity', which is 'the notion that as congregations sing hymns they are engaging in a unique activity (hymnic performativity) in which as they make music through hymn singing, the music is also at work shaping and forming the congregations' communal identity'.[52]

Historical Theology

Many theologians within the region have engaged with historical methodologies in order to deepen their theological gaze. Key
figures in Caribbean church history such as Arthur C. Dayfoot,
The Shaping of West Indian Church 1492 to 1962, and Dale
Bisnauth, *A History of Religions in the Caribbean*, sit alongside
more specific and localized historical reflections.[53] For example,
Sehon Goodridge's *Facing the Challenge of Emancipation*
explores the first bishops of the Caribbean, specifically William
Hart Coleridge of Barbados, and Kortright Davis explores late
nineteenth-century political religion in the Caribbean in his
Cross and Crown in Barbados.[54] Etienne Bowleg looks at the
influence of the Oxford Movement on the Church of England
in the Caribbean.[55] Noel Titus explores the condition of slavery
in the region in his *The Amelioration and Abolition of Slavery
in Trinidad, 1812–1834: Experiments and Protests in a New
Slave Colony*, and *Mission in a Volatile Society: Reflections
on Christian Churches in Caribbean Slave Societies*.[56] Winelle
Kirton-Roberts' *Created in their Image: Evangelical Protestantism in Antigua and Barbados, 1834–1914* remains one of the
most recent historical pieces of research to be published.[57]

Systematic Theologies

While there might be tensions between systematic and philosophical theologies arising from Europe and contextual theologies
arising from the Global South, there is always interplay between
the two. Systematic theologians are always contextually situated, and contextual theologians, in most cases, are reacting
and responding to the European philosophical traditions as they
have shaped non-European contexts. Most Caribbean theologians have had to do their research and reflection in Western
metropoles and have to wrestle with both approaches. With
this said, these are some examples of theologies seeking systematic approaches to Caribbean theological discourse. Lewin
Williams' investigation into Caribbean Theology, in his text by

the same name, begins with the contextual issues of colonialism and neocolonialisms in which Missionary Christianity has played big parts. However, in the second part of his book he looks at the sources of a Caribbean Theology. His sources are history, sociology and philosophy. He seeks to systematize his work. Donald Chambers is an example of a systematic theologian whose PhD and subsequent writings aim to articulate a constructive Christology for the Caribbean.[58] Marjorie Lewis's theological research also merits attention. She explains:

> Against the background of injustice in contemporary British society and the legacy of colonialism, and the inherited values of diasporic African culture and world views, the women's views on God, the nature and vocation of humanity, evil, suffering and salvation, are discussed. An underlying search for truth and belief in the existence of God are unifying motive and assumption in the quest for spiritual development.[59]

Majorie Lewis continues to contribute to what can be described as 'Nannyish Theology', describing it as a Liberation Theology coming out of the experience of Jamaican women, named after Nanny of the Maroons, a Jamaican freedom fighter.[60] Michael Miller takes a philosophical approach to Caribbean Theology through his concept of 'dialectical contextualism', engaging with questions about theological method and how only a dialectical approach to context makes sense within a region as complex as the Caribbean or, in fact, any context.[61]

Towards Interdisciplinary Approaches

Interdisciplinarity, central to contextual theologies, is perhaps *the* characteristic of Caribbean theologies. The complexity of the region requires multiple methodologies and approaches. However, what is needed is an intentional engagement with other disciplines. One of the bigger issues with European theology is the dependence on Western philosophical thought, often at the expense of local knowledges and indigenous epistemologies.

Engaging other disciplines, such as the social sciences, psychological sciences or trauma studies, might prove helpful. There is space to create new and more robust approaches to theological research in the region, especially when considering the innovative thinking there in the works of, for example, Sylvia Wynter, Frantz Fanon, Walter Rodney and Carolyn Cooper.[62] We now move to Part 2 of this book, which attempts to put some of these complex dynamics and diverse scholarship to work in a set of theological reflections.

Notes

1 See Idris Hamid (ed.), *Troubling of the Waters*, San Fernando, Trinidad: W. I. Rahaman Printery Ltd, 1973. See Carlton Turner, *Overcoming Self-Negation: The Church and Junkanoo in Contemporary Bahamian Society*, Eugene, OR: Pickwick Publications, 2020.

2 James H. Cone, *God of the Oppressed*, New York: Seabury Press, 1975. James H. Cone, *A Black Theology of Liberation*, 40th Anniversary edn, Maryknoll, NY: Orbis Books, 2010.

3 Kortright Davis, *Emancipation Still Comin': Explorations in Caribbean Emancipatory Theology*, Maryknoll, NY: Orbis Books, 1990. Lewin L. Williams, *Caribbean Theology*, New York: Peter Lang, 1994. Noel L. Erskine, *Decolonizing Theology: A Caribbean Perspective*, Trenton, NJ: Africa World Press, 1998.

4 Hilary Beckles, *How Britain Underdeveloped the Caribbean: A Reparation Response to Europe's Legacy of Plunder and Poverty*, Jamaica: The University of the West Indies Press, 2021.

5 Davis, *Emancipation Still Comin'*.

6 See CCC website: https://www.oikoumene.org/organization/caribbean-conference-of-churches (accessed 14.7.23).

7 Hamid, *Troubling of the Waters*.

8 William Watty, 'The De-Colonization of Theology', in *Troubling of the Waters*, ed. Hamid. Ashley Smith, 'The Religious Significance of Black Power in the Caribbean', in *Troubling of the Waters*, ed. Hamid. Earl Augustus, 'The Spiritual Significance of Black Power in the Christian Churches', in *Troubling of the Waters*, ed. Hamid.

9 Knolly Clarke, 'Liturgy and Culture in the Caribbean', in *Troubling of the Waters*, ed. Hamid. Gordon Rohlehr, 'Man's Spiritual Search in the Caribbean through Literature', in *Troubling of the Waters*, ed. Hamid. Joseph Owens, 'The Rastafarians of Jamaica', in *Troubling of the Waters*, ed. Hamid. Horace Russell, 'The Challenge of Theo-

logical Reflection in the Caribbean', in *Troubling of the Waters*, ed. Hamid. Robert Moore, 'The Historical Basis of Theological Reflection', in *Troubling of the Waters*, ed. Hamid.

10 Idris Hamid (ed.), *Out of the Depths*, San Fernando, Trinidad: Rahaman Printery Ltd, 1977.

11 Kortright Davis, 'Theological Education for Mission', in *Out of the Depths*, ed. Hamid. Terry Julien, 'Christian Mission, Cultural Traditions and Environment', in *Out of the Depths*, ed. Hamid. Geoffrey B. Williams, 'Classicism and the Caribbean Church', in *Out of the Depths*, ed. Hamid. Patrick A. B. Anthony, 'A Case Study in Indigenization', in *Out of the Depths*, ed. Hamid.

12 Idris Hamid, 'In Search of New Perspectives', Caribbean Ecumenical Consultation for Development, Bridgetown, Barbados, 1971.

13 David Mitchell (ed.), *With Eyes Wide Open*, Barbados: CADEC, 1973.

14 Ashley Smith, *Real Roots and Potted Plants: Reflections on the Caribbean Church*, Mandeville, Jamaica: Eureka Press, 1984. William Watty, *From Shore to Shore: Soundings in Caribbean Theology*, Kingston, Jamaica: Cedar Press, 1981.

15 Roderick R. Hewitt, Hopeton S. Dunn and Jane Dodman, *Caribbean Prophet: The Public Theology of Ashley Smith*, Kingston, Jamaica: Ian Randall Publishers, 2022.

16 Edmund Davis, *Roots and Blossoms*, Bridgetown, Barbados: Cedar Press, 1977.

17 Gerald Boodoo, 'In Response to Adolfo Ham (1)', in *Caribbean Theology: Preparing for the Challenges Ahead*, ed. Howard Gregory, Barbados: Canoe Press, 1995, p. 9.

18 Gregory, *Caribbean Theology*.

19 Burton Sankeralli (ed.), *At the Crossroads: African Caribbean Religion and Christianity*, St James, Trinidad and Tobago: Caribbean Conference of Churches, 1995.

20 Davis, *Emancipation Still Comin'*.

21 Williams, *Caribbean Theology*.

22 Erskine, *Decolonizing Theology*.

23 Charles Jason Gordon, 'Theology, Hermeneutics and Liberation: Grounding Theology in a Caribbean Context', PhD thesis, University of London, 2003.

24 Donald Dean Chambers, 'The Faces of Jesus Christ in the Literary Works of Caribbean Preachers and Theologians: Towards a Constructive Christology for the Caribbean', PhD thesis, Pontificia Università Gregoriana, 2005.

25 Karen Elizabeth Durant, 'Imitation of God as a Principle for Ethics Today: A Study of Selected Psalms', PhD thesis, University of Birmingham, 2010.

26 John Augustine Rogers, 'Siege-Mentality and the Book of Deuteronomy', PhD thesis, University of Birmingham, 2019.

27 Mikie Anthony Roberts, 'Hymnody and Identity: Congregational Singing as a Construct of Christian Communty Identity', PhD thesis, University of Birmingham, 2014.

28 Marjorie Lewis, 'Towards a Systematic Spirituality of Black British Women', PhD thesis, University of Birmingham, 2007.

29 See the published version of her thesis: Winelle J. Kirton-Roberts, *Created in their Image: Evangelical Protestantism in Antigua and Barbados, 1834–1914*, Bloomington, IN: AuthorHouse, 2015.

30 See the published version of his thesis: Oral Thomas, *Biblical Resistance Hermeneutics within a Caribbean Context*, London: Equinox, 2010.

31 Novelle Josiah, 'The Develoment of Calypso in Antigua and its Continuity with Old Testament Traditions', unpublished MPhil thesis, University of the West Indies, 2003.

32 See the published version of my PhD thesis: Turner, *Overcoming Self-Negation*.

33 The Conference on Theology in the Caribbean Today is a group of Caribbean persons of faith who over the last 25 years have struggled to provide a 'free and open space' for theological reflection grounded in the daily lives of ordinary people while forging deep personal and spiritual relationships in an ongoing exploration and sharing of our Caribbean religious experiences. See: https://ctctoday.org/ (accessed 15.7.23).

34 Owens, 'The Rastafarians of Jamaica', p. 166.

35 Barry Chevannes, 'Our Caribbean Reality', in *Caribbean Theology*, ed. Gregory, p. 65. See also, Barry Chevannes, *Rastafari: Roots and Ideology*, Syracuse, NY: Syracuse University Press, 1995.

36 Barry Chevannes, 'Towards an Afro-Caribbean Theology: The Principles for the Indigenisation of Christianity in the Caribbean', *Caribbean Quarterly* 37, no. 1, 1991, p. 46.

37 Nathaniel Samuel Murrell, *Afro-Caribbean Religions: An Introduction to their Historical, Cultural, and Sacred Traditions*, Philadelphia, PA: Temple University Press, 2010. Nathaniel Samuel Murrell, William David Spencer and Adrian Anthony McFarlane (eds), *Chanting Down Babylon: The Rastafari Reader*, Philadelphia, PA: Temple University Press, 1998.

38 Erskine, *Decolonizing Theology*; Noel L. Erskine, *From Garvey to Marley: Rastafari Theology*, Gainesville, FL: University of Florida Press, 2005.

39 Don Saliers et al., 'Ethnography and Theology: A Critical Roundtable Discussion', *Practical Matters* 3, Spring 2010.

40 Dianne M. Stewart, *Three Eyes for the Journey: African Dimensions of the Jamaican Religious Experience*, Oxford: Oxford University Press, 2004.

41 Stewart, *Three Eyes for the Journey*, p. 214.

42 See Dianne M. Stewart-Diakité and Tracey E. Hucks, 'Africana Religious Studies: Towards a Transdisciplinary Agenda in an Emerging Field', *Journal of Africana Studies* 1, no. 1, 2013.

43 Etienne E. Bowleg, 'Liturgical Implications of Junkanoo', in *Junkanoo and Religion: Christianity and Cultural Identity in the Bahamas*, Nassau: Media Enterprises, 2003. Kirkley C. Sands, 'Junkanoo in Historical Perspective', in *Junkanoo and Religion*, p. 17. Turner, *Overcoming Self-Negation*.

44 Walter Brueggemann, *The Prophetic Imagination*, 2nd edn, Minneapolis, MN: Fortress Press, 2001. Mark G. Brett, *Political Trauma and Healing: Biblical Ethics for a Postcolonial World*, Grand Rapids, MI: Eerdmans, 2016. Jione Havea, *Religion and Power: Theology in the Age of Empire*, Lanham, MD: Lexington Books/Fortress Academic, 2018. John Hull, *Towards the Prophetic Church: A Study of Christian Mission*, London: SCM Press, 2014.

45 See Robert Hood, *Must God Remain Greek? Afro Cultures and God-talk*, Minneapolis, MN: Fortress Press, 1990. Erskine, *Decolonizing Theology*. Thomas, *Biblical Resistance Hermeneutics*. Michael Jagessar, 'Spinning Theology: Trickster, Texts and Theology', in *Postcolonial Black British Theology: New Textures and Themes*, ed. Michael Jagessar and Anthony Reddie, Peterborough: Epworth, 2007.

46 George Mulrain, 'Hermeneutics within a Caribbean Context', in *Vernacular Hermeneutics*, ed. R. S. Sugirtharajah, Sheffield: Sheffield Academic Press, 1999, pp. 121–4.

47 Thomas, *Biblical Resistance Hermeneutics*, p. 59. Interestingly, Thomas also speaks of a 'hermeneutic of authentic self-affirmation' being appropriated within the Caribbean context as part of resistance. He traces it in the religiosity and philosophy of Rastafarianism. Thomas, *Biblical Resistance Hermeneutics*, pp. 44–6.

48 Rogers, 'Siege-Mentality'. Durant, 'Imitation of God as a Principle for Ethics Today'.

49 Burton Sankeralli (ed.), *At the Crossroads: African Caribbean Religion and Christianity*, St James, Trinidad and Tobago: Caribbean Conference of Churches, 1995.

50 Stewart, *Three Eyes for the Journey*. See also George Mulrain, *Theology in Folk Culture: The Theological Significance of Haitian Folk Religion*, Frankfurt: Peter Lang, 1984. George Mulrain, 'Is There a Calypso Exegesis?', in *Voices from the Margin: Interpreting the Bible in the Third World*, ed. R. S. Sugirtharajah, Maryknoll, NY: Orbis Books, 1995.

51 Clarke, 'Liturgy and Culture in the Caribbean'.

52 Roberts, 'Hymnody and Identity'.

53 Arthur C. Dayfoot, *The Shaping of the West Indian Church 1492–1962*, Kingston, Jamaica: University of the West Indies Press, 1999. Dale

Bisnauth, *A History of Religions in the Caribbean*, Kingston: Kingston Publishers Ltd, 1989.

54 Sehon S. Goodridge, *Facing the Challenge of Emancipation: A Study of the Ministry of William Hart Coleridge, First Bishop of Barbados, 1824–1842*, Barbados: Cedar Press, 1981. Kortright Davis, *Cross and Crown in Barbados: Caribbean Political Religion in the Late 19th Century*, Eugene, OR: Wipf & Stock, 1983.

55 Etienne Bowleg, 'The Influence of the Oxford Movement Upon the Church of England in the Province of the West Indies', PhD thesis, McGill University, 1986.

56 Noel Titus, *The Amelioration and Abolition of Slavery in Trinidad, 1812–1834: Experiments and Protests in a New Slave Colony*, Bloomington, IN: AuthorHouse, 2009. Noel Titus, *Mission in a Volatile Society: Reflections on Christian Churches in Caribbean Slave Societies*, London: Blessed Hope Publishing, 2017.

57 Kirton-Roberts, *Created in their Image*.

58 Chambers, 'The Faces of Jesus Christ in the Literary Works of Caribbean Preachers and Theologians'.

59 Lewis, 'Towards a Systematic Spirituality of Black British Women'.

60 Marjorie Lewis, 'Diaspora Dialogue: Womanist Theology in Engagement with Aspects of the Black British and Jamaican Experience', *Black Theology: An International Journal* 2, no. 1, 2004.

61 Michael St A. Miller, 'He Said I Was Out of Pocket: On Being a Caribbean Contextual Theologian in a Non-Caribbean Context', *Black Theology: An International Journal* 9, no. 2, 2011. Michael A. Miller, *Reshaping the Contextual Vision in Caribbean Theology: Theoretical Foundations for Theology which is Contextual, Pluralistic, and Dialectical*, Lanham, MD and Plymouth: University Press of America, 2007.

62 See, for example, Katherine McKittrick (ed.), *Sylvia Wynter: On Being Human as Praxis*, Durham, NC: Duke University Press, 2015; Frantz Fanon, *Black Skin, White Masks*, New York: Grove Press, 1967; Frantz Fanon, *The Wretched of the Earth*, Harmondsworth: Penguin, 1967; Walter Rodney, *How Europe Underdeveloped Africa*, London: Bogle-L'Ouverture Publications, 1972; Walter Rodney, *The Groundings with My Brothers*, London: Bogle-L'Ouverture Publications, 1969; Carolyn Cooper, *Noises in the Blood: Orality, Gender, and the 'Vulgar' Body of Jamaican Popular Culture*, 1st US edn, Durham, NC: Duke University Press, 1995.

Part 2

They say that the Caribbean is a sea. Yes!
I am an island in it.
Much blood
has spilled
In
That
Sea.
All the waters of humanity have washed my shores.
I am a Caribbean.
Yes I!
I am
A Caribbean.

Peter Minshall, 'Dear Promoter'[1]

---

1 Peter Minshall, *Dear Promoter (Official Short Film)*, 2020.

4

Columbus's Ghost:
Missionary Christianity
and its Aftermath

This chapter focuses specifically on an enduring and very much unaddressed feature of African Caribbean ecclesiastical life. It is this: Missionary Christianity has shaped the region, but particularly the African Caribbean Church. The depth of this colonial conditioning remains a growing theme within the region. In fact, precisely because of the region's connectedness with Britain's imperial legacies, some fundamental theological questions are asked about the very conceptualization of church in colonial and postcolonial contexts. In thinking about what it means to be church, theology, done anywhere, must be aware of its hidden assumptions. Missionary Christianity, for the most part, failed to recognize notions of superiority and certainty, which created huge problems across the Christian world. Sometimes the consequences were overt and deadly. At other times they were subtle, structural and compounding. What a Caribbean Theology does, and desires to do, is to pay attention to hidden assumptions about God, human beings, church, salvation and so on. This idea of 'paying attention' is key to this text, and to Caribbean theological refection generally.

1492 ...

The Bahamian playwright, author and academic Ian G. Strachan gave a lecture on tourism, art and identity in the Bahamas, referencing the importance of the New World encounter as still operative within contemporary Caribbean life.[1] For Strachan, 'Columbus's Ghost' explains the deep and pervasive power of fifteenth-century European imagination in all spheres of African Caribbean life, including, and perhaps especially, the Church. The year 1492 haunts contemporary Caribbean societies, mostly in costly ways to the peoples of the region. Columbus's landfall on the island of Guanahani (an island of what is now the Bahamas) on 12 October 1492 would set the precedent for all church–culture relations within the region. On encountering the indigenous Lucayans he records in his journal the following day:

> It appears to me, that the people are ingenious, and would be good servants and I am of opinion that they would very readily become Christians, as they appear to have no religion. They very quickly learn such words as are spoken to them. If it please our Lord, I intend at my return to carry home six of them to your Highnesses, that they may learn our language.[2]

This fateful moment led to what only can be considered the mass enslavement and genocide of the indigenous. Who were these people so easily considered as non-religious and servile? Hilary Beckles and Verene Shepherd offer this statement to help more adequately frame the region:

> Three thousand years before the Christian era a distinct Caribbean civilization was established. These civilizations had a strong influence on the peoples of the ancient world. They, together with other communities, helped shape the way society was organized, how work, money and the economy were planned, and how human culture was created and developed. Together with their continental cousins in Mexico, Guatemala, Peru and elsewhere, the ancient Caribbean communities engaged with and used their environment in dynamic and creative ways. The Caribbean, then, was home to an old and ancient cultural civilization that continues to shape and inform our present-day understanding and identity.[3]

Beckles and Shepherd further explain that archaeological excavation suggests a people settled the region as far back as 7000 BC. It is likely that they entered the region from Central America, since similar archaeological sites exist between what is now the Caribbean Islands and Nicaragua. It is also likely that in 1000 BC another group joined the Caribbean from what is now Venezuela. However, a broader question persists: How did people come to the Americas before Columbus in the first place? This has been a matter of debate. Since the sixteenth century it was thought that a migration of Asian people some 25,000 years ago passed over the Beringia land–ice bridge from Northern Europe to North America. However, this theory is being contested since there is some evidence that perhaps millions of years ago there were settlers already, and that during this period the American and African continents were connected, allowing for ease of migration. An important study on pre-Columbian New World civilization is Guyanese scholar Ivan van Sertima's, *They Came before Columbus*.[4]

Columbus's landfall was a traumatic rupture into history, culture, politics, religiosity and spirituality of the entire region. Clearly, civilization existed in the region long before his arrival. The region was configured differently, with complex cultural and political relationships between mainland dwellers and islanders. There were varieties of religious, linguistic and cultural differences. In short, there was pre-history before the arrival of the Europeans! But the question remains: Why so violent and disruptive? Why so traumatic?

These questions are important because when trying to decide upon timelines, or give some historicity to the region, we enter significant political, historical, geographical and cultural debates: Who 'owns' the land? Who demarcated/demarcates the region? Who were the first? Who gets to 'historicize' the region? Whose culture or which culture should be celebrated or prioritized?

At stated in Chapter 1, the coming of Columbus and thus the beginning of European expansion into the New World began a chain of traumatic events that saw the decimation of pre-Columbian people and led to the forced labour of non-Europeans, which in the course of time evolved into the institution of the enslavement of African people on a scale hitherto unknown. The very presentation of the Christian faith within this new and untouched setting was pathologically structured towards violence, since sword (or branding iron) and cross were inextricably linked.

What must be further understood is that the trading and enslavement of African peoples, at least within the mind of seventeenth-century Protestant English society, necessitated a particular kind of evangelization: a forced indoctrination of the Christian faith as practised within England. This is the second traumatic process. The very reception of Christianity itself was traumatic. This meant that hitherto religious systems needed a kind of exorcism through force, if not state-sanctioned capital punishment. In fact, African traditional religions and customs were taken seriously within plantation society. Such was the fear (or respect) of practices such as Obeah and Mayal in the Anglophone African Caribbean that these practices were criminalized, often with the penalty of death. Diana Paton and Maarit Forde explore how Anti-Obeah Laws across the Anglophone Caribbean perpetuated the long-held belief that African Traditional Religious Heritages were dangerous and antithetical to notions of truth, beauty, order and civility essentialized within the Church and colonial governance.[5] While the French *Code Noir* and the Spanish *Siete Partidas* mandated missionary instruction of slaves at the start of their colonial expansion, the English instituted the Jamaican Slave Codes and used it as their pattern for ensuring the instruction of slaves in the Christian faith. Dale Bisnauth explains that the 1696 Jamaican Slave Codes contrasted with the *Code Noir* and the *Siete Partidas* in its practice since, in the British colonies, slaves were not considered worthy of education and Christianization.[6]

Furthermore, England's establishment of itself in the Caribbean in 1624 was both political and ecclesiastical. The royal mandate of King Charles I of England was simultaneously about propagating the Christian religions as well as establishing territories under the direct rule of the crown.[7] Islands were organized into parishes, which reflected the political and ecclesiastical shaping of English society. This means that the final process of trauma was slaves adapting to a society totally alien to their homeland, ingesting the culture, language, thought patterns and religion of their new home: plantation society. Orlando Patterson gives a sociological account of plantation society within the Jamaican context and comes to an important insight that should always be borne in mind: that such societies were 'non-societies'.[8] What Patterson means is that they were not constructed for the flourishing of their inhabitants. These patterns include aspects of flourishing such as building family life and sustaining kinships, participating in the political process, engaging in commerce, and owning land or property. Patterson is clear: plantation society existed solely to produce economic profit. These were factories, not societies. A similar observation is given by Ian Strachan, who argues that the plantation never dissolved but re-emerged in the form of tourism where the myth of paradise still serves the ancient quest of Missionary Christianity and its settling of the New World. That quest was, and has always been, profit, which has always signified disastrous consequences for the indigenous populations and their ways of life.[9] By the mid-eighteenth century, British sugar plantations were doing very well, revolutionized by African slave labour. The demographics of plantation societies were made more complex by planters taking African women as mistresses, introducing what Dale Bisnauth describes as an increasing number of mulatto slaves, and a new class of 'Free people of Colour'.[10] The Church of England in these colonies remained undisturbed by other ecclesiastical bodies, and its outlook on African enslavement can best be described by Arthur C. Dayfoot:

The darkest blot upon the history of the established Church in the West Indies in this era is its failure to do anything effective about the welfare, either physical or spiritual, of the slaves. For the twentieth century it seems incredible that any Christian Church should have acquiesced in the practice of slavery or failed to offer the Gospel to any class of humanity. For the seventeenth century, on the other hand, slavery as an ancient and almost universal institution remained unchallenged either

by churches or national governments and only rare and isolated individuals had dared to question it in principle.[11]

The European Expansionist Christian World View

But, again, what lies behind this tendency towards violence and
domination? What we find thus far is a theology of non-being,
which equals the non-society in which the pre-Columbian
indigenous tribes and subsequent African slaves were to live.
The Western legacy of 'othering' non-European peoples with
their pre-Christian religious beliefs seems a natural consequence
or outworking of this theology of non-being. If the African
slave and his or her descendant is not fully human, then they
must be reminded of this designation in every sphere of their
existence. To understand the complex relationship more fully
between Christianity and indigenous and/or African cultures in
the Caribbean context we must understand some key termin-
ologies, movements or philosophies at the heart of European
civilization and European Christianity. Three movements come
to mind that intertwine to produce this kind of Christianity: the
Enlightenment, Rationalism and the Age of Discovery. While
the Enlightenment, which comes to prominence in the eighteenth
century, argued that reason was the primary source of authority and legitimacy, Rationalism held that human reason was
the way of gaining knowledge. The Age of Discovery, on the
other hand, which included the voyages of Columbus, added
another dimension. Not only were the new philosophies and
technologies of this epoch proof of the rise of reason, science
and European advancement, but it was also important to put
such advancement into action to discover new worlds and pro-
claim the pre-eminence of Europe. In this regard, we find in
Columbus and in missionary Christian expansion a mixture of
religious and theological, scientific and political evangelism. Ian
Strachan further interrogates this European mindset in the Age
of Discovery that has shaped Caribbean plantation societies. In
Chapter 1, entitled 'Paradise and Imperialism', of his *Paradise
and Plantation*, he makes the following arguments: Europeans

were in search of gold, and capital was the chief motivation. Paradise was, within the European imagination, their birthright; it was their right to claim new lands. Untamed territories had to conform to the image of paradise as they imagined it. Hence, paradise quickly became plantation, since it has to remain tamed, controlled, yielding and productive. Such a process required management and control; it required a faultless system. Fundamentally, colonization is about control. It is a mechanism of control in which any deviation is removed, be it a person, a religion or a culture, or even an ethnicity.[12]

Strachan gives us further insight into the theological imagination of plantation society in the Caribbean and how it viewed the religiosity of the enslaved Africans, which was also very connected to how they were treated – as expendable tools and beasts of burden. His examination of the colonial mindset undergirding Crusoe's contact with the Carib, for example, and his ordering of life in Daniel Defoe's (1718) novel, is as much about theology as it is about imperial power. Strachan writes:

> Few masters have ever cared for their slaves to become Christians. Indeed, the Christianizing of the Other has endangered the foundations of the colonial relation in the Caribbean since Las Casas first protested the treatment of the indigenous. One does not admit that the slave-animal has a soul, that the non-Christian will enter the same heaven as the Christian. One certainly does not let the slave-animal think of itself as the Christian's equal. Whereas Crusoe's replacement of the language and the history of the indigenous with his own is consistent with the process of devaluing the culture and past of the indigenous, the Christianizing of the slave was more an accident than a part of the plan of the planter class in the Caribbean.[13]

In expressing how the Bible was used to justify the conquest of the New World, Michael Prior explains that the theology undergirding the subjugation of the indigenous in the New World was ideological; therefore, its concept of sin would have followed the ideological trend. Christendom in the Middle Ages seemed more in line with the Old Testament Hebraic tradition, particularly in its tendency for sinfulness to be accorded to those outside the Israelite religion, whose land needed possession. Prior states:

> Mediaeval Christian theologians shared a common conception with Israelite theologians, involving a radical sacralization of the state and all its institutions, including its land ... As in the Old Testament period, religion invaded every facet of life in the Middle Ages. The majority of theologians and jurists considered the Pope, as the vicar of Christ, to be sovereign of all the earth.[14]

The conclusion would naturally be that God was on the side of Christendom, and not the indigenous. The framing of the social order in the fifteenth- and sixteenth-century New World precluded the indigenous from being understood as worthy of the descriptor 'righteous', or of meriting justice. Such a social order conflated sinfulness with religious and cultural heritage.

Missiological Implications of Christendom

Specifically concerning the Church in the African Caribbean, Lewin Williams attests that 'The Church found colonizing convenient because it did not wish to deal with the paganism it perceived these cultures to contain.'[15] Within the African Caribbean, it is an understatement to say that African Caribbean spiritualties were suppressed within the very place that gave them birth. The colonial expansion of Missionary Christianity was an overwhelmingly violent act. While on the one hand there was a sense of promoting the Christian faith, on the other hand multiple and often deadly means of assault were enacted on those considered heathen, uncivilized or different from those inhabiting European ideals.

Cross-cultural or intercultural aspects of mission are a perennial point of reflection. How the gospel takes root in a culture and how it is interpreted and appropriated are fundamental to missiological thinking.[16] Unfortunately, colonial and imperial models of church and concepts of mission have shaped Caribbean ecclesiology almost entirely. While there have been indigenous expressions of Christianity over time within the region, such as the Spiritual Baptists in Trinidad, or Revivalism in Jamaica, these have, without exception, been vilified. The Christendom model shaping the regions means oppression and exploitation for those who are not part of the 'empire' or those who are 'other' – Black, indigenous and so on. Also, engaging with people of different cultures and world views means that they must abandon all that they are, to become part of said empire. By culture we are talking about the total way of life of a people, which is a dynamic process bound together through signs, symbols, languages, histories and theologies. We cannot simply impose one culture on to another, or one religion on to another! Yet this has been the Christendom way. Examples of these abound throughout history: for example, the Crusades; Europe's expansion into the New World; the legacies of Henry VIII (Catholic vs Protestant England); and modern missions to and in the Global South.

In his introductory text on Christian mission, Stephen Spencer reminds us of the concept of Christendom, which has never been an innocent terminology.[17] He explains that Christendom, where the Church and the government become enmeshed under a Christian monarch, has haunted Christian mission history almost from inception. Spencer states:

> The Christendom paradigm, in other words, had made an initial appearance on the world stage: there was to be one order, with Christ at the head and beneath him the emperor (or, later, the pope) exercising a magisterial authority over the peoples of the earth. Implicit within this was a new understanding of mission: The church was to come into an increasing unity with the state and together do all they could to incorporate more and more people within its jurisdiction. The Church, in other words, was to work for the establishing of Christendom.[18]

Furthering this missiological critique of Christendom, Kwame Bediako asks bluntly: 'Whose Religion is Christianity?'[19] He argues that Christianity should be seen differently, since its centre of gravity has moved from the Jewish to the Hellenistic, then to Northern and Western European, and now to African, Asian, Caribbean and American contexts. Nonetheless, Christendom, particularly in theological discourse, still finds its way into how the Church is conceived and how it operates. Bediako explains that if we are to take the kinds of movements within Christianity seriously, particularly as they have manifested across Africa for example, then there is enough material to rethink Christianity itself. He writes:

> it is important to take seriously that Christianity has now entered a post-Western phase. This makes the category of 'post-missionary' a larger framework, in fact, since it recognises that the Christian faith in Africa is not ultimately determined by Western paradigms of interpretation.[20]

Delving more deeply, we must consider some inherent assumptions of a Christendom model as they relate to the very ecclesiological shaping of the African Caribbean. Fundamental questions about theological truth arise, and who gets to name and frame Christian belief and doctrine. Inherent in this are doctrines around sin and righteousness, and what happens to those considered outsiders. Similarly, this affects how Jesus is interpreted, understood and even visually represented. In terms of how church is organized, who gets to determine worship or mission itself? What we have seen and what is wrestled with in the region to one degree or another is the persistent influence of Christendom or colonial Christianity centred on Whiteness and European identity. African Caribbean and indigenous religiosity and spirituality continue to be disparaged.

Theologies of Domination

A good way of exploring the shaping of the Church in the African Caribbean further is by studying a snapshot of its history. There seems no better example than Codrington College, Barbados, in 1829. This date and location bring together theological education, plantation slavery and transatlantic relationships between Britain's slave colonies and the maintenance and growth of Britain's church structures in the mid-1800s. I want to highlight the life of one Revd John Hothersall Pinder of Barbados, the first principal of Codrington College. Codrington College has a plaque to Pinder, lauding him as its first principal, a plaque that I spent three years looking at, with no clue about this historical figure. I became acutely aware of Pinder when preparing to speak at a conference at Wells Cathedral, England, as they were trying to make the links between their history and transatlantic slavery. Pinder was at the centre of their investigations.[21] Before looking at Pinder and those associated with the following points I will make, it is helpful to be reminded of what is taking place in the mid-1800s for the African Caribbean. The slave trade had been abolished in 1807. Abolitionist movements are underway, and the Slavery Abolition Act will be passed in 1834. Also, and critically important to the argument here, two dioceses are created, and bishops appointed in 1824 – William Hart Coleridge of Barbados, and Christopher Lipscombe of Jamaica. The colonies had, to this point, been under the jurisdiction of the Diocese of London.

John Hothersall Pinder, born in Barbados in 1794, was shaped by this world. He was a colonial, born into the institution of enslavement, to a slave-owning family. He was educated in Cambridge, becoming part of the SPG while at university, returning to Barbados in 1819, now ordained as a priest. He became chaplain to the slaves at the Codrington plantation and in his position he held significant power and carried out a meticulous approach to the 'missionizing' of the slaves under his purview. He was resisted by the slaves due to the brutality of the Codrington plantation. Pinder was pro-slavery and preached in its defence even while vigorous debates were going on regarding the abolition of slavery. He was also appointed as the first principal of Codrington College in 1829, seeing Christopher Codrington's will to fruition. The death of the ex-colonial governor, ex-captain general and commander-in-chief, and plantation owner Christopher Codrington III in 1710 meant the bequeathing of his Barbadian estates to the ownership of the Society for the Propagation of the Gospel in Foreign Parts (SPG), newly formed in 1701, eventually becoming a key mission agency of the Church of England, with an odd condition: that it always hold 300 negroes on the plantation.[22] This was clearly mixed with a desire for the estate to become a college, training in both medicine and divinity. Codrington had a vision, albeit an ambivalent one, which Pinder discharges as a key member of the Barbadian plantocracy, a SPG chaplain and a pioneer theological educator.

John Pinder left Barbados for Wells in 1835, establishing himself there, especially as someone with considerable wealth from his involvement in and defence of chattel slavery in Barbados. He connected with others who were also connected to enslavement in the Caribbean. He set up and headed the first theological college at Wells within five years. He did what he had been doing in the colony of Barbados – theological education and the advancement of Christian society. Furthermore, he set up scholarships for the training of clergy and missionaries back at Codrington College. His passion for colonial Anglican expansion remained undaunted. He spent 25 years as principal and left part of his estate for the sustaining of Wells Theological College. His wealth was also used to purchase property in the Cathedral Close at Wells. He held esteemed positions at Wells Cathedral – Precentor, Prebendary and Canon Residentiary – until his death in 1868.

What became clear, though, is that Pinder pioneered a type of colonial theological education that never questioned its foundations. This kind of education was pro-slavery, and no doubt expansionist and racist. Pinder's pioneering work led to the establishment of St Aidan's (1846), Cuddesdon (1854), Lichfield (1857) and Salisbury (1860). Wells and Salisbury converged in 1971 becoming Sarum College in 1995. Pinder's life was bound up with the different legacies of enslavement. As a colonial he was a political figure, an intellectual figure and, ultimately, an ecclesiastical figure.

But others must be mentioned here. First, the first Bishop of Barbados, William Hart Coleridge, a friend and contemporary of Pinder, must be examined. Coleridge, like Lipscombe of Jamaica, was educated at Oxford, and both were strategically appointed. Kirkley Sands gives three reasons for the appointment of the first bishops, as laid out by Lord Bathurst, and suggests another: character change and reformation of slaves; validation of slave testimony in the court of law; the regulation of Christian marriage among slaves, and also basic social control.[23] In Sands' view, Britain saw itself and its colonies as being a godly and Christian society. Sehon Goodridge explains that Coleridge's ministry in Barbados was to the entire population, across the various classes, and for this he was resisted by the planter class, which included many clergy, unconcerned with the well-being of slaves. There were exceptions, one of whom was a Revd Richard Harte. Goodridge asserts: 'Bishop Coleridge would have been greatly encouraged if other rectors had shown Harte's zeal for the religious upliftment of the slaves.'[24] He explains that even though Coleridge embarked upon a phenomenal building programme to accommodate the influx of slaves in the light of emancipation, those churches still remained racially segregated.[25] Goodridge adds that even though Coleridge instructed his clergy to speak and preach in as much of a vernacular as they could to the slaves, and even though the encouraged worship more appealing to the slaves (congregational singing for example), he was deeply suspicious of their cultural practices:

> Bishop Coleridge constantly faced the challenge of wooing the Negroes away from their practices on Sundays to a strict observance of the Sabbath. Slaves had Sundays to themselves, and they seized this opportunity to dance and sing, work on their gardens, visit slaves and neighbouring estates, trade with them and the poor whites, and participate in the rites of the obeah cult. The obeah men, the priests of the spirit Obi, who

was believed to have come to the West Indies in the minds of the transported Africans, were very powerful. The 'heathen rites' included sacrifices at graves, 'howling and dancing', witchcraft, charms and deadly poisons.[26]

This kind of ambivalence is also seen in perhaps one of the lesser-known abolitionist figures of the early 1800s, Bishop Beilby Porteus. Bishop of London from 1787 to 1809, and before that Bishop of Chester, Porteus also played a key part in the governance and decision-making of the SPG. He was hailed as the first Anglican with significant authority to challenge slavery, and also with a strategic acquaintance of abolitionists such as William Wilberforce, Thomas Clarkson, Henry Thornton and Zachary Macaulay. While he led the way in what was 'An Experiment in Anglican Altruism' and was concerned with the better treatment of slaves on the West Indian colonies, he was instrumental in the publication of the infamous 'Slave Bible', issued in 1807 as *Select Parts of the Holy Bible for the use of the Negro Slaves in the British West-India Islands*. What is interesting is that all of this takes place as the Act for the Abolition of the Slave Trade is being passed.[27]

While Pinder, Porteus and Coleridge are historical characters who intersect in the early to mid-1800s transatlantic world, examining their lives reveals a deep connection between the British imperial expansion, European-centred, Afrophobic and anti-indigenous theological education, and the formation of African Caribbean church and society. Kortright Davis summarizes this relationship and its concrete impact on the Caribbean in his *Emancipation Still Comin'*.[28] He explains that for the African Caribbean, Christianity began as a chaplaincy to the plantation establishment, functioning as a means of social control. It then became a pioneer for education, but this was education for domestication not development. Finally, it evolved to become a collective mode of social identification as the Church became peopled by the poor. However, governance was always White, whether in terms of leadership, the acceptance of aid or generally in terms of its external allegiance.

Caribbean Responses to Missionary Christianity

The people of the African Caribbean have responded to the theology and structures of the Church in complex ways throughout history. It is tempting to believe that the Church in the region simply evolved in natural ways or, perhaps, even flourished. Here again, there must be a more complex reading of history. First, slave rebellions highlighted in Chapter 1 were slave responses to theologies of domination entrenched in colonial Missionary Christianity and its inherent violence towards slaves and their descendants. Rebellions such as the Sam Sharpe rebellion (1832–33) were sparked by the religious convictions that the plantocracy and its reading of Scripture were evil. Slaves, from inception, held a counter-hermeneutic to that of the churches.

Second, it must be asserted that creative religious and cultural resistance movements were birthed in the context of the plantation society and the plantation church. Distinctly anti-Christian and anti-imperial movements such as the Rastafari, or even calypso singing, or stick-fighting traditions, were cultural as well as artistic reactions to Missionary Christianity or colonial Christianity within the region. The music of Bob Marley and its anti-Babylon lyrics serves as a powerful example. This will be further discussed in the next two chapters, first in relation to ATRs and then decolonial hermeneutics in the African Caribbean.

Third, in the context of plantation societies, alternative Christian traditions developed. These are the traditions that have blurred the lines between African Traditional Religions and European Christianity in complex ways. Examples of these are the Spiritual Baptists and Revival Zionism. Again, these will be examined in more detail in the next chapter on ATRs in the African Caribbean.

Finally, there is a need to explore contemporary denominations. We must acknowledge the persistence of the various denominational churches in the region. Most major denominations throughout the world have taken root within the various nations and territories of the African Caribbean, and have for the most part remained stable. The degree to which colonial or missionary roots still remain operative is an important and persistent question. Nonetheless, at the heart of ecclesiastical life in the African Caribbean there is a tension that cannot be ignored. Noel Erskine's latest book, *Plantation Church*, explores the tensions between concepts of sin in Missionary Christianity and in ATRs. His conclusion is instructive for any serious attention to the different legacies of church in postcolonial contexts:

> There is ample evidence that in African religions, as they took root in the Caribbean and were ignited by a hermeneutic of freedom, Christian doctrines of sin, guilt, and the afterlife took root much later and were inspired by the missionary's Church. A majority of Caribbean people who were born in Africa during slavery were steeped in African notions of wholeness that did not make room for sin and guilt. Later, when these doctrines found currency among enslaved people in the Caribbean, they were cast in an African framework ... In an African worldview, human beings were to be seen as sinful, but not 'self-define as sinners'. The plantation kept slaves thinking of themselves as unworthy – compared to Jesus the worthy one. It is this unhealthy degrading of person hood that was key to a missionary theology.[29]

Similarly, Kortright Davis explains that the lower-class concepts of sin and divine grace in African Caribbean plantation society often diverged from the concepts held out to them. Their theology was different. God was present and could be relied upon.[30] They sustained themselves in the established churches, which did not affirm them in return. They had other avenues for sustaining themselves. In short, Christianity in the region has had more than one face, and this has to do with denominations, as well as social stratification. Davis also reminds us that it wasn't until the 1960s that missionaries began to retreat. Black leadership in African Caribbean societies at the time of his book's publication in the 1990s was a recent phenomenon.

A Caribbean Church

The nature of the Church seems a perennial doctrine to explore in the region precisely because of its colonial and imperial foundations. The Caribbean remains a space in which the ecclesiastical shaping of the past – which includes colonial expansion, genocide, denominational and political wars, Eurocentrism, Afrophobia and regional dependency – continues to inform the nature of the contemporary Caribbean church. Within the wider field of theology, the impact of empire and colonialism on the contemporary Church is a growing conversation. There is a growing body of political and postcolonial theological reflections that are challenging the very conception of what it means to be the Church, particularly in the Western tradition. For example, Walter Brueggemann's *Prophetic Imagination* argues for a different kind of consciousness – a prophetic one – that consistently contests royalist, imperial forms of religion and church.[31] For Brueggemann, the structural disposition of the Church has theological consequences, since the process is two-way: the structure of the Church influences theology, and theology influences the structure. The prophetic imagination is wilderness-bound, wild, free, inclusive, and empathizes with the marginalized and wounded in ways that imperial apathy cannot. A similar point is made by John Hull in his *Towards a Prophetic Church*, in which he criticizes historical approaches to mission, concluding that 'following Jesus' is never a static notion.[32] The history of Christian thinking indicates that Jesus has always been seen in different ways, from the militant ones of empire, to pious ones, to sceptical ones. What is needed is a concept of mission and church that is dynamic, inclusive, tended towards justice and true to the prophetic nature of Jesus who, at the core of his ministry, contests imperialist religion. Similarly, Mark Brett and Jione Havea, among other scholars, continue to ask profound questions about the legacies of violence inherent in colonial or imperial Christianity, and how they continue to be reinscribed in contemporary forms of church.[33] There is a growing sense that the depth and pervasiveness of the colonial structuring of the concept of church is something always to take note of.

In the African Caribbean, who we are as a Church, and who we dare to be, remain important points of reflection. Perhaps the two books for further study on the impact of the colonial shaping of the Church in the region are Ashley Smith's *Real Roots and Potted Plants: Reflections on the Caribbean Church*, and Noel Erskine's *Decolonizing Theology: A Caribbean Perspective*.[34] Ashley Smith argues that the Church in the Caribbean has always been a potted plant, which has survived in little containers, brought from nurseries elsewhere. Concerning the Church's urgent need for a new self-perception and a new anthropology, he writes:

> It is hardly possible for a Caribbean church to become fully autonomous unless those who are its leaders and constituents experience a transformation of their consciousness. At the present time most of our Caribbean peoples see themselves as they were seen and defined by their captors, masters and colonizers nearly three centuries ago.[35]

Out of the Depths is perhaps the earliest collection of papers wrestling with multiple legacies of misisonary expansion into the region and its significance for any formation of church.[36] Both Kortright Davis and Noel Erskine propose that the development of the Church in the region has followed a fourfold trajectory. Davis refers to 'The Church and the People', 'The Church for the People', 'The Church of the People' and 'The People's Church'; Erskine frames it as 'Church as Friend of Plantocracy', 'Church as Friend of the Black People', 'Church and the Black Experience' and 'Church as the Bearer of Identity'.[37] For both scholars, it is the last phase that remains unattained.

The very nature of the Church is something that the African Caribbean has had to wrestle with significantly. There are deep challenges to Western, European and missionary forms of church, since the very institutionalizing of church has led to profound experiences of violence and spiritual and psychological abuse of the different identities in the region, especially those of African and pre-Columbian indigenous heritages. To become a church in the African Caribbean means that 'church' itself must be reconceived. Plantation societies were and are static, capitalistic and in every way orientated towards the flourishing and well-being of the European. Could it be that Christianity in the region was never intended to celebrate African or indigenous cultural heritages, but always to replicate the image of the European? Dianne Stewart has, perhaps more than most, been employing a hermeneutic of suspicion against Missionary Christianity in the region and for good reason![38] The very notion of church must be disentangled from the legacies of colonialism and empire, and this process is a significantly challenging one.

When speaking to the wider field of theology and other postcolonial contexts, the African Caribbean experience asks the following profound questions as we collectively attempt to reimagine the concept of church in our contemporary world: Can Christianity be expressed in one way, or an 'ideal' way? Who or what determines how Christianity should look? How should the 'gospel' engage with those of pre-Christian beliefs and practices? Are Christianity and our concepts of church unfolding? Should they be? Or is there a type that endures always? These are questions being faced in the region, but they are also significant for the rest of the Christian world and for Christian theology. While the Church in the African Caribbean remains significant, and has become quite powerful, it still must do a lot of work in disentangling its colonial, imperialist, missionary heritage. In the next chapter I will shift focus from the Church towards an exploration of the African and other indigenous cosmologies and religious and cultural heritages in the region. The African Caribbean must not only deal with the Church that came but with the lives that were profoundly disrupted because of its coming.

Notes

1 See Ian G. Strachan, 'Columbus's Ghost: Tourism, Art and National Identity in the Bahamas', a lecture given at the Inter-American Development Bank in Washington, DC, 30 June 2000, as part of the IDB Cultural Center Lectures Program.

2 See Christopher Columbus, *The Journal of Christopher Columbus (During His First Voyage, 1492–93) and Documents Relating the Voyages of John Cabot and Gaspar Corte Real*, ed. and trans. Clements R. Markham, Cambridge: Cambridge University Press, 2010. DOI: http://dx.doi.org/10.1017/CBO9780511708411, Cambridge Library Collection, Hakluyt First Series, 1893.

3 Hilary McDonald Beckles and Verene A. Shepherd, *Liberties Lost: Caribbean Indigenous Societies and Slave Systems*, Cambridge: Cambridge University Press, 2004, p. 1.

4 Ivan van Sertima, *They Came before Columbus: The African Presence in Ancient America*, New York: Random House, 1976.

5 Diana Paton and Maarit Forde, *Obeah and Other Powers: The Politics of Caribbean Religion and Healing*, Durham, NC: Duke University Press, 2012. See also Jerome S. Handler and Kenneth M. Bilby, *Enacting Power: The Criminalization of Obeah in the Anglophone Caribbean 1760–2011*, Jamaica: University of the West Indies Press, 2012.

6 Dale A. Bisnauth, *A History of Religions in the Caribbean*, Kingston: Kingston Publishers Ltd, 1989, p. 199.

7 Francis J. Osborne and Geoffrey Johnston, *Coast Lands and Islands: First Thoughts on Caribbean Church History*, Jamaica: UTCWI, 1972.

8 Orlando Patterson, *The Sociology of Slavery: An Analysis of the Origins, Development and Structure of Negro Slave Society in Jamaica*, Studies in Society, London: MacGibbon & Kee, 1967.

9 Ian G. Strachan, *Paradise and Plantation: Tourism and Culture in the Anglophone Caribbean*, New World Studies, Charlottesville, VA: University of Virginia Press, 2002.

10 Bisnauth, *A History of Religions in the Caribbean*, ch. 8.

11 Arthur C. Dayfoot, 'The Shaping of the West Indian Church: Historical Factors in the Formation of the Pattern of Church Life in the English-speaking Caribbean 1492–1870', ThD thesis, Emmanuel College, Victoria University, 1982, p. 275.

12 Strachan, *Paradise and Plantation*, ch. 1.

13 Strachan, *Paradise and Plantation*, p. 48.

14 Michael Prior, *The Bible and Colonialism: A Moral Critique*, Sheffield: Sheffield Academic Press, 1997, p. 52.

15 Lewin L. Williams, *The Caribbean: Enculturation, Acculturation, and the Role of the Churches*, Gospel and Cultures, Geneva: WCC Publications, 1996, p. 14.

16 For example, see such key missiological texts as David Jacobus Bosch, *Transforming Mission: Paradigm Shifts in Theology of Mission*, American Society of Missiology Series, Maryknoll, NY: Orbis Books, 1991; Stephen B. Bevans and Roger Schroeder, *Constants in Context: A Theology of Mission for Today*, American Society of Missiology Series, Maryknoll, NY: Orbis Books, 2004; Stephen Spencer, *SCM Studyguide to Christian Mission: Historic Types and Contemporary Expressions*, London: SCM Press, 2007; Andrew Walls and Cathy Ross (eds), *Mission in the 21st Century: Exploring the Five Marks of Global Mission*, Maryknoll, NY: Orbis Books, 2008.

17 Spencer, *Christian Mission*.

18 Spencer, *Christian Mission*, pp. 93–4.

19 Kwame Bediako, '"Whose Religion is Christianity?" Reflections on Opportunities and Challenges in Christian Theological Scholarship: The African Dimension', in ed. Walls and Ross, *Mission in the 21st Century*, p. 107.

20 Bediako, '"Whose Religion is Christianity?"', p. 115.

21 For more information, including some of the history of John Hothersall Pinder, see https://wellsandtransatlanticslavery.com/ (accessed 17.7.23).

22 For further reading on the history of Codrington College, see John Holder, *Codrington College: A Brief History*, Bridgetown, Barbados: Codrington College, 1988. See also https://codringtoncollege.edu.bb/history/ (accessed 17.7.23).

23 See Kirkley C. Sands, 'Missionary Bishops and Education in the British Caribbean 1824–1841: Christopher Libscomb and William Hart Coleridge', *Vox Collegii Codringtoniensis*, 22 October 2015. Bathurst was Secretary to the Colonies and naturally the mediator in colonial matters.

24 Sehon S. Goodridge, *Facing the Challenge of Emancipation: A Study of the Ministry of William Hart Coleridge, First Bishop of Barbados, 1824–1842*, Bridgetown, Barbados: Cedar Press, 1981, p. 35.

25 Goodridge, *Facing the Challenge of Emancipation*, p. 25.

26 Goodridge, *Facing the Challenge of Emancipation*, p. 74.

27 *Select Parts of the Holy Bible for the use of the Negro Slaves in the British West-India Islands*, derived from the King James Version 1611, London: Law & Gilbert, 1807. See the recent publication, Joseph B. Lumpkin, *The Negro Bible – the Slave Bible: Select Parts of the Holy Bible, Selected for the Use of the Negro Slaves, in the British West-India Islands*, Blountsville, AL: Fifth Estate, 2019.

28 Kortright Davis, *Emancipation Still Comin': Explorations in Caribbean Emancipatory Theology*, Maryknoll, NY: Orbis Books, 1990.

29 Noel L. Erskine, *Plantation Church: How African American Religion was born in Caribbean Slavery*, Oxford: Oxford University Press, 2014, p. 168.

30 Davis, *Emancipation Still Comin'*, ch. 3.

31 Walter Brueggemann, *The Prophetic Imagination*, 2nd edn, Minneapolis, MN: Fortress Press, 2001.

32 John Hull, *Towards the Prophetic Church: A Study of Christian Mission*, London: SCM Press, 2014.

33 Mark G. Brett, *Political Trauma and Healing: Biblical Ethics for a Postcolonial World*, Grand Rapids, MI: Eerdmans, 2016. Jione Havea (ed.), *Religion and Power: Theology in the Age of Empire*, Lanham, MD: Lexington Books/Fortress Academic, 2018.

34 Ashley Smith, *Real Roots and Potted Plants: Reflections on the Caribbean Church*, Mandeville, Jamaica: Eureka Press, 1984. Noel L. Erskine, *Decolonizing Theology: A Caribbean Perspective*, Trenton, NJ: Africa World Press, 1998.

35 Smith, *Real Roots and Potted Plants*, pp. 44–5.

36 Idris Hamis (ed.), *Out of the Depths*, San Fernando, Trinidad: Rahaman Printery Ltd, 1977.

37 Davis, *Emancipation Still Comin'*, p. 72. Erskine, *Decolonizing Theology*, p. 99.

38 Dianne M. Stewart, *Three Eyes for the Journey: African Dimensions of the Jamaican Religious Experience*, Oxford: Oxford University Press, 2004.

5

Revitalization or Rejection: The Persistence of African Traditional Religions and Culture

This chapter wrestles specifically with the ambivalent presence of mainly African Traditional Religions and cosmology within any consideration of a Caribbean Contextual Theology. On the one hand, an argument can be made that they have always rejected Missionary Christianity; on the other hand, they have reinterpreted and reformed Missionary Christianity. The point here is that African Traditional Religious Heritages (ATRs) or indigenous spiritualities within the region have always been 'reformational'. They have always been reinterpreting Christianity towards liberation and authenticity for all. In doing so they have also been asking fundamental questions about the nature of God's people, and whose culture can or cannot contain the Christian revelation.

Examining 'Culture' and 'Gospel'

A good place to begin this reflection on the African Traditional Religious Heritages in the African Caribbean context is Lewin Williams' distinction between 'enculturation' and 'acculturation'. While the former is the 'natural process of socialization that belongs to a particular culture', the latter 'is the imposition of one culture upon another'.[1] Williams notes:

> Unfortunately, to move beyond the harmony of culinary art, and to add the European segment, is to move from

89

enculturation to acculturation. This assessment is based on the fact that the European segment introduced colonialism, slavery and racism, making it responsible for the cultural stratification and domination which have made disengagement a viable alternative to what could otherwise have been a harmonious amalgamation. This is the basic problem with Caribbean identity.[2]

A big question remains of how the Christian gospel becomes rooted in the region and how African Traditional Religious Heritages, the dominant feature of the region, are either integrated or vilified.

African Traditional Religious Heritages (ATRs) and Indigenous Spiritualities

In 1992 the Caribbean/African American Dialogue (CAAD) met in Barbados and produced the Verdun Proclamation, which clearly highlighted, among other things, indigenous clergy disparaging their ancestral heritages.[3] This consultation produced a statement, worth quoting in full, about the need to:

Recognize the equal dignity and rights of all cultures, religions and traditions; Believe that the perception of traditional religions and cultures as a priori defined as 'superstitious and pagan' is erroneous and must be rejected; Affirm and celebrate the ongoing contributions being made by people of traditional religions and cultures to instill a sense of worth and dignity in those among whom they minister; Celebrate also the emergence of a liberating Christianity which has abandoned triumphalism in relation to traditional religions; Realize that many Christians affirm and live the rituals, beliefs and tenets of other religions, cultures and traditions, seeing this as essential for the wholeness of self and development; Recognize the Caribbean as having the potential to become an example of interreligious dialogue and action; Call for active engagement in further dialogue to develop mutual respect and understanding among people of different religions, cultures and traditions; *Commit* ourselves to establishing a creative partnership among the peoples of religions, cultures and traditions of the region; *Commit* ourselves to continue the process of reflection with a view to articulating a righteous and spiritual vision for the region; *Recognize*, in view of our finding that terminology has been a hindrance to dialogue, that language and concepts be revised and fashioned to reflect the interfaith realities; and *Urge* governments of the region to give equality of opportunity and official representation to religions, cultures and traditions, and to repeal any legislation which inhibits the practice of religion.[4]

In 1994 the Caribbean Conference of Churches (CCC) held the Ecumenical Consultation on Popular Religiosity in Suriname, published as *At the Crossroads: African Caribbean Religion and Christianity*.[5] This consultation sought to increase awareness of the religious and cultural diversity of the region and the need for the Church to dialogue with this reality. For our purposes, it's important to present the religious and cosmological background to the diversity of identities in the region. At the risk of being too simplistic, I will group this reflection into two broad categories that have been radically affected by the coming of Christianity into the region. These are pre-Columbian and West/Central African cosmologies. The risk is that this does not cover many other identities and cosmologies, such as Asian, Chinese, Syrian, Middle Eastern, Greek, Jewish, East African and so on. It is hoped that the two groupings offered will suffice.

Pre-Columbian Cosmology

Hilary Beckles and Verene Shepherd give us a good background to the pre-European settlers of the region in their *Liberties Lost* text.[6] When the Europeans came they identified three groups in the Caribbean and labelled them Arawaks, Caribs and Maya, although these groups had their own names. We now know the following: there were the *Ciboney* or the *Guanahacabibe*; the Europeans called them 'wild and as fleet as deer'. There were the *Taino*, who were called Arawak by the Europeans. And finally, there were the *Kalinago*, called Caribs by the Europeans.

The Ciboney

These were the smallest of the Caribbean inhabitants. They were nomad hunter-gatherers. It was thought that they were from pre-farming cultures that entered the Antilles from South America in small waves over a long period of time. They were not technologically advanced people and were often dominated by the *Taino*.

The Taino

Generally, the *Taino* were expert seafarers who navigated the chain of islands. There were two language groups here – Arawakan and Cariban, both of which were widely spread across the region. They were also a highly developed agricultural people with industrial technology and textiles. Their main cultivation was cassava. They hunted green turtle throughout the Caribbean waters, farmed tobacco and built canoes. They were also creative workers of gold and engaged in trade and commerce. They had a religion that was based on respecting the environment, and believed in peaceful co-existence rather than hostile war. They were very religious and had distinct theological ideas with attendant rituals and ceremonies. They held to a spiritual world in which both humans and gods were classified and ranked. Gods were called *Zemis* and were carved from gold, wood, stone and bones. Some of the *Zemis* were fertility gods, being explicitly sexual in design.

The Kalinago

This was the group that Columbus met and branded as 'Caribs', a negative term. The *Taino* and *Kalinago* were in conflict but their differences were of degree rather than kind. The *Kalinago* conquered and expelled the *Taino* in the Lesser Antilles and integrated their women and children into their communities. With the coming of the Spanish, the *Taino* tried to secure support for this resistance against the *Kalinago*. The *Kalinago* did not have spirit gods called *Zemis*. Their spirituality was centred on the individual's relationship with the spirit self. The world was divided between good and evil spirits that fought for supremacy, and the individual mind was a battlefield of this struggle. Their society had priests and shamans, whose duty was to help with reconciliation. Their societies were much less hierarchical than the *Taino*. They were more nomadic and concentrated on their military objectives.

West African Cosmology

When thinking of the African presence in the Caribbean, or African Caribbean cultures, we must consider the West African religious and cultural origins. Nathaniel Samuel Murrell's *Afro-Caribbean Religions* gives a good introduction to the transatlantic cultural and religious connections undergirding African Caribbean popular religions.[7] The presence of Africans in the region is largely due to enslavement, and to such a significant degree that the largest African population in the world outside of Nigeria is Brazil. The African presence in the Americas is not only in the Caribbean, but in South, Central and North America. African culture has deeply, structurally, shaped the modern Americas. To understand contemporary popular religions in the region, we must consider the following:

West Africa

The Yoruba People

Dwelling in present day Nigeria, Ghana, Togo and Benin (Dahomey), they constitute the second-largest language group in Nigeria, with 25 ethnic subgroups, including the languages Ewe, Ga, Akan, Igbo and Kru. Ile-Ife and Oyo function as both religious and political centres of Yoruba culture. Yoruba myths make the *ooni* a direct descendant of Oduduwa, an African divinity and founder of Ile-Ife (Ife).

Akan and Fanti-Ashanti

These people occupy regions of southern Ghana, a large eastern section of Ivory Coast and much of Togo. Twi is a family of dialects that these people speak. The Akan is constituted by 12 kingdoms of whom the Ashanti is a member with its city, Kumasi.

Fon-Ewe (Dahomey)

This group hails from Benin, formerly Dahomey, Togo and Eastern Ghana, and share linguistic and cultural traditions with the Yoruba. They were originally part of Yorubaland but broke away to settle in what is called the Republic of Benin. 'There they built the capital city and kingdom, Abomey, in central Benin, and the city-kingdom of Allada; this is the root word from which the Haitian Vodou Rada spirits get their name.'[8]

Central Africa

Kongo

The diverse cultures of the modern Kikongo-speaking people of what is now the Democratic Republic of the Congo in Central Africa, and Angola (Niger-Congo), have their roots in the Kongo Kingdoms. This region in Central West Africa was conquered and divided by France, Portugal, Belgium and Britain. The Kongo Kingdom was founded in the fourteenth century. Many Congolese, Angolan and others from West Central Africa, and even from South-East Africa, were brought to Brazil, Cuba, Haiti and other Caribbean states.

What is important to note is that while people and cultures were extracted from these regions of sub-Saharan Africa, they disembarked across the Americas in heterogenous ways, as shown in Table 1.

Cuba	Jamaica	Haiti
Yoruba	Yoruba	Kongo
Kongo	Kongo	Yoruba
Dahomey	Akan-Ashanti	Igbo
Bantu		Fon-Dahomey
		Bambarras
		Mandingos
		Fulas
		Polards
Puerto Rico	**Brazil**	**Trinidad and Tobago**
Yoruba	Yoruba	Yoruba
Kongo	Dahomey	Kongo
Fon-Dahomey	Bantu	Mandingo
Bantu		Egbo/Eba
Mandingos		Efik
Hausa		Calabari
Fanti-Ashanti		Kramanti
Bantu/Kongo		

Table 1: West/Central African Presence in the Americas.[9]

The religious cosmologies vary across the different cultures of West and Central Africa. However, 'among the many theological perspectives in African life and thought, belief in the one supreme deity is primary'.[10]

> God in Africa is no different from the benevolent, compassionate, and merciful Judeo-Christian God who created the World and sovereignly controls it, but Africans' view of God is not monolithic. To some Africans, God is an all-pervading reality and an active participant in human affairs. The divine, who may be male or female, is accessible to all, irrespective of race, tribe, gender, or religion, and is approached directly through sacrifices, worship, and prayers or indirectly via intermediaries.[11]

With this background, what we have is a rich tapestry of traditions that can be described as New World syncretic traditions. There is a mixture of indigenous pre-Columbian, African, European, Asian and even Middle Eastern traditions. These manifest in all areas of African Caribbean religious and cultural life – music, religions, carnivals and street festivals, proverbs, healing traditions, language and so on. Examples of maximum syncretism in the region are Trinidad and Tobago, Guyana and Belize (formerly British Honduras).

Assault on African Caribbean Religions

In African Caribbean plantation societies, ATRs have had to endure extensive and multiple forms of assault. It is helpful to parse these out for a better appreciation of the degree to which vilification and stigmatization have happened. First, there is what I refer to as an epistemological assault. Dianne Stewart traces the philosophical assumptions of pre-slavery and colonial life in the African Caribbean. Even before black people were transported to the new world, there was an epistemological assault on them. She uses Michel Foucault's work on epistemology to explain that the epistemological framework of post-Enlightenment rationalistic Europe didn't allow for subjugated or disqualified knowledges.[12] That which could not be proved by reason and logic, which constituted truth, was disqualified as invalid. Black culture was considered heathen; expressivism was considered evil and irrational; and African spirituality was considered hocus-pocus. Ronald Nathan states:

> The dichotomy between, for example, Good and Evil, Secular and Spiritual, Heaven and Earth and Male and Female and so on does not exist within the world view of African societies and certainly not within an Afrocentric philosophy. These Hellenistic mythological imports were incorporated within the European Enlightenment and later Reformation Christian thought.[13]

This imposition of a sacred/secular divide allowed for a Neoplatonic political, cultural and theological framing of society: White vs Black; Christian vs Heathen; Civilized vs Uncivilized; and Good vs Bad.

Second, there is religious assault. The very formation of the colonies was religious, but it was a religiosity that conflated the growth of Christianity with European imperial and economic expansion. Colonies within the Caribbean were not meant to be societies. They were meant to be production houses. The only permissible religion was Missionary Christianity, and any derivation was either ignored, vilified or penalized. Christianizing the slaves was as much about making them subjects as it was about making them better, more obedient labourers. Slaves were taught, by the Church, to obey. Across the Anglophone Caribbean, there are varied responses to the slaves. In large measure, the Established Church detested Christianizing the slaves. Their churches were almost totally white; the Methodists were largely mulatto and the Baptists were usually black. Other denominations came in the twentieth century, for example the Pentecostals. Perhaps the best treatment of slaves came from the Moravians, who had a totally different approach to this.

Third, there is legal and political assault. Diana Paton explains that in the colonial framework, African religiocultural retentions such as Obeah and Junkanoo have not only been branded as heathenish practices, but also as criminal offences. Largely based on the Obeah Law in Jamaica (1760 and 1898), till now the only countries to have removed Obeah laws from their legal codes are Anguilla (1980), Barbados (1998), Trinidad and Tobago (2000) and St Lucia (2004). It is important to note that the Bahamas is not among these nations. Diana Paton explains that post-emancipation anti-Obeah laws were culture-forming. They fostered certain social and cultural conventions about the place and significance of African religiocultural activities, usually casting them as barbaric, harmful or even evil or demonic.[14] During the slave period the fear of the Obeah Man or Woman was so great that those who were charged as such were tried and hung. There are many testimonials of court cases to this effect.[15]

The final and continual assault is the lasting Afrophobia within the region. In my own work I have traced the reality of self-negation within African Caribbean societies through the writings of some key theorists.[16] First, Frantz Fanon has helped elucidate this, that in the colonial context the colonized are not human at all. In his *The Wretched of the Earth*, he states: 'Because it is a systematic negation of the other person and a furious determination to deny the other person all attributes of humanity, colonialism forces the people it dominates to ask themselves the question constantly: "In reality, who am I?"'[17] W. E. B. Du Bois also notes this deeply engrained reality, that central to the psychology of oppression is the oppressed seeing themselves through the lens of the oppressor. Du Bois explains:

It is a peculiar sensation, this double consciousness, this sense of always looking at one's self through the eyes of others, of measuring one's soul by the tape of a world that looks on in amused contempt and pity. One ever feels this twoness – an American, a Negro; two souls, two thoughts, two unreconciled strivings; two warring ideals in one dark body, whose dogged strength alone keeps it from being torn asunder.[18]

The lasting Afrophobia that I speak of is an internalized reality wherein non-European religious and cultural practices and cosmologies, particularly African ones, are disparaged by African Caribbean people themselves.

Theorizing ATRs

Ennis Edmonds and Michelle Gonzalez's book *Caribbean Religious History: An Introduction* is helpful as it positions ATRs and pre-Columbian indigenous religions and spiritualities in the region alongside Christianity.[19] After historicizing early colonial Catholicism and Protestantism, they explore the following traditions as potent and legitimate ones in the African Caribbean. These include *Creole African Traditions*, which pervades the region, such as Santería, Palo Monte, Abakua, Vodou and Espiritismo; *Afro-Christian Faiths* such as Revival Zion and the Spiritual Baptists; *Mainline Protestantism vs Pentecostalism*; and other *Religious Movements*, such as Hinduism, Islam and Rastafarianism. In this work they consider the complex processes of legitimation, indigenization and contextualization involved in making any sense of religiosity in the region.

I am employing the term African Traditional Religious Heritages to signify a wide range of indigenous religiocultural productions across the region as a whole.[20] These include the more formal African traditional religious forms found mostly on the larger Islands (Haitian Vodou, Cuban Santería, Trinidadian Shango, Brazilian Candomblé); African-based spiritualties (Obeah, Myal); African-influenced Christianities (the Native Baptists and Revival Zionism, Jamaica; and Spiritual Baptists, Trinidad); religiocultural and political movements (Rastafari); and religiocultural art forms (Junkanoo, Carnival, Reggae, Calypso, salsa, merengue, capoeira, stick fighting and so on); and Black missionary churches and denominations (Anglican, Roman Catholic, Baptists, Methodists, Pentecostals). In short, ATRs pervade every sphere of African Caribbean life, and have functioned in multiple ways, including as theological devices. These include the following:

Reggae/Dancehall

Bob Marley is by far the most iconic musical artist that the region has ever produced. His music is informed by his Rastafarian roots and function as socio-political critique, as well as Rastafarian theological hermeneutics. One only needs to process the lyrics of 'Jump Nyabinghi' and 'Babylon System' to see this clearly. Both are simultaneously descriptions of Rastafarian worship, and also call to a new kind of African-centred consciousness, as well as theological reflections based on Old Testament imagery. Anna Perkins has contributed work on Rastafarianism where she engages in dialogue with Ras Dermot Fagan to clarify church and Rastafari conceptions of sin. But her work on Dancehall deserves attention, in particular her engagement with the work of Tanya Stephens. She critically engages with Stephens' music and lyrics, seeing them as grass-roots theological discourses. Perkins explains that Tanya, through her matured Dancehall lyrics, challenges both the dehumanizing, misogynistic, male practices endemic in Dancehall and the Caribbean patriarchal system, and the self-important contradictory religion of the Church, which lacks a deeper spirituality.[21] Anette Brown looks at the Church in Jamaica's rejection of Dancehall and argues for engagement with Dancehall, using a 'Dancehall Hermeneutics of Mission'. While the anti-Dancehall rhetoric is rife within the churches, a rhetoric undergirded by conceptions of Dancehall as 'low culture, unfit to be embraced and incorporated into Christian life', it connects with the lived realities of Jamaicans generally, but particularly young people, who seem more and more absent from established churches. She challenges the Church to overlook its bias against Dancehall and embrace it as a potent resource for mission in the Jamaican context.[22]

Gospel Music

Dulcie Dixon McKenzie challenges the lost historiography of Black British Gospel, which has largely come to be seen as emanating from North America, but really has equally or more been influenced by its African Caribbean historical roots and routes. In doing so, she points out the exploitation of Black British Gospel music by white mainstream churches and artists. They have been drawing from Black British musical traditions without acknowledging their indebtedness. Sadly, do Black British Christians know and own their own history and spiritual traditions? She contends that they have been denying their own histories and needlessly borrowing from other traditions. For the first generation of African Caribbean migrants, their theology was embodied in their music.[23]

Calypso

George Mulrain highlights the need for a Calypso exegesis. If we were to look at how Calypso functions, there is a method to decoding and encoding the truth of Caribbean suffering. It interprets the text of life and the text of the Bible. It also allows for multiple readings of the biblical text, something that Caribbean people are used to.[24] Richard Burton sees Calypso as part of the Carnival complex, functioning to comment on daily life, the struggles of black people and the hypocrisy of those in power, by using double talk, ambivalence and subversion.[25] Kortright Davis argues that music is the Caribbean voice of God. Much of Caribbean heritage has been sustained in its music and dance, and religion. Calypso functions as a creative challenge to oppression, it reduces political power and speaks for the people. The calypsonian is a national hero who, like Anancy, majors in double talk, in ambivalence, in creative criticism.[26] The most recent text to make similar connections looking at Carnival, and therefore Calypso, is Clifford Rawlins' *A Theology of Carnival and Other Provocations: Realigning Christian Thought for a Post-Modern World.*[27]

Stick Fighting

In the book *Afro-Creole*, Richard D. E. Burton reminds us that 'stick fighting' or Kalinda/Calenda was pivotal to Carnival countries. Territories such as St Vincent, Dominica and Trinidad had it as their ritual within the Carnival. In fact, when Carnival was banned due to riots in 1884, it was the Kalinda that went underground. There were traditions of crowning the Kalinda king. Eventually stick fighting would find its manifestation in the region's love for cricket. The way cricket was played by the West Indians was buttressed by the ancestral participation in Kalinda.[28]

Myalist Traditions

Myal, like Obeah, Vodou or Kumina, are ATRs that form the bedrock of many African Caribbean cultures, spiritualities and religiosities. Kenneth Bibly conducted research on Myal practices in four parishes in Jamaica and came to the conclusion reached by Martha Beckwith in the 1920s. He documents Myal as a product of the *Jonkunnu* (Junkanoo) masquerading institution and its Gumbay drumming rituals in modern south-western Jamaica. The dancing and the drumming are pneumatological in nature and are meant to conjure up something from the depth of African Caribbean people. Whenever the drum in invoked, ATRs are being reappropriated within African Caribbean societies.[29] I have noted the same phenomenon in my exploration of Junkanoo in the Bahamas and it's Myalist roots. It invokes the spirit, and functions to contest and even reform colonial forms of Christianity.[30]

For African Caribbean people living under dislocation, slavery, colonialism and perpetual dispossession, African religiocultural productions like Junkanoo, Reggae, Calypso, stick fighting are simultaneously religious, playful and martial. In simultaneously being these three things, they become one liberative means of doing theology. They also function to bring the mystery of God into the daily realities of African Caribbean life. And when all three are employed, they debunk the persistent myth that indigenous religiocultural productions like these are ineffective cultural trappings – rather they have always been potent means of doing theology.

Theologizing ATRs

But how do ATRs in the African Caribbean function theologically? Anthony Reddie, writing in the Black British context, and being of Black Caribbean heritage, suggests that Black Theology and Caribbean Theologies should be participative if they are to be liberative or allow the voiceless to have their say. He uses ethnography and participant observation to access the experiences of young black people in Birmingham. He sees the exercise of Black Theology as needing an interactive, interdisciplinary and constructive approach in order to allow black people to critically, theologically reflect on their black subjectivity in the midst of white normativity. He uses an imaginary barn dance to emphasize the point.[31] Furthermore, whether one talks of Rastafarians, Vodou, Calypso or Carnival, these, as suggested by Reddie, are Caribbean dialectical spiritualties, which have functioned in the context of slavery and colonialism constantly to expose and resist the colonial myth that there is a standard, universal way of doing 'God', a way that just happens to be European. He uses jazz music as a way of emphasizing the participative, dialectical nature of African Caribbean religiocultural productions.[32]

Michael Jagessar uses the pan-Caribbean trickster Anancy as a way of mediating a culturally authentic, liberative theology. He suggests that the ambivalence Anancy employs, and 'is', and the way he/she moves in between worlds, allows for multiple perspectives for critiquing and liberating biblical and theological truth from long-held colonial chains. Anancyism as trickster theology leaves space for the imagination, a place long denied within classical theological circles. He writes:

Having inherited Christianity with all its Western Eurocentric baggage, I suggest that we have become locked into a largely Protestant theological mindset that has relegated the act of imagination to the realm of 'hocus-pocus' which is viewed with suspicion. While Black theological discourses (and contextual theologies) emphasize experience, there is still much to be done in the area of imagination.[33]

In his ground-breaking research on Haitian Vodou, George Mulrain concludes that it is inherently theological and functions theologically as a 'spirit religion'. It challenges injustices, consistently asserting the idea that God as revealed in Jesus Christ is interested in every aspect of his people. God is a God of justice, and Vodou is principally concerned with this theological claim.[34]

Dianne Stewart presents another view. She traces the trajectory of Myalism in Jamaican religiosity and culture, arguing that there is a systematic renewal of the culture towards wholeness.[35] Beneath the history of vilification and suppression, Myalism transforms into various cultural traditions and experiences, including Revivalism, Native Baptists, Kumina, Rastafari and Dancehall. There is an impulse within ATRs consistently to 'remember' themselves. There is a deep sense of religiocultural anamnesis within the region.

Other Caribbean theologians, myself included, have been highlighting another perspective. There is a sense in which ATRs are pneumatological acts which have been reappropriating Christianity pneumatologically. Taking events such as 'speaking in tongues' and trance/possession seriously, Barry Chevannes associates ATRs with the potent pneumatology emphasized within African cultures and theologies. He states:

Where Christianity is transfixed on Jesus as mediator Myal was transfixed on the Spirit as possessor and sought [the Spirit] in dreams and secluded retreat. Whereas Christianity placed its emphasis on transmitted *knowledge* (doctrine, Bible, catechism) for conversion, Myal placed its emphasis on the *experience* of the Spirit. When followers found [the Spirit] it was to be filled by [the Spirit], to be possessed. Possession by the Spirit thus became the quintessential experience of myalized Christianity.[36]

Timothy McCartney argues the Obeah Man (or Woman) speaks in more tongues than the Christian. What we think is mumbled nonsense is the effect of trance/possession that the Obeah Man knows much better than those in church. In fact, the Obeah Man knows the Bible better than the good church man.[37] I go a step further in my work to argue that far from simply contesting colonial Christianity in the region, ATRs were and continue to reconceive and reappropriate Christianity to connect more deeply with the African or indigenous roots of the culture.[38]

Finally, there is a strong link between ATRs and the prophetic tradition and motif within the scriptural tradition. Kortright Davis asserts that the spirit of prophecy is deeply imbedded within African religiocultural retentions. Looking at the multiple roles of Calypso, he likens it to the dual roles of the Hebrew prophets of critiquing injustice and oppression and also calling God's people back to their religious roots.[39] Novelle Josiah links Calypso to the role of Old Testament prophetic figures. His research on Calypso remains key for the region and deserves attention.[40] Kirkley Sands describes Junkanoo in the Bahamas as fulfilling a prophetic role in contesting injustice against the Black majority within post-emancipation Bahamian society.[41]

A Caribbean Christ

ATRs challenge theology in the Caribbean in multiple ways, pneumatologically, Christologically, soteriologically and so on. Perhaps it's best to reflect on an important anthropological and Christological question: Who bears the image of God in the Caribbean context? For centuries the image of God has been foreign, white and male, and often, as Kortright Davis asserts, 'Absentee'.[42] The very image of Christ has been a process of acculturation, and Christ has been understood in the region as White European. This question of the image of God can be traced in formative Caribbean reflections such as *Troubling of the Waters* and *Out of the Depths*, as well as the works of the most well-known Caribbean theologians.

Teasing out an image or concept of Christ for the Caribbean that has not been imposed is always tricky based on our conversation above. Perhaps a good discussion of these issues would result from exploring the following theologians as they specifically wrestle with the question of a Caribbean Christ. First, Donald Chambers' PhD 'proposes that the plural nature of the Caribbean contextual reality is a critical lens in the interpretation and re-reading of the Christ-event and its liberating/emancipating consequence for the Caribbean'.[43] The African Caribbean presents a unique locatedness from which to reflect on the person and ministry of Jesus. While the lens insists on liberation – for Chambers associates the African Caribbean with Third World and Liberation theological perspectives – it must disentangle from the complex internalized processes of Missionary Christianity. In proposing a constructive Christology, Chambers suggests three guidelines based on the African Caribbean context: an exploration of the mystery of God as revealed in the plural context; the significance of the cross in the Caribbean context; and the meaning of liberation in the Caribbean context. The conclusion to these three areas is that more or different approaches are needed than have been offered before within the Christian tradition. For example, the significance of the cross and the resurrection require deeper meaning if Christology is to be effective. Also, for the region the question of authenticity is relevant. How does Christ become appropriated in a plural context, especially when some of those identities are mutually contested? Chambers proposes:

> the continuing process of redemption in the Caribbean means the power to break the cycle of inauthentic-being-with-the-other and following an authentic way of relating to suffering humanity in the cross of Jesus. Any other way, means meaninglessness of the peoples of the Caribbean, because they know only God who is a friend of the suffering poor.[44]

Similarly, Lewin Williams suggest that while it might not be the most reflected upon theme in Caribbean Theology, 'Christology in the Caribbean context is the most crucial area in the Caribbean perspective.'[45] He too notes the importance of the complex religious and cultural nature of the African Caribbean and suggests that the Caribbean Christ must be Afro- and Indo-Caribbean. Williams also suggests that the universality of Christ isn't rejected by the region, but because of the pervasive influence of colonial ideas about universality, there must be a concerted effort to keep the universal and the particular together. Finally, the Caribbean Christ must be connected to Christ's soteriological acts, which are always about liberation and justice. He states: 'In the final analysis, the liberation that the Caribbean seeks is the right to build its community and develop its dream. If this is the main perspective shared within the pluralism of the Caribbean, the Caribbean Christ is already at work within that same pluralism.'[46] A similar observation is made by Gabriel Malzaire, whose work is perhaps the latest attempt to engage Christological thinking in the complexity of the African Caribbean.[47]

George Mulrain, unlike Chambers and Williams, engages the Person of Christ from a contextual theological perspective and suggests that Christ be considered as a Calypsonian. He states that Caribbean people 'are trying desperately to project the figure of Jesus today in ways that are meaningful'.[48] He considers a *Cricketer Christ*, but settles with the image of the Calypsonian, the popular artist of the musical genre. For Mulrain:

Calypso is much more than a song. It is expressive of a culture or a way of life. This culture is also captured in reggae, the Jamaican musical equivalent in the sense that its traditional songs also have features that include a carefree, easygoing approach to issues and the ability to laugh in the face of difficulties. Calypso also performs a political and prophetic function and in so doing offers a subtle challenge to authority, just as Jesus challenged the political and religious leaders of his day.[49]

Mulrain also asserts that Calypso provides a therapeutic function, and therefore a Calypso Christ is both prophetic and therapeutic. Thorough liberation and deep healing are essential in this conception of Christ. In considering gendered imaging of Christ in Christian history and theology, Mulrain states:

> Some would, because of gender, scoff at the idea of a feminine Christ. But should the fact that Jesus the Jew was male necessarily mean that the female image of Christ cannot be acceptable? In fact, when we acknowledge how Caribbean women have been mistreated and given a raw deal by their menfolk, we note how they more than anybody else embody suffering and rejection. They, more than their male counterparts, display a closeness to and a dependence upon God, very much in keeping with the Christ who is all one with the Creator and the Holy Spirit.[50]

It is clear from the scholars highlighted that Christological questions in the region are not straightforward. Images of Christ imported as universal have been used as weapons against the non-European ethnicities, cosmologies and religiosities. There is the sense in which new images and concepts of Christ must continually be employed. There is space for engaging the imagination of ATRs to bring to the surface images of Christ that are both liberative and healing. In the next chapter we further engage the inherent decolonial hermeneutics of ATRs and a further exploration of the Person of the Holy Spirit in the African Caribbean.

Notes

1 Lewin L. Williams, *The Caribbean: Enculturation, Acculturation, and the Role of the Churches*, Gospel and Cultures, Geneva: WCC Publications, 1996, pp. 1, 5.

2 Williams, *The Caribbean*, p. 3.

3 Oscar L. Bolioli (ed.), 'Reclaiming Identity: The Verdun Proclamation', in *The Caribbean: Culture of Resistance, Spirit of Hope*, New York: Friendship Press, 1993. This document, also quoted in the Intro-

duction, brought self-negation and African religiocultural retentions to the forefront of Caribbean and African American diasporan concerns.

4 Bolioli, 'Reclaiming Identity: The Verdun Proclamation'.

5 Burton Sankeralli (ed.), *At the Crossroads: African Caribbean Religion and Christianity*, St James, Trinidad and Tobago: Caribbean Conference of Churches, 1995.

6 Hilary McDonald Beckles and Verene A. Shepherd, *Liberties Lost: Caribbean Indigenous Societies and Slave Systems*, Cambridge: Cambridge University Press, 2004, pp. 2–27.

7 Nathaniel Samuel Murrell, *Afro-Caribbean Religions: An Introduction to their Historical, Cultural, and Sacred Traditions*, Philadelphia, PA: Temple University Press, 2010, ch. 1, pp. 13–36.

8 Murrell, *Afro-Caribbean Religions*, p. 19.

9 Murrell, *Afro-Caribbean Religions*, p. 24.

10 Murrell, *Afro-Caribbean Religions*, p. 25.

11 Murrell, *Afro-Caribbean Religions*, p. 26.

12 Dianne M. Stewart, *Three Eyes for the Journey: African Dimensions of the Jamaican Religious Experience*, Oxford: Oxford University Press, 2004.

13 Ronald Nathan, 'Caribbean Youth Identity in the United Kingdom: A Call for a Pan-African Theology', *Black Theology in Britain: A Journal of Contextual Praxis* 1, October 1998, p. 10.

14 Diana Paton, 'A Legacy of Emancipation in the Diaspora', *StabroekNews.com*, 18 March 2013, http://www.stabroeknews.com/2013/features/in-the-diaspora/03/18/a-legacy-of-emancipation/ (accessed 17.7.23). See also Diana Paton and Maarit Forde, *Obeah and Other Powers: The Politics of Caribbean Religion and Healing*, Durham, NC: Duke University Press, 2012.

15 See Diana Paton's website giving the history and the facts: https://obeahhistories.org/ (accessed 17.7.23)

16 Carlton Turner, *Overcoming Self-Negation: The Church and Junkanoo in Contemporary Bahamian Society*, Eugene, OR: Pickwick Publications, 2020.

17 Frantz Fanon, *The Wretched of the Earth*, Harmondsworth: Penguin, 1967, p. 200.

18 W. E. B. Du Bois, *The Souls of Black Folk*, Signet Classics, New York: New American Library, 1969, p. 3.

19 Ennis B. Edmonds and Michelle A. Gonzalez, *Caribbean Religious History: An Introduction*, New York: New York University Press, 2010.

20 The use of the words 'African retentions' is not new to Caribbean theological discussion. See Stephen Jennings, 'Caribbean Theology or Theologies of the Caribbean', *Caribbean Journal of Religious Studies* 8, no. 2, 1987, p. 4. He employs the term to highlight the need for any form of Christian theology within the region to critically and constructively correlate with African Survivals of one kind or another. His examples

of such African retentions are Vodou, Shango, Myalism, Revivalism and Pocomania, as wells as Rastafariansim, Garveyism and the Black Power movement, all of which he sees as synthesized expressions, to one degree or another, of European cultural theology and African inculturation theology.

21 Anna Kasafi Perkins, 'The Wages of (Sin) is Babylon: Rastafari Versus Christian Religious Perspectives of Sin', in *Rastafari in the New Millennium: A Rastafari Reader*, ed. Michael Barnett, Syracuse, NY: Syracuse University Press, 2012. Anna Kasafi Perkins, '"Tasting Tears and [Not] Admitting Defeat": Promoting Values and Attitudes through the Music of Tanya Stephens?', Inaugural Lecture of the Centre for Social Ethics, St Michael's Theological College, Academia.edu, 12 January 2008.

22 Annette Brown, 'Church and Dancehall: Challenges to Mission Among Young People in the Churches in Jamaica', *Rethinking Mission*, April 2011, https://d3hgrlq6yacptf.cloudfront.net/uspg/content/pages/documents/1596109978.pdf (accessed 17.7.23).

23 Dulcie A. Dixon McKenzie, 'Black British Theology in Gospel Music', in *Postcolonial Black British Theology: New Textures and Themes*, ed. Michael Jagessar and Anthony Reddie, Peterborough: Epworth, 2007.

24 George Mulrain, 'Is there a Calypso Exegesis?', in *Voices From the Margin: Interpreting the Bible in the Third World*, ed. R. S. Sugirtharajah, Maryknoll, NY: Orbis Books, 1995.

25 Richard D. E. Burton, *Afro-Creole: Power, Opposition and Play in the Caribbean*, New York: Cornell University Press, 1997.

26 Kortright Davis, *Emancipation Still Comin': Explorations in Caribbean Emancipatory Theology*, Maryknoll, NY: Orbis Books, 1990, p. 44.

27 Clifford Rawlins, *A Theology of Carnival and Other Provocations: Realigning Christian Thought for a Post-Modern World*, San Fernando, Trinidad and Tobago: Trinity Hill Publishing, 2021.

28 Burton, *Afro-Creole*, pp. 173–86.

29 Kenneth Bilby, 'Gumbay, Myal, and the Great House: New Evidence of the Religious Background of Jonkonnu in Jamaica', *ACIJ Research Review* 4, 1999, p. 64.

30 Turner, *Overcoming Self-Negation*.

31 Anthony G. Reddie, 'An Interactive Methodology for Doing Black Theology', in *Postcolonial Black British Theology*, ed. Jagessar and Reddie, 2007.

32 See, Anthony Reddie, 'Dramatic Improvisation: A Jazz Inspired Approach to Undertaking Theology with the Marginalized', in *Reading Spiritualities: Constructing and Representing the Sacred*, ed. Dawn Llewellyn and Deborah F. Sawyer, Aldershot: Ashgate, 2008.

33 Michael Jagessar, 'Spinning Theology: Trickster, Texts and Theology', in *Postcolonial Black British Theology*, ed. Jagessar and Reddie, 2007, p. 134.

34 George Mulrain, *Theology in Folk Culture: The Theological Significance of Haitian Folk Religion*, Frankfurt: Peter Lang, 1984.

35 See Stewart, *Three Eyes for the Journey*.

36 Barry Chevannes, *Rastafari: Roots and Ideology*, Syracuse, NY: Syracuse University Press, 1995, pp. 18–19; emphasis original.

37 Timothy McCartney, *Ten, Ten, the Bible Ten: Obeah in the Bahamas*, Nassau, Bahamas: Tinpaul Publishing Company, 1976, pp. 113–14.

38 Carlton Turner, 'Taming the Spirit? Widening the Pneumatological Gaze within African Caribbean Theological Discourse', *Black Theology: An International Journal* 13, no. 2, 2015.

39 Davis, *Emancipation Still Comin'*, p. 44.

40 Novelle Josiah, 'The Develoment of Calypso in Antigua and its Continuity with Old Testament Traditions', unpublished MPhil thesis, University of the West Indies, 2003.

41 Kirkley C. Sands, *Early Bahamian Slave Spirituality: The Genesis of Bahamian Cultural Identity*, Nassau, Bahamas: The Nassau Guardian Ltd, 2008, p. 65.

42 Davis, *Emancipation Still Comin'*.

43 Donald Dean Chambers, 'The Faces of Jesus Christ in the Literary Works of Caribbean Preachers and Theologians: Towards a Constructive Christology for the Caribbean', PhD, Pontificia Università Gregoriana, 2005, p. 6.

44 Chambers, 'The Faces of Jesus Christ in the Literary Works of Caribbean Preachers and Theologians', p. 304.

45 Lewin L. Williams, *Caribbean Theology*, New York: Peter Lang, 1994, p. 151.

46 Williams, *The Caribbean*, pp. 154–5.

47 Gabriel Malzaire, *Christ & Caribbean Culture(s): A Collection of Essays on Caribbean Christology and its Pastoral Implications*, Philadelphia, PA: Parchment Global Publishing, 2019.

48 George Mulrain, *Caribbean Theological Insights: Exploring Theological Themes within the Context of the Caribbean Region*, London: Blessed Hope Publishing, 2014, p. 51.

49 Mulrain, *Caribbean Theological Insights*, p. 53.

50 Mulrain, *Caribbean Theological Insights*, p. 56.

6

'Chanting Down Babylon':
An Anti-imperial Hermeneutic

'Chanting Down Babylon' is both an important theological work in the region, as well as the title for one of Bob Marley's songs. This chapter argues that at the heart of a Caribbean Contextual Theology is a challenge to empire and colonialism using a theological hermeneutic deeply influenced by the Christian Scriptures and pro-African and pro-Caribbean motifs. It seeks to be inclusive, African-centred, identity-affirming, justice-seeking and God-expanding. The chief theological idea promoted is that God is bigger than the concept the missionary brought. While the last chapter helped us to frame ATRs more clearly, it can be argued that ATRs have always employed decolonial or anti-colonial methods, hence giving Caribbean Contextual Theologies a decolonial or anti-colonial edge.

Hermeneutics and Decoloniality

First, it's important to establish what we mean by 'hermeneutics', or 'decolonial', or 'anti-colonial'. By 'hermeneutics', we simply mean the way texts are interpreted or the factors involved in the interpretative exercise. Paying attention to how texts are interpreted, particularly biblical texts, is crucial within the African Caribbean region, where the Bible has been used in multiple ways, either for perpetuating violence and oppression or for resisting the same. The term 'anti-colonial' is an earlier term associated with thinkers such as Aimé Césaire, Frantz Fanon and Walter Rodney, among others.[1] 'Anti' suggests a counter or a direct contradiction to the colonial agenda with its anti-African hermeneutics. For example, in Aimé Césaire, 'negritude' is championed to counteract the black hatred inherent in colonialism. For Césaire, the colonizer is not innocent, but barbarous and pathologically violent.[2] For Marcus Garvey, the solution for diasporan black people in the Americas is to return to Mother Africa, to live out a counter-history, spirituality, culture and political and economic system rather than what was provided in the racist Euro-American world order as he saw it.[3] 'Decolonial' and 'postcolonial' are more contemporary terms that highlight the complex dialectical relationship between the colonizer and the colonized in colonial situations. They interrogate the substructures of the colonial machinery, its language, psychology, and philosophical and theological assumptions. Some of these thinkers will be explored below, but before examining the Caribbean, something must be said about the tradition of postcolonial theology and its rise in recent decades.

Postcolonial theology is very connected to Liberation Theology and Black Theology, but its focus is particularly on all the deceptive ways in which the colonial agenda and narrative have shaped both the Church and the world. Originally, postcolonial theory came to prominence in literature as persons like Edward Said (*Orientalism*, 1978), Gayatri Spivak (*Can the Subaltern Speak?*, 1988) and Homi Bhabha (*The Location of Culture*, 1994) contested the ways in which the 'West' or 'Europe' got to frame the world.[4] Why is the West, West? Bhabha extended Said's insights to open up conversations around notions such as 'hybridity', and even the concept of postcolonialism. In short, colonization has never been something innocent, but rather a narrative, story or discourse, which dictated who the main characters were, who the supporting casts were and how the plot would conclude.

Perhaps a key theological voice and pioneer for postcolonial theology is R. S. Sugirtharajah's *Postcolonial Reconfigurations* (2003), whose deep reading of theology and Christian texts is informed by his cultural upbringing in the British colonial world. Sections of this book give us an idea of what he is doing. First, he re-positions Christian discourse. Second, he relocates biblical studies. Third, he re-maps Christian theological discourse.[5] In other words, the ways in which we understand theology have been framed by the West or by Europe for so long, but what would it look like if it were framed by an Asian? An African Caribbean person? A Nigerian? A Fijian? Through Sugirtharajah's work we see a space open up to interrogate the Scriptures or construct theology in other ways, with other insights, seeing the narrative differently. Other edited works have become important for their postcolonial insights: for example, Gerald West, *Reading Other-Wise: Socially Engaged Biblical Scholars Reading with their Local Communities* (2007) and Michael Jagessar and Anthony Reddie, *Black Theology in Britain: A Reader* (2007).[6]

A Note about Liberation Theology

It is common to speak of Liberation Theology as if it were unified, but for now let's think in terms of theologies of liberation that appear across the globe and across Christian denominations. Key thinkers such as Gustavo Gutiérrez, Leonardo and Clovodis Boff and Jon Sobrino theologically reflect out of the Latin American context, where the history of European expansion has created a situation of class structures, the systemic oppression of the poor and the marginalized, and the continued accumulation of power by the wealthy.[7] Unfortunately, 'the Church' has been deeply complicit in these pervasive practices of injustice. Such thinkers have challenged the theological agenda, shifting the hermeneutical focus of theology from the oppressor to the oppressed. They have challenged the way God is read in the Scriptures, coming to the realization that God is the God of the poor and the oppressed, and that God, and the Church, should resist systems of injustice and impoverishment. Also, such scholars challenge the idea of 'the expert' in theology, arguing that theology should be read by and in conjunction with those who are the poor and the marginalized. This is the only way for the gospel to emerge as liberative. Furthermore, they emphasize practice, that there should not be a disconnect between what is preached or taught and what is enacted.

However, it is not fair to say that Liberation Theology belongs only to the Latin American context. Legacies of reading the Bible through the lens and framework of liberation have been central to oppressed people seeking to live out the gospel in the context of oppression. For example, we can argue that slave revolts in the African Caribbean were powerful examples of Liberation Theology in the persons of Sam Sharpe, Nanny of the Maroons and Nat Turner. When we think about the development of Black Theologies, or Black Theologies of Liberation in the USA, South Africa and the UK, through the likes of academics and activists such as James Cone, Steve Biko, Anthony Reddie and Robert Beckford, we see consistent attention to the sin of racism deeply embedded in Western societies. But this must never be separated from Womanist theologians, who have consistently argued that even within these movements of liberation, women of colour have still been oppressed and marginalized. Theologians such as Delores Williams, Jacqueline Grant, Katie G. Cannon and Dulcie Dixon McKenzie have been making black women's voices heard, and with a powerful emphasis not just on liberation but on healing also.

African Caribbean Hermeneutics

The Caribbean has a rich and developed decolonial or post-colonial tradition outside theology that must be considered before surveying some of the Caribbean theological works. First, the French Caribbean has produced a few thinkers such as the Martinicans Aimé Césaire and Frantz Fanon, who have looked at, in different ways, the psychology and political structure of colonialism. Perhaps Fanon has been the most enduring thinker for the Francophone and wider African Caribbean, and even globally, with his two famous works, *Black Skin White Mask* and *Wretched of the Earth*. Fanon considers the colonial system as a totalizing situation that is undergirded by violence, and should be read as such. Experiencing the inherent racism in the French Caribbean, in France and in Algeria, he concludes:

As long as he remains among his own people, the little black follows very nearly the same course as the little white. But if he goes to Europe, he will have to reappraise his lot. For the Negro in France, which is his country, will feel different from other people. One can hear the glib remark: The Negro makes himself inferior. But the truth is that he is made inferior.[8]

In my article 'Deepening the Postcolonial Theological Gaze', where I engage with Fanon as a way of exploring the psychological nature of colonial oppression, I argue:

What we see in Fanon is diversity of critical tools with which to view coloniality, hence there are different ways to read and interpret this French Caribbean revolutionary. On the one hand, he can be seen as a political anti-colonial activist and theorist. It is often the case that he is seen as a freedom fighter, but this side-lines the other way in which Fanon should be read which is that of a postcolonial theorist of the specifically psychological dimensions of the colonial situation. He describes the unseen psychological, social, and religious dimensions of the inherent violence of colonialism, without compartmentalizing these different aspects.[9]

Sylvia Wynter is another name that deserves attention here. Her academic output as a philosopher, anti-colonial thinker, dramatist and novelist covers Caribbean, Latin American and Spanish history and insights. In essays such as 'Towards the Sociogenic Principle: Fanon, Identity, the Puzzle of Conscious Experience', 'What it is Like to be "Black"', 'Unsettling the Coloniality of Being/Power/Truth/Freedom: Towards the Human', and 'After Man, its Overrepresentation – an Argument', Wynter is one of the earlier thinkers exploring and exposing the philosophical substructures of coloniality, particularly in how it perpetuates itself through signs and symbols.[10]

Walter Rodney is another voice deserving attention. His radical and revolutionary deconstruction of Western neo-liberal capitalism and its continued effects on colonized territories remains significant. His *How Europe Underdeveloped Africa* is a work that has inspired many political thinkers since his assassination in his native Guyana in 1980.[11]

Theological thinking in the region, including formal theological works, inevitably stems from this kind of anti-imperial critique. Long before the publication of Noel Erskine's *Decolonizing Theology*, the Baptist deacon Sam Sharpe was touring various Jamaican plantations preaching and teaching a kind of gospel that led to slaves fighting for their lives and freedom in the Christmas Day riots (Baptist War) of 1831–32.[12] Deeply influenced by Afro-cultures in the Atlantic world, including the Caribbean, Robert Hood asked the perennial question: *Must God Remain Greek?* This book by the same title argues that the Graeco-Roman framework informing European Christianity in the West continues to shape the religious thoughtforms of black people in Afrophobic ways. He presents the issue this way:

> Hence, a crucial question for the worldwide Christian church as it tries to take seriously Third World cultures, particularly those in Africa and in the African diaspora (e.g., in the Caribbean), is whether Greek metaphysics will continue to be used as a filter to authenticate its claims and understanding of God in Jesus Christ. For the Third World cultures in Africa and the Caribbean, must God remain Greek?[13]

Noel Erskine's assessment of hermeneutics in the African Caribbean context is worth repeating here:

> The point of departure for reflection on the Caribbean experience will be my own background within the church in Jamaica. My knowledge of theological education and life as a pastor in the church in Jamaica indicated that theology as it was practiced within the church did not address the identity problem that slavery created among Caribbean peoples. God as presented within the Caribbean church was often on the symbol of freedom but, rather, the extension of the European and the North American church experience.[14]

Other Caribbean theologians have written specifically about theological hermeneutics in the Caribbean. Oral Thomas has argued that the biblical reading strategies often employed in the African Caribbean still conform to literary-rhetorical models that prioritize the social world of the biblical text, with little regard for transformation of the present context of the reader. He argues for a biblical resistant reading strategy that takes both the African Caribbean context and that of the biblical world seriously. He writes:

> A resistant reading strategy necessitates giving self-conscious attention to the world or interests of practices in which the text was produced (behind the text), the writer's vision of reality (on the text), and the influences and experiences that shape the reader's interpretation (in front of the text) or the particularities and peculiarities of the context of the inter-preter. Both the production and reading of biblical texts are modes of social action. It is out of these modes of social action in which all three hermeneutical moves are involved – behind the text, on or within the text and in front of the text – that a biblically resistant hermeneutic within a Caribbean context will take shape.[15]

Thomas maintains his commitment to an interdisciplinary post-colonial and decolonial tradition with his engagement with the scholarship of, for example, R. S. Sugirtharajah, Itumeleng J. Mosala and Gerald O. West.[16] Through these insights, hermen-eutics begin to challenge the colonial narratives that have shaped the received understandings of biblical texts, the ideological framing of texts and their reception, unearth the social, gender, class and social practices of the text, and ultimately expose the power dynamics involved in how texts are interpreted. Thomas explores historical examples of this in the writings and activism of Sam Sharpe, Paul Bogle and Marcus Garvey, revolutionary freedom fighters in Jamaica in their respective historical time periods. Their agitation was informed by a deep understanding of a God of justice who suffers and cares about the plight of his people. The same central approach to reading and understanding Scripture is also traced in the tradition of the Rastafari and in historical figures such as Philip Potter.[17] Interestingly, Thomas also looks at African Caribbean cultural productions such as cricket and Carnival as hermeneutical practices of resistance.[18] For Thomas, Carnival and cricket provide insight into the Caribbean use of place for resistance and subversion. They bring social struggle into public display, providing accessible ways of critiquing, questioning and contesting often unvoiced realities.

George Mulrain is another Caribbean theologian who has paid particular attention to the importance of hermeneutics within the Caribbean context. He contributed to Sugirtharajah's *Vernacular Hermeneutics* using the framework of Black theological hermeneutics.[19] Caribbean hermeneutical techniques, according to Mulrain, involve the use of the historico-critical methods to understand the original context of the Bible, the interpretative lens of the reader and his/her community context, and the interaction between the text of Scripture and the lived experiences of Caribbean people. This hermeneutical approach in the Caribbean, Mulrain argues, inevitably includes 'slavery, oppression, colonialism, suffering, victimization, marginalization, anonymity'; the awareness of the multi-faith reality of Caribbean life; a commitment to liberation; and an insistence on hope.[20] In his most recent work, *Caribbean Theological Insights*, he devotes a chapter to theological hermeneutics in the region and suggests several considerations.[21] First, the Bible has always been central to Caribbean self-understanding whether it be the established churches or the African Traditional Religious Heritages. Second, there has always been suspicion over how the Bible has been expounded in such a postcolonial and postimperial context. Third, along with Mulrain's general thesis that theology in the region is done orally and narratively, African culture dominates theological hermeneutics. Fourth, it is not an individualistic but a communitarian exercise. And fifth, it is always directed towards salvation, liberation and emancipation.

Michael Jagessar is yet another Caribbean theologian and postcolonial thinker for whom hermeneutics is central to his decolonial work. He employs the pan-Caribbean figure of Anancy to articulate a hermeneutical approach patterned after the trickster figure. His chapter in *Postcolonial Black British Theology: New Textures and Themes*, his work co-edited with Anthony Reddie, unavoidably engages the Caribbean, and his chapter on Anancy, perhaps better than most, reveals a compelling and engaging take on how Caribbean people interpret texts and contexts.[22] Jagessar confesses:

> As one whose life has been shaped in the Caribbean, my theology, my theologizing and hermeneutics reflects its Caribbean heritage – especially its rainbow nature. This is one of the reasons why I find it difficult to theologize with *a* view. Like Anancy, my proclivity is to do theology from a multiplicity of views, that is, 'with eight legs tapping epics from the cosmic floor'.[23]

Anancy, the West African figure prominent in Caribbean literature, folk tales and folk traditions, employs trickery and subversion amid brutal colonial oppression to provide a kind of counter-imagination, one that continually contests the deep psychic and theological anti-African and colonial imaginations of empire. Anancy provides a counter-hermeneutic of resistance, and does this by weaving multiple stories together, inevitably subverting dominant narratives. Anancy engages in mimicry, ambivalence and sarcasm, asserting strategies of power for otherwise disempowered people. Anancy transgresses accepted codes and dogmas to loosen complex and more nuanced readings of texts and situations. These strategies are true across Caribbean life, whether the calypsonian, the carnival dancer or the thunderous preacher. Jagessar writes: 'Be it in the Caribbean or in the Caribbean diaspora around the North Atlantic world, Caribbeans can reel out stories of the demonic, of triumphs and defeats, and of promises realized, hopes smashed and dreams held on to.'[24]

In a more recent reflection, Anna Kasafi Perkins and I explore the place of drumming traditions within the Caribbean and their theological significance. Using qualitative research methods into the experience of drumming practitioners, Rastafarian and Baptist, we conclude that the liberatory and anti-imperial impulse within African Caribbean religious and cultural productions is still alive across the region. There is still a deep-seated contestation against colonial forms of Christianity that continue to be anti-African. We state:

> Such contestations, we argue, are grounded in a colonized theological aesthetic, which too often rejects beauty in the African form, body, worship and play. Perhaps the crucial question of theological aesthetics when accounting for Caribbean concerns is whether, and to what extent, the Afro-Caribbean person truly reflects divinity. Rastafari, an Afro-Christian movement originating in Jamaica, presents a response to such contestations, which is still perceived as radical today. The theological aesthetics of Rastafari divinizes the Black man as God because he appeared in the form of Emperor Haile Selassie I of Ethiopia. This connection valorizes the African – including African ways of worship, where drumming and chanting are central.[25]

We progress our reflection towards pneumatology, arguing that such aesthetics and hermeneutics are always grounded in African traditional spiritualty and pneumatology. We further state:

> It is our contention, however, that theological aesthetics in a Caribbean key, particularly drumming, pounds out 'rhythms on the heart of God' and leads directly to a consideration of the work of the Spirit, which liberates.[26]

A Revolutionary Spirit: Resistance, Affirmation, Wholeness

From the theology explored above, it becomes clear that liberation, emancipation and affirmation are not separate desires in the region. Decolonialization is not simply a political or a theological event, it is also a psychological and existential one.

Theological hermeneutics in the region continue this tripartite function of simultaneously resisting violence and oppression using political subversion and critique; affirming the identity and the image of God within the African person; and consistently working towards greater wholeness within African Caribbean persons and their societies. Following Perkins and Turner, I suggest that Caribbean Theology naturally proposes a pneumatology that is revolutionary, especially in these three dimensions.

Before proceeding, it must be asserted that pneumatology remains an underexplored area of theology generally. In my article, 'Taming the Spirit', in the *Black Theology in Britain* journal, I have argued that the African religious and cultural heritages of the Caribbean are inherently pneumatocentric and have consistently functioned to contest missionary forms of Christianity that were more Christocentric.[27] I advanced the thesis that, in many respects, Africanized forms of Christianity within the region were pneumatological reformations of Missionary Christianity.

Within the Christian tradition the Third Person of the Trinity has remained elusive, both doctrinally and in the Revivalist and Pentecostal movements across Christian history. Jürgen Moltmann invites us to be critical of Western Christianity and its Platonic influence because it has yet to reconcile the Spirit of Jesus and the Spirit of creation. He states:

> One reason is certainly the continuing platonization of Christianity. Even today this still puts its mark on what is termed 'spirituality' in the church and religious groups. It takes the form of a kind of hostility to the body, a kind of remoteness from the world, and a preference for the inner experiences of the soul rather than the sensory experiences of sociality and nature.[28]

This has a lot of implications for how we approach pneumatology within a multi-religious and multi-cultural context such as the African Caribbean. Robert Murphy surveys the African Traditional Religions across the region and how they theologically reconcile their monotheism and their expanded cosmologies or, more specifically, the relationship between the 'One God' and the many 'spirits'. He writes:

> Each of the traditions speaks of one God who is the first principle of the universe: Vodou's Grand Maitre or Bondye; Olodumare or Olorun in Candomblé and santeria; and God Almighty in Revival Zion and the Black Church. In each case the focus of the service is on the incarnation of one or more spirits which partake of the essence of the single, supreme being, but which also represent more localized or concretized forms of the abstraction ... The Christian metaphors of several persons or hypostases of one God might be applied to diasporan ideas of spirit.[29]

In a similar vein, George Mulrain makes the following challenge when considering Vodou in Haiti:

> Sometimes God chooses methods other than Jesus Christ, His Supreme Revelation, or the Church, to testify to His existence. His Holy Spirit cannot be limited, for He is at work everywhere in the world. How God chooses to make His will known through a spirit may be inconceivable to the western mind. But to people within folk culture, this is quite normal.[30]

It is precisely this elusive, untamed, supra-doctrinal nature of the Spirit that allowed for an African Caribbean pneumatology embracing African Caribbean Traditional Religious Heritages and cultures. Furthering Moltmann's criticism of the Western Christian tradition and applying it to the African Caribbean context, I state:

> Firstly, one must dispense with a rigid separation between Black Christianity within the African Caribbean and African Traditional Religions and their variants within the region. African culture permeates both. Secondly, Africans slaves and Liberated Africans were reinterpreting and significantly influencing Christianity, even within the Protestant Churches.

Though church as an institution may have rejected their spiritual expressivism, they were tapping into a pneumatology already deep within their culture. Thirdly, African slaves and Liberated Africans were not disparaging their African roots when they became vibrant Christians; they were simply adopting another, equally valid spiritual system, one which had attractive power. They did not abandon the former because of notions of inferiority; they choose the latter because it related to them. There was something about the Person and acts of the Holy Spirit in the Bible with which they identified. In fact, it can be argued that these early African Caribbean Christians had a deeper grasp of biblical pneumatology than did the hierarchy of the established or missionary churches, which disparaged such expressive forms of Christianity.[31]

In fact, it can be argued that within the African Caribbean context, where the common conception is that slave and indigenous peoples were converted to Christianity by the Church, the reverse might also be true. Dianne Stewart, in her book *Three Eyes of the Journey*, argues that, within the Jamaican slave plantation context, the slaves and their descendants were Africanizing Christianity. When considering the history of pneumatocentric traditions such as Revival Zion and the Native Baptists, she suggests that they masked Christianity for their social acceptance. They were concealing their Obeah and Myal against the backdrop of censorship and annihilation. She writes: 'Rather than viewing them as syncretism, I prefer to name them innovations or christianisms responsible for transforming African traditional Myalism into Native Baptist and Revival Zion traditions "antibodies".'[32]

Barry Chevannes makes a similar observation about the Myal religious trajectory in Jamaica as pneumatologically reinterpreting Christianity. It challenged Western preoccupations with the Trinitarian Persons of the Father and the Son, and instead asserted the Person of the Spirit. It's worth requoting him here:

Where Christianity is transfixed on Jesus as mediator Myal was transfixed on the Spirit as possessor and sought [the

Spirit] in dreams and secluded retreat. Whereas Christianity placed its emphasis on transmitted *knowledge* (doctrine, Bible, catechism) for conversion, Myal placed its emphasis on the *experience* of the Spirit. When followers found [the Spirit] it was to be filled by [the Spirit], to be possessed. Possession by the Spirit thus became the quintessential experience of myalized Christianity.[33]

It was this pneumatological version of classic Christianity that African Jamaicans, and other African Caribbean people, clung to, and which provided foundation for attempts at liberation. It brought them closer to agency during anthropological impoverishment.

Given the unique history of the region and the continued contestation between African Traditional Religious cultures and heritages and Missionary or Western Christian traditions, let us return to this idea of a tripartite understanding of the Holy Spirit within Caribbean Theology. First, and naturally, the Third Person of the Trinity is the Spirit of Resistance. In the beginning the Spirit moves over the waters of creation, bringing new life into being. The Spirit empowers the prophets and contests violence and oppression. In the Spirit, Jesus asserts in Luke 4 the famous mandate:

> The Spirit of the Lord is upon me, because he has anointed me to bring good news to the poor. He has sent me to proclaim release to the captives and recovery of sight to the blind, to let the oppressed go free, to proclaim the year of the Lord's favour.[34]

The movement of the Spirit within the biblical tradition is never without contestation and transformation. This is naturally part of an African Caribbean understanding and explains beginnings of revolutionary movements such as the Sam Sharpe rebellion or the Haitian Revolution.

Resistance and liberation are not the only characteristics of the Spirit within Caribbean Theology. There is, secondly, the Spirit of Affirmation. The anthropological impoverishment of

African people within the region, and the persistent anti-African hermeneutic across the region, has significantly impacted a sense of dignity and worth within African Caribbean life. Caribbean theological reflections have had to address the idea that sinfulness was projected on to the indigenous, or the African, or simply the non-European identity, an issue that persists today. In *Overcoming Self-Negation*, I argue that what the Spirit does, as evident in religiocultural productions across the region, is to affirm African Identity as equally valid and divine within the post-plantation context.[35] Whether we are thinking of possession rituals or musical traditions, the consistent plea is for a deep sense of self-love. The Spirit crosses boundaries and, as in Acts 11, continually contests norms and ideas around who might be deserving of inclusion within the Jesus movement. Identity, whether Jew or Gentile, is the central focus in this gospel narrative. Through the leading of the Spirit, the Gentiles find a place; in fact, it had always been the case that all had a place within God's economy of grace. Similarly, from Marcus Garvey to Sam Sharpe, or from Walter Rodney to Kortright Davis, the Spirit isn't only about resistance: the Spirit also deeply affirms identity. In the colonial and plantation context where African identities were marginalized and deemed sinful and unimportant, African Caribbean ways of pneumatologically reconceptualizing Christianity served the purpose of deeply affirming the identity and worth of African Caribbean people themselves.

Finally, there is the Spirit of Wholeness. This conception of the Spirit within Caribbean Theology must also be asserted. In a region that has, from inception, known persistent violence and trauma, healing or wholeness must be at the heart of its theological articulations. An important part of the prophetic tradition within the biblical tradition in the life of the Hebrew prophets, and also in the life of Jesus, was healing and wholeness. Walter Brueggemann's *The Prophetic Imagination* helps us with this insight.[36] For him, the prophetic consciousness, fully embodied in Jesus, ultimately exists for the healing and wholeness of the oppressed and downtrodden. While there is criticism and resistance in Jesus' confrontations with religious and political systems, there is also healing for the oppressed and broken. This kind of healing is intimate and deep, and involves identification with the oppressed ones. In the same vein, African Caribbean religious and cultural productions have always functioned simultaneously to criticize, to affirm, but more importantly to heal. Myal, Vodou, Shango, for example, were not only pneumatologically orientated harming traditions; more fundamentally, they were healing traditions. They functioned to help the enslaved and their descendants survive slavery and genocide.

Conclusion

Decolonization and hermeneutics within the African Caribbean pre-date and extend beyond any formal sense of theology. Caribbean people, including African Caribbean ones, living in the legacies of plantation slavery and colonial oppression, have always employed strategies of critiquing, resisting and surviving such experiences. They have always preserved healing traditions to accompany the resistance efforts. In a sense, they're part of what it means to be Caribbean and manifest across religious and cultural life. Ultimately, a Caribbean Theology that is birthed in the revolutionary spirit of the region can help renew and supplement our understanding of the Spirit of God. The Spirit is reformational and revolutionary. The Spirit resists and disrupts oppressive and dehumanizing systems. Finally, the Spirit brings new life, wholeness and peace.

Notes

1 Aimé Césaire, *Discourse on Colonialism*, New York: Monthly Review Press, 1972. Frantz Fanon, *The Wretched of the Earth*, Harmondsworth: Penguin, 1967; *Black Skin, White Masks*, New York: Grove Press, 1967. Walter Rodney, *How Europe Underdeveloped Africa*, London: Bogle-L'Ouverture Publications, 1972. Walter Rodney, *The Groundings with My Brothers*, London: Bogle-L'Ouverture Publications, 1969.

2 Césaire, *Discourse on Colonialism*.

3 See Marcus Garvey and Amy Jacques Garvey, *The Philosophy and Opinions of Marcus Garvey*, Dover, MA: Majority Press, 1986.

4 Edward W. Said, *Orientalism*, 1st edn, New York: Pantheon Books, 1978. Gayatri Chakravorty Spivak, 'Can the Subaltern Speak?', in *Marxism and the Interpretation of Cultures*, ed. Cary Nelson and Lawrence Grossberg, Urbana, IL: University of Illinois Press, 1988. Homi K. Bhaba, *The Location of Culture*, 1st edn, New York: Routledge, 1994.

5 R. S. Sugirtharajah, *Postcolonial Criticism and Biblical Interpretation*, Oxford: Oxford University Press, 2002.

6 Gerald O. West, *Reading Other-Wise: Socially Engaged Biblical Scholars Reading with their Local Communities*, Society of Biblical Literature Semeia Studies, Atlanta, GA: Society of Biblical Literature, 2007. Michael Jagessar and Anthony Reddie (eds), *Postcolonial Black British Theology: New Textures and Themes*, Peterborough: Epworth, 2007. See also Mark G. Brett, *Political Trauma and Healing: Biblical Ethics for a Postcolonial World*, Grand Rapids, MI: Eerdmans, 2016, p. 5.

7 See, for example: Gustavo Gutiérrez, *A Theology of Liberation: History, Politics, and Salvation*, Maryknoll, NY: Orbis Books, 1981; Clodovis Boff, *Theology and Praxis: Epistemological Foundations*, Maryknoll, NY: Orbis Books, 1987; Lornardo Boff and Clodovis Boff, *Introducing Liberation Theology*, Maryknoll, NY: Orbis Books, 1987; Jon Sobrino, Paul Burns and Francis McDonagh, *Jesus the Liberator: A Historical-Theological Reading of Jesus of Nazareth*, Alexandria, VA: Alexander Street Press, 2014.

8 Fanon, *Black Skin, White Masks*, p. 115.

9 Carlton Turner, 'Deepening the Postcolonial Theological Gaze: Frantz Fanon and the Psychopathology of Colonial Christianity', *Modern Believing* 62, no. 4, Autumn 2021, p. 346.

10 For a more thorough discussion of her work, see Katherine McKittrick (ed.), *Sylvia Wynter: On Being Human as Praxis*, Durham, NC: Duke University Press, 2015.

11 Rodney, *How Europe Underdeveloped Africa*.

12 Noel L. Erskine, *Decolonizing Theology: A Caribbean Perspective*, Trenton, NJ: Africa World Press, 1998.

13 Robert Hood, *Must God Remain Greek? Afro Cultures and God-talk*, Minneapolis, MN: Fortress Press, 1990, p. 9.

14 Erskine, *Decolonizing Theology*, pp. 1–2.

15 Oral Thomas, *Biblical Resistance Hermeneutics within a Caribbean Context*, London: Equinox, 2010, p. 8.

16 R. S. Sugirtharajah, *The Bible and the Third World: Precolonial, Colonial, and Postcolonial Encounters*, Cambridge: Cambridge University Press, 2001. Itumeleng J. Mosala, *Biblical Hermeneutics and Black*

Theology in South Africa, Grand Rapids, MI: Eerdmans, 1989. Gerald O. West, *Biblical Hermeneutics of Liberation: Modes of Reading the Bible in the South African Context*, The Bible and Liberation Series, Maryknoll, NY: Orbis Books, 1995.

17 Philip Potter, a Caribbean intercultural theologian and intellectual, served in the World Council of Churches (WCC) from 1967 to 1983. See also Michael N. Jagessar, 'Pan Recipe: Philip Potter and Theology in the Caribbean', *Black Theology: An International Journal* 3.1, no. 5, November 2000.

18 Thomas, *Biblical Resistance Hermeneutics within a Caribbean Context*.

19 George Mulrain, 'Hermeneutics within a Caribbean Context', in *Vernacular Hermeneutics*, ed. R. S. Sugirtharajah, Sheffield: Sheffield Academic Press, 1999.

20 Mulrain, 'Hermeneutics within a Caribbean Context', pp. 121–4.

21 George Mulrain, *Caribbean Theological Insights: Exploring Theological Themes Within the Context of the Caribbean Region*, London: Blessed Hope Publishing, 2014. See ch. 2, 'Hermeneutics Gone Mad?'.

22 Michael Jagessar, 'Spinning Theology: Trickster, Texts and Theology', in *Postcolonial Black British Theology*, ed. Jagessar and Reddie, 2007.

23 Jagessar, 'Spinning Theology', p. 125; emphasis original.

24 Jagessar, 'Spinning Theology', p. 143.

25 Ana Kasafi Perkins and Carlton Turner, '"Monotonous Rhythm on the Heart of God?" Drumming, Theological Aesthetics and Christianity in the Caribbean', in *The T&T Clarke Companion to Theology and the Arts*, ed. Imogen Adkins and Stephen Garrett, London: Bloomsbury, 2024.

26 Perkins and Turner, '"Monotonous Rhythm on the Heart of God?"'

27 Carlton Turner, 'Taming the Spirit? Widening the Pneumatological Gaze within African Caribbean Theological Discourse', *Black Theology: An International Journal* 13, no. 2, 2015.

28 Jürgen Moltmann, *The Spirit of Life: A Universal Affirmation*, Minneapolis, MN: Fortress Press, 1992, p. 8.

29 Joseph Murphy, *Working the Spirit: Ceremonies of the African Diaspora*, Boston, MA: Beacon Press, 1994, p. 181.

30 George Mulrain, *Theology in Folk Culture: The Theological Significance of Haitian Folk Religion*, Frankfurt: Peter Lang, 1984, p. 373.

31 Turner, 'Taming the Spirit?', p. 131.

32 Dianne M. Stewart, *Three Eyes for the Journey: African Dimensions of the Jamaican Religious Experience*, Oxford: Oxford University Press, 2004, p. 221.

33 Barry Chevannes, *Rastafari: Roots and Ideology*, Syracuse, NY: Syracuse University Press, 1995, pp. 18–19; emphasis original.

34 Luke 4.18–19.

35 Carlton Turner, *Overcoming Self-Negation: The Church and Junkanoo in Contemporary Bahamian Society*, Eugene, OR: Pickwick Publications, 2020.

36 Walter Brueggemann, *The Prophetic Imagination*, 2nd edn, Minneapolis, MN: Fortress Press, 2001.

7

Nannyish Sass:
Gender, Sexuality and the Body

The term 'Nannyish' is gaining some traction among Caribbean women theologians to distinguish themselves from Womanist traditions rooted in the North American context. It draws inspiration from the military feats of Nanny of the Maroons in her cunning leadership in rebelling plantation slavery in Jamaican society during the Maroon Wars. This chapter focuses on dimensions of African Caribbean theological conversations that women have been addressing. These would include gender, sexuality and continuing reflections on the body in light of the unique history of chattel slavery and its aftermath. Gender, sexuality and the body remain under-discussed and are perennially difficult topics within the region, especially when it comes to Christian theology and praxis.

Let's begin with rather sizeable and significant grounding excerpts from two theological thinkers in the region, Barry Chevannes and Winelle Kirton-Roberts. First Chevannes:

What annoys the mind for whom Europe is the model and ideal, is the fact that the visiting and common-law unions are broken at will, leaving women without husbands; children without fathers; children, women and children with grand-mothers; children with stepmothers; women with multiple baby-fathers and fathers with multiple sets of children. Instability is what such a person sees.

What is overlooked is the movement towards stability. By the time they get married, most couples would have been visiting or cohabiting for a long period; they seldom if ever divorce. From the unstable, people progress to the stable.

What is also overlooked is the fact that only a minority of families are female-headed, the overwhelming majority being male-headed; or that even in the latter, it is the mother on whom the affective life of the family is centred. Overlooked also is the fact that most children are raised by fathers and stepfathers. In other words, what is overlooked is the fact that there is a system.[1]

Second, Kirton-Roberts:

Protestant theology hinged upon the notion that there was punitive action to be taken as a result of sin. As in the African context, sin was a new component in Caribbean sexuality. Diane Austin-Broos was right in pointing out that 'The Christian notion of sin and the guilt that was meant to accompany sin were alien to the slaves.' With thorough instruction, the formerly enslaved Africans came to associate sexuality not only with sin but also with punishment. This instruction, together with punishment, comprised the disciplinary strategy of the evangelicals. It was a discipline which they hoped would inform and transform the behaviour of the followers.[2]

Kirton-Roberts continues:

The missionaries discovered that females were not waiting for marriage to have sexual relations and have children. Women were having sexual intercourse with men who were married and were not satisfied to stay solely in a single relationship. Efforts to curb the unrestricted sexuality of the African female not only exhausted the missionaries but also steered their attention away from other areas of the mission ...

The attempt to amend the sexuality of the African male was just as enervating. Unlike the black female, who was sexualized but not as sexually appealing as her coloured sister, the black male had been stereotyped from slavery as a 'black stud'. Kempadoo noted that 'the darker the man is, the more sexually attractive he is considered ... It is in an image that harks back to older notions in both European and US culture of black African man as an embodiment of insatiable sexual appetite and uncontrollable lust.[3]

Conversations around gender and sexuality within the Caribbean region require deep nuance, and if they are theological conversations of one kind or another there needs to be a deep engagement with other spheres of knowledge, such as sociology and history. Between Chevannes and Kirton-Roberts above, theological conversation around gender and sexuality in the region is informed by sociology and history respectively. When reading these extracts from their work, one can discern that these are deeply complex issues and have always been. As with every area of African Caribbean life, theological conversations around sexuality and gender are never divorced from: European Enlightenment rationalism and its shaping of the processes of empire and colonialism; Missionary Christianity and its hermeneutics around sin and the body, particularly the non-white body; the traumatic impact of the institution of enslavement on every aspect of African Caribbean sexuality – gender relations, mating practices, intergenerational dynamics; and the continued struggle for survival that continually contests European ideals around how life, particularly sexuality, should be ordered within the region.

In the following sections I will attempt to make some sense of sexuality in the Caribbean, and do so by highlighting the contributions of women theologians who have, arguably, been foregrounding this conversation. The conversation will be guided by the following: first, a survey of the works of some Caribbean women scholars and theologians as they comment on gender and sexuality in the region, summarizing general themes that come to the surface. Second, I look at what Marjorie Lewis has branded 'Nannyish Theology', patterned after the liberatory militancy of Nanny of the Maroons. Nannyish Theology in the Caribbean is what would be called Womanist Theology in the African American context. Third, I engage the concept of embodiment, which is gaining ground in theological conversations worldwide. The Caribbean is a site in which the body has been central to theological reflection, whether, on the one hand, it was to disparage the African body or, on the other hand, it was ATRs' attempts at accessing divinity and engaging spirituality through the same body. Fourth, I return to writers such as Chevannes and Kirton-Roberts and try to make some sense of sexuality in the region, including conversations around homophobia and transphobia. Finally, I reflect on the notions of 'sin' and 'salvation', asking the question, a perennial one for theology in any context: Who or what gets to shape approaches to sin and salvation? It is clear that the body and sexuality were quintessential for Missionary Christianity's framing of sinfulness, purity and salvation.

Caribbean Women Doing Theology

Caribbean women have been doing theology from its earliest articulations in the contributions of persons such as Theresa Lowe Ching, and in more recent decades in the work of scholars and activists such as Marjorie Lewis, Nicqui Ashwood, Dianne Stewart, Rachelle Evie Vernon and Anna Kasafi Perkins, to name but a few. Collectively, their work foregrounds the experience of women in the Caribbean, not as isolated from but as central to discerning the complex theological issues and questions facing the region. Through their work they employ a wide range of theological and social scientific tools to uncover the realities of gender injustice, sexuality and ultimate survival in a region that has, from its inception, seen the interconnections of Blackness, sexuality, gender and the body as deeply and even theologically problematic.

A good place to begin this discussion is with a collection of Bible studies featuring Caribbean women, ordained and lay, reading the Bible and reflecting theologically from their standpoint. The collection, *Righting Her-Story: Caribbean Women Encounter the Bible* (2011), covers a range of topics:

• Theology of gender justice and partnership
• Sexuality
• Marriage and family

- Violence against women
- Women's resistance
- Leadership and power
- Women as channels of grace
- Caregivers and nurturers of life
- Women, beauty and personal empowerment
- Culture
- Healing and building community.[4]

In the Introduction to the volume, editor Revd Patricia Sheerat-tan-Bisnauth states:

> *Righting Her-Story: Caribbean Women Encounter the Bible Story* is a Bible study book on women, which provides re-freshing ways to read the Bible, enabling women and men to rediscover its richness and its ability to help them reflect theologically on their faith and experience. It is envisioned as an instrument that will contribute to building the critical consciousness of women and men and in fostering women's leadership. The book includes stories of women who have played significant roles in their churches and communities. Caribbean women have contributed greatly to the survival of their families and communities by finding ways to resist in-justices, bringing healing, providing food, shelter, hospitality, comfort as well as avenues for peace and reconciliation. They have acquired survival skills in situations of poverty, violence and social decay. There are many examples of how women have found ways and means to be resilient in the face of harsh economic times, very often working beyond the boundary of state mechanisms.[5]

The volume is also very interesting in its hermeneutical approach. It employs a biblically resistant strategy that:

> uses the tools of remembering and imagination. It is remem-bering which embraces the historical context of the Caribbean reader as it considers the narratives of courageous women and men who led revolutions for freedom from slavery; visionary

leaders who have led communities, churches and nations; marginalized groups, especially women who struggle for recognition, rights and justice; and persons whose prophetic voices and actions are significant for justice, for right relations and for betterment of communities and families.[6]

Judith Soares traces the issue of gender injustice in the Caribbean to its deep roots in Missionary Christianity and colonialism. For her, the Church has always been an overseer of justice and thus a supporter and dispenser of gender injustice, precisely because of its missionary and European roots. She states:

Patriarchal ideology was critical in the structuring of the state precisely because it had to locate all women, particularly black women, in a uniquely subordinate position. As slaves, black women shared the status of commoditization with black men, but after slavery, they became subordinate to white men, white women, and black men. The struggle for black women in the Caribbean was from the outset one of racism, classism, and sexism. They had to fight the racism and sexism of the white man, the racism of the white woman, and the sexism of the black man. Note, however, that the white woman was subject to the sexism of the white man to whom she belonged according to British common law. Thus, a gender system, a system of racial discrimination, and a system of economic discrimination operated simultaneously in the period of colonialism and beyond. And the church continues to preserve that order throughout the Caribbean. (In the same way, the church justified and legitimized the segregating of whites and nonwhites through the system of apartheid in South Africa and isolating the native people of Canada and the United States on reservations.)[7]

Another among Caribbean women theologians, Dianne Stewart, in her article 'Womanist Theology in the Caribbean Context: Critiquing Culture, Rethinking Doctrine, and Expounding Boundaries', interrogates the spirituality of women in the Kumina tradition of Jamaica, particularly trance/possession and the special role women play within it, and how it continually contests the patriarchal and doctrinal constraints of Missionary Christianity that have formed the region. Using a Womanist lens, she reconceptualizes trance/possession:

as *recurring incarnation* in African-derived religions such as Kumina. By reflecting upon the first-order religious experiences of Kumina women in ritual performance, I hold that incarnation (as opposed to divine death) defines *the cross* in Kumina and other African-derived religions as the locus of transformative healing power. Indeed, the Kumina religion is a site for subversive perspectives on the cross that contest the propensity in Christian theology of associating suffering with redemption and ascribing positive value to the experience of suffering. Thus, the Kumina cross of recurring incarnation lends much to current womanist/feminist responses to normative characterizations of human suffering in the history of Christian thought.[8]

In this work she explores 'the paradoxical status of female Kumina priests as simultaneously prominent and impoverished in Jamaican society'.[9] In classical contextual theological style, using a Womanist theological approach, she begins her construction of doctrine from the experience of African Caribbean women. In doing so, she both attends to the religious experiences of African Caribbean women while also critiquing and contesting the European Missionary Christianity that has shaped their lives in invalidating ways. Out of this reflection she suggests 'Four Avenues of Empowerment' for women within African-Derived Caribbean Religions: the nurturing of black female agency; the empowerment of black women as official leaders and teachers in their religious traditions; female personifications of the divine; and divine revelation via incarnation in female bodies as a recurring event.

Taking the contesting power of African Caribbean women seriously, particularly in the arts and musical traditions, the Roman Catholic theologian Anna Kasafi Perkins uses Dancehall and the music of Tanya Stephens to do her theological reflection. She sees within the genre a potent contribution by women to consistently respond to and critique the misogyny and violent anti-female lyrics usually associated with Dancehall music. She writes:

> Without a doubt, Tanya refuses to buy into the Jamaican dancehall culture where male identity is concerned with sub-duing and conquering female sexuality. Rather, she attempts to cleverly turn that on its head and calls it into question. Her in-your-face no-holds-barred feistyness makes both men and women uncomfortable, particularly when she is explicit about female sexual desire and sexual needs and performance.[10]

In parsing Stephens' lyrics further, Perkins suggests that the dancehall is an ambivalent space in which complex issues, sexuality being one of them, are addressed. One such clear com-mentary is that women's bodies are sacred, and that sexuality and violence need to be uncoupled. In fact, the right to free-dom and pleasure for the African person is asserted, even in the face of church and cultural censorship. Perkins' observations of the dancehall is corroborated by Carolyn Cooper, who reveals the counter-hermeneutic within the dancehall that works to reshape sexuality and sexual politics away from violence and oppression and towards pleasure and freedom, particularly the freedom of identity. She writes:

> Arguing transgressively for the freedom of women to claim a self-pleasuring sexual identity that may even be explicitly homoerotic, I propose that Jamaican dancehall culture at home and in the diaspora is best understood as a potential-ly liberating space in which working-class women and their more timid middle-class sisters assert the freedom to play out eroticized roles that may not ordinarily be available to them in the rigid social conventions of the everyday. The dance-hall becomes an erogenous zone in which the celebration of female sexuality and fertility is ritualized as men pay homage to the female principle.[11]

Anna Perkins and Nicqui Ashwood have looked at the hermeneutics within African Caribbean churches around sexuality and violence in their reflections on violence (of all kinds) against women in the region. In commenting on Intimate Male Partner Violence and its prevalence in the region, Perkins suggests:

> Among the reasons surfaced are the silence of the church on the matter oftentimes in a bid to maintain membership or preserve the image of individual members living as a truly Christian life, the implicating of male Church leaders themselves in IPV, and the belief that divorce is a dangerous trend for family life and men's role in the family (the Bible is against divorce).[12]

Perkins identifies church hermeneutics as problematic, and therefore a change in hermeneutics is vital for any kind of deep address of sexual violence within the African Caribbean context. Nicqui Ashwood reflects on clergy sexual misconduct and problematizes the way that it is perceived and addressed across the region. She states:

> Clergy sexual misconduct continues to be a troubling issue in the Caribbean region and in Jamaica in particular. There have been at least three cases of ministerial sexual abuse which have made the headlines in the Jamaican papers ... The public responses to these incidents are varied, especially in relation to other 'newsworthy' items that seem to cloud or overshadow these, not make them less bothersome; for one is aware that for every crime which is reported, there are several others which gain less prominence. And the problem will only persist if we as clergy and laity remain silent.[13]

For both women, the kinds of hermeneutics around sexuality inevitably lead to victim shaming, which is quite acute given the history and cruelty of slavery wherein victims of slave sexual abuse and oppression were deemed as non-human and beasts of burden.

Nannyish Theology: A Theology of Survival

The suggestion thus far has been that women in the Caribbean have been articulating a counter-hermeneutic in their theological conversations, one that is militant and resistant to the received theological traditions of Missionary Christianity that have been injurious to the Black body and the Black person in the region, particularly women. The term 'Nannyish' is gaining some traction among Caribbean women theologians to distinguish themselves from Womanist traditions rooted in the North American context. It draws inspiration from the heroic feats of Nanny of the Maroons in her cunning leadership in rebelling plantation slavery in Jamaican society during the Maroon Wars.

Marjorie Lewis suggests that African Caribbean Womanist theological reflection should be considered Nannyish precisely because of its resistant quality. In her article 'Diaspora Dialogue: Womanist Theology in Engagement with Some Aspects of the Black British and Jamaican Experience', Lewis engages with and critiques African American Womanist Theology, eventually suggesting what for her could serve as a more adequate framing of African Caribbean women's theological construction.[14] While there are themes in Womanist Theology – such as *survival and liberation, Jesus as co-sufferer, self-esteem and self-actualization, solidarity with the community*, and *sexuality* – that are common to the Caribbean experience, there are criticisms as well, particularly about the very naming and framing of Womanist Theology. Lewis writes:

> The most important criticisms are that the concept 'womanism' is inadequate to represent the perspectives of all Black women across the many locations of the world. Secondly, it argues that Black women's theology does not reside only in Christianity, nor in isolation from the cultural communications among Black people in the diaspora. This article offers 'Nannyish T'eology' as an appropriate nomenclature to describe the experience of Black Jamaican women, and identifies this theology as an influential strand in the experience of Black British women. While noting the influence of

'Nannyish T'eology' on Britain, the need for further research to accurately document and describe a contextualized Black British feminist/Womanist theology is identified.[15]

Lewis proceeds to relate Nannyish T'eology to the Jamaican context and how it engages the complexities of that society, and also the region, pertinent to women's experiences. These include: Colourism; (Homo)Sexuality; Polygamy (Womanizing); and The Female Body Performed.

Ultimately, Nannyish T'eology seeks to allow African Caribbean women to speak on issues that often remain constrained by the Church. It is a movement that employs imagination, fierce criticism, sass and deep attention to the lived experiences of African Caribbean women. She concludes her article in this way:

> Dialogue among Black women of faith from different traditions may have the potential for refining the mechanisms for the empowerment of Black women, and forging sustain-able Black communities. 'Nannyish T'eology' is thus justified as a nomenclature for Jamaican Womanist theology, as Nanny is recognized nationally as a heroine for both male and female Jamaicans. She is seen as preserver and transmitter of African traditions, and as an inspiration and example for women of different religious traditions and among people of different ideologies. It acknowledges the many 'Voices of God' in different religions, and rejects the approach that only privileges Christian theology. Nannyish T'eology, therefore, has some similarities to African-American Womanist theology, but acknowledges that Womanist theology is inadequate to express the experience of Black women in Jamaica.[16]

Thus far we have been discussing the contribution of Caribbean women to theological conversations around gender, sexuality and the body. We now turn our attention to teasing out some further theological reflections around concepts of sin and salvation in Caribbean theological discourse. However, we cannot do this without considering the body, or the notion of embodiment, which is central to a more nuanced discussion of such theological concepts.

Embodiment, Sin and Salvation

Engaging the Body

As an approach to theological discourse, embodiment has been gaining prominence as a way of foregrounding the body precisely to engage the real lives of people, particularly in contexts of colonial and racial trauma. The noted African American Black Theologian, Anthony Pinn, engages with the concept of embodiment to approach theology, not as a disembodied exercise but looking to the body as a site of theological discourse and reflection.[17] Engaging with Michel Foucault's conceptual frameworks, Pinn states:

> In short, the body is the location for the arrangement and display of power, producing a certain 'art of the body'. Through power, subjects are produced and these subjects come to present various arrangements of power. The discursive body is 'inscribed' by power relationships and modalities of discipline.[18]

He continues:

> The reminder to engage with the 'fleshy' body is important for theology. Any effort to change the situation of embodied people must have litmus tests, benchmarks, and only attention to the concrete conditions faced can give a sense of the 'felt' consequences of struggle. We cannot step outside of power relationships and the workings of discourse; it is only through engaging the markers of materiality that resistance can be assessed and strategies revised as necessary.[19]

Pinn reminds us that Black Theology, and by extension Caribbean Theology, must take the body seriously. In the history of sin and salvation it is the axis upon which much theology about sinfulness, holiness, purity and salvation has been framed. These deeply engrained theological presuppositions have significantly conditioned cultural, political and ecclesiastical attitudes towards sex, sexuality, gender, the body. The ultimate question is to what degree the shaping of a society within a European colonial imagination informs every aspect of theology and practice in this regard.

The Trauma of Plantation Life in the Caribbean

In a Caribbean contribution to a volume on sexual violence and assault and their theological implications, I have asserted what is well known in the region but often little appreciated:

> Plantation slavery as it manifested in the African Caribbean was the most brutal experience of that institution. Sexual violence was pervasive. Acts of sexual abuse and terror were not isolated and individual events, but were legally and culturally part of the plantation society. Sex was a weapon used to maintain a White European power structure that permitted atrocious acts towards Black and Brown people collectively. Within the African Caribbean, control over the sexual lives of slaves was so acute and severe that it was the intention to introduce 'breeding farms' into Caribbean plantation life.[20]

I suggest that there is something pathological about levels of sexual abuse and violence, and scholars such as Frantz Fanon and Orlando Patterson have commented on this. For Fanon, the persistent and calculated sexual, psychological and bodily violence meted out to black persons within colonial societies bred other maladies such as hostility, self-hatred, anger, depression, anxieties, toxic relationships, toxic community secrecies that ignore or even further permit ongoing sexual violence and assault. The trauma of this creates cycles of violence.[21] The sociologist Orlando Patterson has argued convincingly that slave societies were never meant to be 'societies' in the usual sense of the word. They were meant solely for producing capital and furthering the agenda of the plantocracy. In summarizing the thoughts of both Fanon and Patterson, I state: 'The idea of sexual freedom and dignity for slaves, male or female, parents, or children, were inconsequential. Slaves were non-persons and non-persons could not claim to be sexually abused or assaulted.'[22] As an example of this ongoing embodied conversation around Caribbean sexuality in light of the historic trauma of the plantation, Carolyn Cooper explains that the African Caribbean carnivalesque tradition, of role-play and -reversal, is also found within the Dancehall aesthetic and works specifically to address the deep wounds inflicted by slavery and colonial oppression and their attendant theologies of domination and power. She states:

> There are, it is all too true, profound psycho-sociological underpinnings of this desire to be/play the other that cannot be simply written off as mere entertainment. Role-play both conceals and reveals deep-seated anxieties about the body that has been incised with the scarifications of history.[23]

The Black Body as Site of Vilification

The African American Womanist theologian Kelly Brown Douglas has written extensively on the extent of the trauma that the construct of Whiteness has inflicted on Black life – Black culture, Black spirituality, Black sexuality, Black family systems and so on. Like Anthony Pinn and Carolyn Cooper above, the Black body and how it has been problematized historically within the White European imagination is something that has been central to Douglas's theology. Her book *Stand Your Ground: Black Bodies and the Justice of God* delineates the connection between the contemporary wanton killing of black bodies by police officers, as in the case of Trayvon Martin in the United States, and a long history of criminalizing, villainizing and ultimately demonizing Blackness and black bodies within the Western Christian tradition.[24] For Douglas, the philosophical, scientific and theological traditions and their convergence in utterly stigmatizing black bodies run deep. There is a deep belief within Euro-American White exceptionalism that the Black body is chattel, a commodity, to be used and abused at will, and for the purposes of Whiteness. It was, and continues to be, easy to equate Blackness with sin, hypersexuality, perversion and criminality. This examination of the deep cultural, philosophical and theological roots of White (American) exceptionalism and anti-Blackness is equally evident, if not more so, within the African Caribbean contexts, where slavery has been arguably more pervasive and more brutal.

The Black Body as Site of Resistance

Furthermore, in her book *Sexuality and the Black Church: A Womanist Perspective*, Douglas highlights the deeply entrenched and pervasive nature of White assault upon Black sexuality in all forms. Using Michel Foucault's discourse on power and its exposure of how silence is used by power to legitimate itself, Douglas suggests that Black sexuality must be proactive and provide a discourse of resistance, not simply react to White versions of Blackness but provide healthy and comprehensive understandings of Blackness, sexuality and the body. She suggests: 'A sexual discourse of resistance has two central goals: first, to penetrate the sexual politics of the Black community; and, second, to cultivate a life-enhancing approach to Black sexuality within the Black community.'[25]

She further states:

Without a sexual discourse of resistance the legacy of one woman's pain cannot be confronted. The absence of such a discourse means far too many Black men and women are left to feel ashamed of their bodies. They have limited avenues for discovering that the pain, ambivalence, and/or shame they feel are shared experiences generated by a history of exploitation.[26]

Making Sense of Sexuality in the African Caribbean

The reason why the body is central to theological conversations around sin and, inevitably, salvation within the region, is because Blackness and black bodies have for far too long been equated with sinfulness, particularly in areas of sexuality. In the imaginations of Missionary Christianity, sexuality and bodies became the linchpin on which concepts of sin and salvation hinged. I want to argue that Black sexuality generally was and continues to be formed within a Western, Missionary Christian imagination, let alone complex realities around gender, different kinds of sexuality and lifestyles. In fact, it's difficult to make sense of these complex issues since the trauma of Caribbean history has informed every aspect of approaches to gender and sexuality. Going back to Barry Chevannes, we are reminded that sexuality, mating practices and family structures within the African Caribbean experience need careful attention. When sociologically analysing family systems and mating practices, there can be the assumption that no system or structure is present. Chevannes concludes:

> It is an irritating fact that official society, in which the church must be included, remains still blinded by European prejudice, failing to come to terms with African-Caribbean social reality, in this respect its family forms. The failure is no more than an irritant, however, because the mating patterns and social and sexual values that produce these forms not only perdure unmolested by the sermons and moral oustings, but are penetrating into the circles of the very guardians of morality, the middle class.[27]

In short, how sexuality, mating practices and family structures have evolved in the Caribbean context has been heavily regulated by Missionary and Plantation Christianity. Before looking at the theological concepts of sin and salvation in the Caribbean context, it is helpful to try, briefly, to make some sense of sexuality in the region.

Sexuality is not a straightforward conversation in the region, which has long been associated with escapism, sexual fantasy, virility, and has also been the touristic sexual destination for many. It is also a region associated with homophobia, sexual assault and violence. At the same time, sexualities, particularly those deemed illegitimate, stigmatized and illegal, are often suppressed, having to find refuge from drastic cultural and theological policing. Furthermore, political pressure from Western nations around LGBTQIA+ issues amid a history of Western external control and coercion does not help the complexity of the situation. I suggest that disentangling and theologically reflecting on sexuality in the region require a consideration of the following realities.

First, in a region where sexuality is inextricably linked to violence, and in which church praxes and hermeneutics carry significant power, sexuality is generally ambivalent. Reflecting on sexual abuse and general theological and cultural approaches to sexuality in the region, I have stated the following in the recent theological work, *When Did We See You Naked? Jesus as a Victim of Sexual Abuse*:

> The ambivalence towards Black bodies, towards sexuality, concomitant with the quest for an absolute and neutral Christianity, creates a culture that denies and casts a blind eye to the real lives of ordinary people within the region, particularly those who have been sexually abused and exploited. But even more than this, it allows for an institution that will not confront its own complicity in perpetuating and legitimizing sexual assault and abuse.[28]

Tara L. Atluri reminds us that the ambivalence and utter confusion around homo/hetero sexism in the region is further confounded by the hermeneutics of the Church. While there is generally fierce policing of homosexuality, and the perpetuation of violent homophobic rhetoric within cultural life, there is equally a pervasive lack of attention to domestic violence and assault against women. She states:

It is clear from both the Trinidadian and Bahamian legislation, that the criminalization of homosexuality and the policing of women's bodies fall under the same fictions of the 'superior', 'respectable' nuclear family, around which these nations have been constructed. Even in its most violent expression (i.e. rape, abuse) the heterosexual family is not interrogated. It is only when this abuse interferes with the site of reproduction and capitalist production that it becomes criminal. The failure to criminalize heterosexuality is constructed in dialectic with the criminalizing of homosexuality.[29]

She further states: 'Within a binary construction of hetero and homosexuality, violent disruptions within the heterosexual home are beyond legislation, while consensual homosexual sex is not differentiated from same-sex rape, as all are perversions.'[30] She continues:

The categorization of homosexuality as 'private' and therefore out of the realm of public discussion is highly contradictory, considering that the criminalization of homosexual practices interferes with this supposed privacy. This contradiction is highlighted when one examines the way in which hetero-sexuality, even in its most misogynistic forms of rape and vio-lence, is often left uncriminalized in the private domain. Male heterosexual power is the only sexuality that remains truly discrete.[31]

Second, we can further interrogate sexuality in the region through the issue of silence or silencing. Earlier we discussed Anna Kasafi Perkins and Nicqui Ashwood and their observation of how silence is used in Caribbean theological discourse pre-cisely to perpetuate sexual abuse and assault, mainly because of Christian hermeneutics around sex and the body. But silence and secrecy were also how black people have survived the plan-tation sexually, spiritually and existentially. Dwight Hopkins, when reflecting on black people in the context of the slave plantation, explains that slaves used secrecy as a means to reconstitute and heal themselves in the context of the trauma of the plantation. In his exploration of slave religion and its importance for Black Theology, Hopkins argues two important points. First, slave secret meetings were for the purpose of reinterpreting Missionary Christianity's hermeneutics that denied their personhood. He writes: '"Stealin' the meetin," what enslaved religious blacks called the secret (reinterpreted) Christian gathering – commonly termed Invisible Institution – reflected the institutional location out of which a future black theology of liberation emerged. Such surreptitious congregations often reached huge numbers.'[32] Second, part of their theological strategy of reimagining freedom was by seizing the domain of pleasure.

Winelle Kirton-Roberts makes a related observation when researching concepts of African sexuality coming into the plantation context of the Caribbean before the imposition of strict moral standards by Christian missionaries. She notes:

> To further suggest that African sexuality was only heterosexual is, according to researchers, inaccurate. Arnfred has noted that homosexuality was present within African communities. There were woman-to-woman sexual relations which were known as *mati*. Interestingly, male same-sex relations, he noted, were not as covert in the African culture. In addition, there were other expressions of sexual pleasure, including *ngwiko*, which allowed for sexual expression without penetration. This was practised by young females before they felt ready for sexual intercourse … Sexual pleasure for the African was evident in his or her having more than one partner. There was widespread acceptance of the practice of polygamy by men. While women could not have more than one husband, it was not unusual for them to participate in extramarital affairs. This became a critical issue that was difficult, if not impossible, to curb in the Caribbean.[33]

A third way of exploring this issue is through the reality of stigma. Sexuality as a topic and as a reality is imbued with much stigma. Missionary Christian norms steeped in Victorian sensibilities have dictated that any overt sensuality, or what seems to be over-sexualization, because of the association with the body, a symbol of baseness, sexual frivolity and licentiousness, should inherently be stigmatized. In my book *Overcoming Self-Negation* I have explored this phenomenon, suggesting that stigma, especially around sexuality, has its genesis in continued colonial hermeneutics around the body, particularly the Black body, as the site of untamed passions and sinfulness.[34]

Sin and Salvation in the African Caribbean

Taking Winelle Kirton-Roberts' historical work into evangelical Protestantism in the shaping of modern African Caribbean societies seriously, concepts of sin and salvation have always needed sharp attention. In her chapter on Black sexuality and sin she analyses Black sexuality in the context of plantation slavery and the evangelical mission's response to it.[35] Through her and others' insights thus far, we get to see just how much missionary hermeneutics around marriage and sexuality was used to police and civilize black bodies, sexualities and relationships in the light of plantation economy and slavery. The Christian concepts of sin and salvation within the African Caribbean context, from inception and to a significant degree, have always been shaped by plantation slavery, anti-Black hermeneutics, and racism. This question of 'who' or 'what' shapes theologies of sin and salvation is fundamental to contextual theologies, especially Caribbean Theology. Sin and salvation are not cerebral or moralistic concepts that can be solved through doctrinal precision or following legalistic codes. In the Caribbean, notions of sinfulness and stigma often have deadly consequences. Or, conversely, ideas of salvation are often used as a means of power for the privileged few.

I have argued elsewhere that sin and salvation within colonial contexts such as the Caribbean must be interrogated deeply before any meaningful and holistic solutions can be brought to deep social and cultural issues.[36] While the theological imagination shaping the region was Western, European and missionary, with deeply entrenched views on Blackness and otherness, attention must now be given to how concepts of sin and salvation were arrived at from such a complex biblical tradition. There is a disconnect between colonial concepts of sin, which are inherently dichotomous, and the plethora of narratives and symbols employed within Scripture. As Mark Biddle states, Western Christianity has not interrogated its narrow view of the biblical conceptions of sin and salvation. The Bible presents sin as a complex picture; sin as crime/juridical model and metaphor are not exhaustive. He argues:

> This 'sin as crime' metaphor, with its emphases on the juridical, the individual, and wilful rebellion, and its interests in assignment of guilt and exaction of punishment, addresses certain aspects of the problem of human existence. Yet, although dominant in the Western popular mind, it does not fully reflect the biblical witness, nor provide a sufficient basis for the church's ministry in addressing human wrongdoing and its consequences, nor take account of the insights of contemporary theological movements, philosophies, and social sciences that do not confirm its validity as a thorough description of the problem of being human.[37]

With this in mind, I have argued that this issue undergirds most, if not all, of the contemporary conceptions of sin within the region, which continue to shape approaches and views on sexuality, indigenous cultural heritages, popular religions and African Caribbean religiocultural productions. Missionary Christianity, particularly that affecting the Caribbean with roots in the dualistic post-Enlightenment, rationalistic philosophical tradition, defined sin more as one's beliefs over and above one's actions.

> Black, Womanist, Third World, and Caribbean theological discourses have rejected this singular image of sin, and have highlighted the social and systemic aspects, recovering other imagery from the biblical text. They highlight the concrete, structural, and existential nature of sin, seeing it as also socially constructed.[38]

This is consistent with Black Theology and the insights of James Cone, for whom sin is seen as an always concretely situated social construction, and for the Black person, racism is that social construction that denies them personhood and freedom.[39] His argument is also that Blacks and Whites are two communities when it comes to sin, the former being the oppressed and the latter being the oppressor. In his estimation, the latter cannot speak about the sinfulness of the former in an attempt to ease their own guilt for the sins their community perpetuates against black people.

Caribbean theologians have been consistent with their contextual framing of sin in the light of the experience of plantation slavery and colonialism. Like Cone, Kortright Davis views sin as socially constructed, and in the Caribbean context it is 'non-responsibility' or one's neglect of the community. This is to be differentiated from one's duty to one's master, which the missionary taught. To resist this was not sinful, but righteous.[40] In Lewin Williams' estimation, sin for the Caribbean person is the 'failure to struggle for an affirmation of the image of God within the oppressed self'.[41] But these understandings of sin are undergirded by two kinds of theology at work within the Caribbean context. On the one hand, there is a missionary theology, which Williams refers to as a theology of domination; on the other, there is grass-roots, indigenous theology steeped in African oral tradition, in folklore and in the cultural productions of the region, such as Junkanoo, Calypso and Dancehall. Anna Kasafi Perkins offers an example of how such cultural productions challenge colonial and patriarchal notions of transgression with respect to the female body in the Caribbean. Theologically reflecting on the Trinidad and Tobago carnival, where women are deemed transgressive, lewd, sinful because of their overt sexuality, she asserts that it is precisely their overt sexuality, their 'playin mas', their parody, mimicry and subversion that seek to expose oppressive social and cultural structures.[42] And, taking a pan-African view, Ronald Nathan rejects the sinful dichotomy characteristic of colonial society and colonial Christianity:

The dichotomy between, for example, Good and Evil, Secular and Spiritual, Heaven and Earth and Male and Female and so on does not exist within the world view of African societies and certainly not within an Afrocentric philosophy. These Hellenistic mythological imports were incorporated within the European Enlightenment and later Reformation Christian thought.[43]

But what about salvation? Reflecting on the first Jerusalem Council in Acts 11, which was preceded by the Peter and Cornelius passages in the Acts of the Apostles, chapters 9 and 10, I have argued for this pattern to be replicated in colonial contexts where notions of sinfulness and salvation are centred on identity markers.[44] We see this foundational stage in the formation of the early Christian communities as a dismissal of sinfulness based on ethnic and religious cultural markers, but also as a reconceptualization of the idea of salvation. The Holy Spirit in Acts 11 works to transcend all that takes away from an integrated Christian community. Peter is rebuked by the Holy Spirit to see that his distinction between Jews and Gentiles is sinful. The council at Jerusalem is moved to repent of their critique of Peter's 'sinful act' of eating with Gentiles (Acts 11.2–3; Acts 11.18). There is a movement from exclusion to embrace through the direct operations of the Holy Spirit. But again, embrace does not mean total acceptance. Just as the Jewish believer is now open to a new revelation through the Holy Spirit (that the covenant is open to Gentiles), the Gentile now confesses a new Lord, Jesus Christ. Both are renewed. Both become part of the kingdom of God. Harmony and embrace then are pneumatological acts ultimately about the renewal of people and relationships within the kingdom of God through, to use Brueggemann's terminology, prophetic criticism of royal consciousness and prophetic energizing.[45] In fact, harmony and embrace are foundational soteriological images in the Bible that have been overlooked in Protestant theology.

'Salvation' is also a tricky word within the Christian tradition, and our theological task is continually to draw from the wealth of resources offered to us within Scripture while simultaneously critiquing and monitoring the restrictive views and images we employ when thinking soteriologically. Brenda B. Colijn explains that within the Western Christian tradition, an over-insistence on justification by faith has led to an under-emphasis on reconciliation as a way of interpreting the biblical narrative. She writes:

> Reconciliation is closely related to peace, in that it describes the establishment of peace between parties that were at enmity. To reconcile is to make peace (see Eph 2:15–16). In biblical terms, peace means far more than lack of conflict; it is a state of wholeness and well-being, expressed as [shalom] in the Old Testament and eirēnē in the New. Peace is the most comprehensive biblical term for the goal of salvation.[46]

In other words, salvation can be reconceived in ways other than simply 'going to heaven'. Salvation must be this-world orientated, and function to issue God's peace and wholeness, especially within contexts such as the African Caribbean that have been not so much 'shaped in sin and iniquity' but rather by trauma, genocide and annihilation. I suggest that Caribbean Contextual Theology is well placed to expand our theological imagination around sin and salvation and explore the biblical and doctrinal traditions for the purpose of pursuing wholeness and harmony in an otherwise traumatized world. We will continue our reflection on trauma as Chapter 8 shifts our attention to ecology and lament.

Notes

1 Barry Chevannes, 'Our Caribbean Reality', in Caribbean Theology: Preparing for the Challenges Ahead, ed. Howard Gregory, Barbados: Canoe Press, 1995, pp. 69–70.

2 Winelle J. Kirton-Roberts, Created in their Image: Evangelical Protestantism in Antigua and Barbados, 1834–1914, Bloomington, IN: AuthorHouse, 2015, p. 182.

3 Kirton-Roberts, Created in their Image, p. 175.

4 Patricia Sheerattan-Bisnauth (ed.), Righting Her-Story: Caribbean

Women Encounter the Bible, Geneva: World Communion of Reformed Churches (WCRC), 2011.

5 Patricia Sheerattan-Bisnauth, 'Editorial', in *Righting Her-Story*, ed. Sheerattan-Bisnauth.

6 Patricia Sheerattan-Bisnauth and Doreen Wynter, 'Bible Study Training Guide', in *Righting Her-Story*, ed. Sheerattan-Bisnauth, p. 6.

7 Judith Soares, 'Gender Justice and the Christian Mission', *Journal of Religious Thought* 57, no. 2, 2001, p. 74.

8 Dianne Stewart, 'Womanist Theology in the Caribbean Context: Critiquing Culture, Rethinking Doctrine, and Expounding Boundaries', *Journal of Feminist Studies in Religion* 20, no. 1, 2004, p. 62; emphasis original.

9 Stewart, 'Womanist Theology in the Caribbean Context', p. 62.

10 Anna Kasafi Perkins, '"Tasting Tears and [Not] Admitting Defeat": Promoting Values and Attitudes through the Music of Tanya Stephens?', Inaugural Lecture of the Centre for Social Ethics, St Michael's Theological College, Academia.edu, 12 January 2008, p. 11.

11 Carolyn Cooper, 'Sweet & Sour Sauce: Sexual Politics in Jamaican Dancehall Culture', The Sixth Jagan Lecture, October 2005, York University, North York, ON: CERLAC, November 2007.

12 Anna Kasafi Perkins, 'Christian Norms and Intimate Male Partner Violence: Lessons from a Jamaica Women's Health Survey', in *The Holy Spirit and Social Justice: Interdisciplinary Global Perspectives – History, Race and Culture*, ed. Antipas L. Harris and Michael D. Palmer, Lanham, MD: Seymour Press, 2019, pp. 242–3.

13 Nicqui Ashwood, 'Self-Questioning from the Caribbean', in *When Pastors Prey: Overcoming Clergy Sexual Abuse of Women*, ed. Valli Boobal Batchelor, Geneva: World Council of Churches, 2013, p. 117.

14 Marjorie Lewis, 'Diaspora Dialogue: Womanist Theology in Engagement with Aspects of the Black British and Jamaican Experience', *Black Theology: An International Journal* 2, no. 1, 2004, pp. 85–109.

15 Lewis, 'Diaspora Dialogue', p. 96.

16 Lewis, 'Diaspora Dialogue', p. 108.

17 Anthony B. Pinn, *Embodiment and the New Shape of Black Theological Thought*, New York: New York University Press, 2010.

18 Pinn, *Embodiment*, p. 5.

19 Pinn, *Embodiment*, p. 10.

20 Carlton Turner, 'Conceal to Reveal: Reflections on Sexual Violence and Theological Discourses in the African Caribbean', in *When Did We See You Naked? Jesus as a Victim of Sexual Abuse*, ed. Jayme R. Reaves, David Tombs and Rocío Figueroa, London: SCM Press, 2021, pp. 153–4.

21 Frantz Fanon, *Black Skin, White Masks*, New York: Grove Press, 1967.

22 Turner, 'Conceal to Reveal', p. 154. See also Carol Marie Webster, 'Body as Temple: Jamaican Catholic Women and the Liturgy of the Eucharist', *Black Theology: An International Journal* 15, no. 1, 2017, pp. 21–40.

23 Carolyn Cooper, *Noises in the Blood: Orality, Gender, and the 'Vulgar' Body of Jamaican Popular Culture*, 1st US edn, Durham, NC: Duke University Press, 1995, p. 3.

24 Kelly Brown Douglas, *Stand Your Ground: Black Bodies and the Justice of God*, Maryknoll, NY: Orbis Books, 2015.

25 Kelly Brown Douglas, *Sexuality and the Black Church: A Womanist Perspective*, Maryknoll, NY: Orbis Books, 1999, p. 69.

26 Douglas, *Sexuality and the Black Church*, p. 74.

27 Chevannes, 'Our Caribbean Reality', p. 68.

28 Turner, 'Conceal to Reveal', pp. 157–8.

29 Tara L. Atluri, *When the Closet is a Region: Homophobia, Heterosexism and Nationalism in the Commonwealth Caribbean*, Centre for Gender and Development Studies (CGDS), The University of the West Indies, 2001, p. 314.

30 Atluri, *When the Closet is a Region*, pp. 314–15.

31 Atluri, *When the Closet is a Region*, p. 316.

32 Dwight N. Hopkins, *Down, Up, and Over: Slave Religion and Black Theology*, Minneapolis, MN: Fortress Press, 2000, p. 135.

33 Kirton-Roberts, *Created in their Image*, pp. 169–70. She cites the work of Signe Arnfred, whose anthropological and sociological research focused on pre-Christian African cultural norms. See Signe Arnfred, '"African Sexuality"/Sexuality in Africa: Tales and Silences', in *Re-thinking Sexualities in Africa*, ed. Signe Arnfred, Uppsala: Nordiska Afrikainstitutet, 2004, pp. 59–76.

34 Carlton Turner, *Overcoming Self-Negation: The Church and Junkanoo in Contemporary Bahamian Society*, Eugene, OR: Pickwick Publications, 2020.

35 Kirton-Roberts, *Created in their Image*, ch. 8.

36 Turner, *Overcoming Self-Negation*.

37 Mark E. Biddle, *Missing the Mark: Sin and its Consequences in Biblical Theology*, Nashville, TN: Abingdon Press, 2005, p. viii.

38 See Turner, *Overcoming Self-Negation*, p. 126.

39 James H. Cone, *A Black Theology of Liberation*, 40th anniversary edn, Maryknoll, NY: Orbis Books, 2010, pp. 53, 110.

40 Kortright Davis, *Emancipation Still Comin': Explorations in Caribbean Emancipatory Theology*, Maryknoll, NY: Orbis Books, 1990, p. 78.

41 Lewin L. Williams, *The Caribbean: Enculturation, Acculturation, and the Role of the Churches*, Gospel and Cultures, Geneva: WCC Publications, 1996, p. 9.

42 Playing Mas refers to participating in the masquerade aspect of Carnival celebrations. It is synonymous for Rushin' within Junkanoo. Both refer to participation through dance movements, costuming and enjoyment.

43 Ronald Nathan, 'Caribbean Youth Identity in the United Kingdom: A Call for a Pan-African Theology', *Black Theology in Britain: A Journal of Contextual Praxis* 1, October 1998, p. 10.

44 Turner, *Overcoming Self-Negation*.

45 Walter Brueggemann, *The Prophetic Imagination*, 2nd edn, Minneapolis, MN: Fortress Press, 2001. In his work, Royal Consciousness refers to human-centred, state/static power that left no room for the movement of the Spirit of God. Prophetic critique was the word of the Lord proclaimed against a kingdom-centred tradition that refused change and renewal; that is, the relationship between Pharaoh and Moses. This kind of static, hierarchically centred, socially constructed and dichotomous thinking is characteristic of what I have explored as a colonial legacy within African Caribbean societies.

46 Brenda B. Colijn, *Images of Salvation in the New Testament*, Downers Grove, IL: InterVarsity Press, 2010, p. 177.

8

Roll Jordan Roll:
Salvation to Land, Sea and People

'Roll Jordan Roll' is a New World African spiritual that references the place and meaning of the River Jordan across the biblical literature.[1] In the Old Testament, Jordan is the river that must be crossed before entering the Promised Land in Joshua 3. It is where Elijah crosses and is subsequently taken up, presumably into heaven, in 2 Kings 2. It the place where Elisha heals Naaman in 2 Kings 5. In the New Testament, it is the place in which Jesus is baptized by John the Baptist. Within the Judaeo-Christian tradition it is multiply symbolic. First, it is a space in which God's promises of freedom are ratified. It is the ultimate sign of reaching freedom. It is the beginning of attaining the Promised Land. Second, Jordan represents that liminal space. It is a decisive point between traumatic and exhausting wilderness wanderings and peace. And third, Jordan is the space of encounter with the holy. It is where God reveals God's self. Whether the discussion is of the Ark of the Covenant rolling back the waters in Joshua 3, or Elijah being caught up by chariots of fire in 2 Kings 2, or Jesus being ratified as the Beloved Son of the Father in Mark 1, the Jordan remains a place of a stark encounter with God.

As a spiritual within the African American slave tradition, and one that Caribbean people know very well, these multiple significances of Jordan rolling back make sense. Spirituals within the African Atlantic world have always been ways of doing theology that seek to do many things simultaneously. They act as liturgical pieces that recount and re-enact God's salvation amid ordinary life. They recount, but also reframe, the traumatic history of oppression and despair. For oppressed peoples, the spiritual is equally a cry amid helplessness and danger, and also an assurance of hope. Spirituals also create space for the holy, the miraculous and the otherworldly newness that God brings, to be ushered in. Moreover, they served a praxiological function. They were covert ways of concretely responding to the political systems of slavery and oppression. 'Roll Jordan', and 'Wade in the Water', among others, were encoded messages for ensuring freedom for persons escaping slavery.[2]

In this chapter, I suggest that a Contextual Theology of the Caribbean is liturgically and melodically orientated and has space to bring together reflections on the ecological, environmental, political and spiritual vulnerability of the region. The fluidity, fragility and danger to those within the region is clearly manifested in the natural environment. In terms of politics, social relations, economics and general health, the overall precarity of the region is without question. Furthermore, as can be argued, tensions between the cultural history of the region and the role of the Church within it remain unresolved. In a sense, like 'Roll Jordan Roll', the region remains in a state of lament. Lament is heard, perhaps, in the two most popular songs associated with the Caribbean diaspora: Bob Marley's 'Redemption Song' and Boney M.'s, 'Rivers of Babylon'. It is important to note that both songs draw heavily on the Old Testament biblical tradition, filtering African Caribbean experiences of exile, despair and desired hope through the mood of lament.

To further this discussion, I will explore a unique occasion in the region where hymnody has been used to frame a Caribbean Contextual Theology. Second, I will explore in a bit more depth the ecological crises of the region that run through such musical and hymnic traditions. Similarly, the same can be said of the political crises in the region that have always had deep theological roots. In this regard, Haiti remains an important case study for the region. Finally, I will explore this theme of lament. It is deeply embedded in the experience of the region and is latent in most, if not all, African Caribbean theological articulations. The cry of lament opens up a space for new and imaginative ways of doing theology in such post-trauma contexts.

Musicality and Hymnody in the Region

When thinking of the Caribbean, hymnody has always been significant. And when thinking of a Caribbean Theology that is contextual, we must consider the lyrical and melodic nature of African Caribbean life and faith. While theologians such as George Mulrain are correct in framing Caribbean theologizing as primarily narrative, more can be said.[3] The stories that testify to our experiences of God are not just poetry or prose, they're also set to music! To be fair, Mulrain does argue that in the region, musical genres such as Calypso are the voice of God and the vehicle for articulating theologies that are rooted in the concrete lives and desires of the people.[4] Looking into the popular music scene of the region there can be no sharp distinction between popular and religious music. An example of this is the lyrical range of key Dancehall artists. Let's consider the musical range of the controversial artist Buju Banton, whose homophobic and violent lyrics led to him being banned from performing in some international scenes, including some in the UK. But songs such as 'Boom Bye Bye' are not his only offerings. One must take into account his rendition of the 23rd Psalm or the Our Father prayer, or the conscious lyrics of his songs on *'Til Shiloh* (1995) and *Inna Heights* (1997).[5] The same can be said of Beenie Man, whose erotic and violent imagery in songs such as 'Girls Dem Sugar' and 'Murderer' must be held alongside his 'Gospel Time', 'Blessings Pon Blessings' and 'Who God Bless'.[6] In fact, the cultural foundations that produce both kinds of lyrics remain the same. The religious roots and spirituality of popular Caribbean artists are embedded within the melody and aesthetics, as well as the lyrics. Carolyn Cooper gives us insight into this when exploring the violence and sexual imagery in, for example, Dancehall music. She reminds us that:

> sex and violence, however primal, are not the only preoccupations of Jamaican dancehall culture. There is a powerful current of explicitly political lyrics that articulate the struggle of the celebrants in the dance to reclaim their humanity in circumstances of grave economic hardship that force the

animal out of its lair. Indeed, Jamaican dancehall culture celebrates the dance as a mode of theatrical self-disclosure in which the body speaks eloquently of its capacity to endure and transcend material deprivation.[7]

She does not leave it there. She also reminds us that much of what is articulated is an exposure or critique of the kinds of Christian discourse existing within the society. In analysing the work of Lady Saw, she notes: 'The flamboyantly exhibitionist DJ Lady Saw epitomizes the sexual liberation of many African-Jamaican working-class women from airy-fairy Judeo-Christian definitions of appropriate female behaviour.'[8]

Hymnody, the music of the Church in the region, deserves attention too. The Caribbean theologian and liturgist Mikie Roberts' invaluable exploration of the Caribbean's only ecumenical hymnal resulted in his suggestion that, when considering the African Caribbean context, hymns function to form congregations. He refers to this as *hymnic performativity*.[9] The hymnal *Sing a New Song*, comprised of 133 hymns grouped into three sections, 'Liturgical', 'The Christian Life', 'Seasonal and General', reveal a consistent theme of liberation using ecological images steeped within Old and New Testament imagery.[10] One popular hymn included and sung internationally is Patrick Prescod's 'The Right Hand of God'.[11] Roberts notes:

In Patrick Prescod's hymn *The Right Hand of God*, the metaphoric 'right hand' – a biblical symbol of God's power, is declared to be at work in varied ways within the Caribbean. Each verse specifically demonstrates what God is doing and how God's power is manifested in the Caribbean church. Through the creative use of repetition, Prescod paints an image of God that conveys six specific actions of God's divine engagement (*writing*, *pointing*, *striking*, *lifting*, *healing*, and *planting*) within the region. The community is invited to partner with God and share in the exercise of God's power as the last verse asserts 'In these Caribbean lands / Let His people all join hands / And be one with the right hand of God'. The church community therefore becomes the symbolic 'right hand of God' being empowered to do all that God is doing in the Caribbean.[12]

Furthermore, Roberts points us in an ecological direction when considering all the other hymns. He states:

An examination of the hymn texts draws attention to God's creative power in these Caribbean lands. The text themselves underscore the power of God at work within the Caribbean community. They highlight that God's power is at work both in the Church itself and in the Caribbean community. Furthermore, they also reveal the nature of God's power that is represented in creation and more especially through the person of the Holy Spirit. The hymns communicate that the creative power of God is reflected in the beauty of these Caribbean lands and the richness of their productivity. There is the suggestion that the same creative power of God which is displayed in the creation continues in the work of the third person of the God-head. Because God's power is visible in nature then God's people who live in these lands share in and have access to that power. As such the community's sense of power rests not in the hands of its political leaders but ultimately power resides with God. Since God is present, then the hymns call on the ecumenical community to both recognize this power and to ensure that it is activated in their living.[13]

Ultimately, what we find is an implicit theology within African Caribbean musical traditions, and also hymnody, that is grounded simultaneously in a political, historical, theological, as well as ecological, reflection. For Caribbean people ecology, economics, culture, spirituality and liturgy are all intricately connected. Caribbean people, arguably, sing or perform their theology. They dance it. They worship with their bodies, and the physical or anthropological body is not removed from the environmental body. Land and sea shape life, and shape theological reflection significantly. Furthermore, there is a deep link between the liturgy, the experience of the peoples of the region, and their land. Michael Jagessar invokes Derek Walcott in his assertion that these things are inseparable within the Caribbean imagination:

> One may be tempted to say that Caribbean living is located between the devil and the deep blue sea. Caribbeans live between the fragile assurance of dry land and the terrifying mystery of the sea. Therefore, we understand paradox: 'We are a paradox.' It is the seascape, that open island space, more than landscape that shapes Caribbean identities. No wonder identity is for us a process, not a product. The site that represents the production of empire becomes the amorphous coordinates for doing theology and rereading texts. Derek Walcott got there first in his poem 'The Sea is History', in which he develops the idea that the Caribbean Sea offers the alternative history that locates the lived experiences of the region's people.[14]

Ecological Crises in the Region

To say that the Caribbean region is ecologically vulnerable is an understatement. The United Nations Office for the Coordination of Humanitarian Affairs (OCHA) report on natural disasters in Latin America and the Caribbean classes the region as the second most disaster-prone region in the world.[15] Between 2000 and 2019 there were 548 floods, 330 storms, 75 earthquakes and 74 droughts, 66 landslides, 50 instances of extreme temperature, and 38 volcanic events. When considering the Caribbean in particular, an average of 17 hurricanes per year took place during this time, 23 of which have been category 5. The 2017 hurricane season was the third worst on record in terms of number of disasters and countries affected, as well as the magnitude of the damage. In 2019, Hurricane Dorian became the strongest Atlantic hurricane on record that directly impacted a landmass, and the 2010 Haiti earthquake ranks among the top ten deadliest earthquakes in human history. According to the report, 'the storms affecting Central America and the Caribbean are becoming increasingly more powerful, producing increased rainfall and higher storm surge due to climate change'.[16] An example of this is the island of Dominica, which, in 2015, was damaged significantly by floods and landslides resulting from Tropical Storm Erika. In 2017, Hurricane Maria devastated the island, killing 64 persons and almost completely displacing the population of some 71,000 persons. Two years later the Bahamas came to global attention. The following excerpt gives a good description of the multiple effects of such a natural disaster:

> At its peak strength, Dorian, a category 5 hurricane, brought winds in excess of 220mph and 23ft storm surge as it barrelled over north-western Bahamas. During its path of destruction, Dorian slowed to a crawl over Grand Bahama (pop. 51,000), remaining nearly stationary for some 36 hours. Abaco, the most severely affected island, suffered thousands of flattened homes, downed powerlines and damaged roads and water wells. Abaco residents were left badly in need of water, electricity, sanitation and shelter. Dorian all but destroyed two Central Abaco settlements of mostly undocumented migrants. A total of 67 deaths have been reported across affected islands in the Bahamas.[17]

As we have discussed before when considering Haiti, natural disaster is also socio-economic and political. The loss of life is but one aspect. We must equally consider the loss of livelihoods, community life, economic stability, political stability and, in many cases, national and political sovereignty. Matthew Bishop and Anthony Payne have proposed the following when considering the reality of climate change in the region:

> It has been recognized for some time that environmental issues are coming to have a significant impact upon Caribbean development. In particular, climate change has moved rapidly up the agenda to become a defining feature of the region's development landscape. Moreover, given its intrinsic trans-boundary nature, it will, over time, come to impact upon the political economy of every territory of the region

in broadly similar and possibly dramatic ways. In this sense, it is the ultimate Pan-Caribbean issue. Despite this growing salience, a number of gaps exist in both the general and the specifically Caribbean academic literature on the subject. The former has tended to be technical in nature, focusing on the 'science', rather than the wider 'social science', of climate change. The latter has been sparse, with the consequence that practical attention to the amelioration of problems has been, at best, piecemeal.[18]

Politicizing and Theologizing Natural Catastrophe in the Region

To further explore the interrelationship between political, theological and ecological crises in the region, it is perhaps best to use Haiti as an example.

Kortright Davis uses Haiti as an example of a perpetual history played out within Caribbean nations struggling for self-determination. While the Haitian Revolution deserves respect as one of three such revolutions in the same historical period – the other two being the American Revolution (1776) and the French (1789) – Haiti's history of continued dependence and impoverishment remains astounding. Theirs has been a history of powerful landowning interests, military might and external forces all designed 'to maintain repressive and rigid control of the people and the country's meagre resources'.[19] The Duvalier regimes, 1957–86, witnessed killings, tortures, disappearances, unjust imprisonments, abject poverty and deprivation of the majority of Haitian people. While Duvalier was overthrown in 1986 and exiled to France, with the army taking over afterwards, the brutality remained. Considering the place of Haiti in the context of the rest of the Caribbean, Davis states explicitly: 'The poverty of Haiti has been compounded by the impotence of the Caribbean as a whole to bring about any form of liberation from the historically entrenched structures of bondage.'[20] What is most interesting, however, is that Davis, in articulating his emancipatory theology for the Caribbean, links the political fragility of Haiti to the ecological and economic vulnerabilities of the region. In connecting what we have discussed above about Haiti with the devastation of Jamaica by Hurricane Gilbert in 1988, and the oil crisis in Trinidad and Tobago in the mid-1980s, Davis states:

> Such is the nature of the Caribbean sandscape. The three experiences described – hurricane gilbert, economic collapse, and political upheaval – portray the realities endemic in the region. The rapid shifts of promise and regression have been frequent in much of Caribbean life.[21]

Then there is the earthquake in Haiti in 2010, which brought Haiti back into international political and theological conversation some 20 years after the publication of Davis's book. This time, the unspeakable calamities brought on by the earthquake sparked big questions and conversations around Haiti's misfortune. Beside the expected questions around aid dependence and international exploitation of the nation, Bois Caïman and long-held stigmas and vilifications of Vodou also surfaced on international media and television.[22] Elizabeth McAlister discusses how international television and evangelical Christianity have publicly attributed Haiti's misfortunes to its relationship with Vodou:

> The deadly earthquake that shook the Haitian capital of Port-au-Prince and its environs on the 12th of January 2010 killed an estimated 300,000 people, making it the worst disaster in the history of the Americas. The next day television evangelist Pat Robertson, while hosting his news talk show *The 700 Club* on the Christian Broadcast Network, said that the earthquake could be best understood by a little-known event that 'people might not want to talk about.' Haitians were cursed, he said, because they long ago 'swore a pact to the devil.'[23]

In fact, his exact words are worth a full citation here:

> Something happened a long time ago in Haiti and people might not want to talk about it. They were under the heel of

the French, you know, Napoleon the Third and whatever ... and they got together and swore a pact to the devil. They said we will serve you if you get us free from the prince ... true story ... so the devil said okay, it's a deal. And they kicked the French out. Ever since, they have been cursed by one thing after another.[24]

What McAlister notes and challenges is the historicizing and villainizing of the nation and its people by mainly American evangelicals using hermeneutics very much intertwined with North American neo-liberal capitalism. What is present is a simple theological conversation, one that is steeped in imperial exceptionalism, akin to the kinds of expansionist Missionary Christian hermeneutics used throughout the long history of the region. In the advent of the earthquake in Haiti, an already politically and economically fragile and dependent nation was made more so through spiritual and theological devices.

Two Haitian decolonial and ecological thinkers help us in this regard. First, Malcom Ferdinand's recent publication brings the multiple issues in this chapter into clear focus as he uses the complex realities of the Caribbean to help us think through the ecological crises of the world as more than natural, biological and environmental events. He states:

Environmental collapse does not impact everyone equally and does not negate the varied social and political collapse already underway. A double fracture lingers between those who fear the ecological tempest on the horizon and those who are denied the bridge of justice long before the first gusts of wind. As the eye of the storm, the Caribbean makes it necessary to understand the storm from the perspective of modernity's hold. Through the Caribbean's Creole imaginary of resistance and its experiences of (post)colonial struggles, the Caribbean allows for a conceptualization of the ecological crisis that is embedded within the search for a world free of its slavery, its social violence, and its political injustice: a decolonial ecology.[25]

Ferdinand bases these reflections mainly on the observation that there is a divide or fracture between ecological or environmental movements, and postcolonial or anti-racist ones. There is also a divide between nature and culture in the long history of colonial thinking, further perpetuated through modernity. Ferdinand is also quick to remind us that the colonial project did not happen to people or social networks alone; it profoundly affected and continues to affect the environment. There is a need to continually bridge these, not just in terms of praxis but also conceptually. But why the Caribbean? Ferdinand sees it as the best scene for exploring this ecological thinking:

> It was here that the Old World and the New World were first knotted together in an attempt to make the Earth and the world into one and the same totality. Eye of modernity's hurricane, the Caribbean is that center where the sunny lull was wrongly confused for paradise, the fixed point of a global acceleration sucking up African villages, Amerindian societies, and European sails.[26]

The kind of decolonial ecology Ferdinand envisages rejects binary thinking and offers a reflection from those who are trapped within the hurricane, the hold of the slave ship or the eye of the storm; those who cannot escape, destined to suffer along with the land and the rest of the biosphere.

The second thinker, the Methodist theologian and minister Marcus Torchon, in his PhD, explores the historical reality of aid-dependency in Haiti and the significance of this for the Protestant Church in the nation.[27] He argues that aid dependency as a phenomenon has disempowered Haitian Protestantism (HP) through inhibiting self-sufficiency. He argues also that aid-dependency contributes to ineffective poverty alleviation. This is precisely due to the underlying unequal power relations between the giver and the receiver. Torchon reminds us that modern attempts at development aid cannot be divorced from historic wealth extraction from the nation. He states:

Wealth extraction from Haiti is the extension of wealth extraction from St. Domingue. In either case, they represent a major challenge to Haiti's economic growth. The literature highlighted different strategies of wealth extraction. These include (a) independence indemnity, (b) trade deals, and (c) United States Occupation (1915–34). Each created albeit unique setbacks.[28]

Torchon reflects on the dual realities of 'development aid' and 'foreign presence', stating that in the literature on aid, a sense of powerlessness is always instilled within the receiving nation and its key institutions such as governments, parliaments, civil society and also the churches. For Haiti, 'the debt-crisis and the resource curse are cases in point. Haiti's productivity stalled as its government's fiscal adjustments further dis-incentivized local productivity.'[29] The aftermath of the 2010 earthquake is a particular example of this. Torchon further explains that what was evident was a monopolization of relations. Foreign mission agencies established unilateral relations with their denominational counterparts in the mission fields. Baptists related only to Baptists and Methodists to Methodists, for example. Torchon further states:

> The data suggested that each foreign church-mission maintained, in a protected way, a paternalistic relationship within HP. Related missional issues have emerged such that aid-recipients' negotiating rights have been subjugated in the particularity of their loyalty to mother-churches in a paternalistic monopolization. In parallel with this, converging missional initiatives of leading foreign aid-providers to help to tackle a national problem in HP have been non-existent. In fact, in circumstances where a mother-church has been unable to bring a development project to completion, another mother-church will not intervene.[30]

To be clear, Torchon does not argue against the giving of aid, seeing it as a moral obligation and a divine mandate. However, in his own words, he highlights that:

another reality of aid-giving has revealed the operational frameworks of its functionality. I refer to aid-modalities. The bureaucratic procedures of budgeting, delivering, and reporting on aid. They include policy implementations and project supports while facilitating fragmentation, project proliferation and overlaps among donors. They are set up to benefit aid-agencies, their intermediaries, more than they benefit aid-receivers, since, for example, aid-givers' rights to totally withdraw from sponsored projects cancel out receivers' rights of redress. Evidence suggests that they are characterized by the principles of the identified victim effect, case-based advocacy, neo-patrimony, and a political economy of trauma, delivered through paternalistic parlances and practices. As such, palliative economics and deprivation of dignity have been two recurrent outcomes.[31]

The Continued Cry of Lament

How shall we live amid natural and human-made crises? Thus far, the point has been made that any Caribbean theological conversation inevitably has an ecological dimension. The ecological and environmental crises of the region, including earthquakes, floods, hurricanes and potential tidal waves, echo the long history of political, economic, cultural and theological trauma of its people. Haiti is a good example of this, and Haitian and wider Caribbean scholars have helped us to see this clearly. What we also discern after careful reflection is that hermeneutics and how the region is framed theologically is something that Caribbean Theology must pay attention to. While patronizing and racist concepts and tropes, in liturgies, church practices and songs, have been employed to vilify African Caribbean people and their traditions, the region has responded in a similar vein. The Caribbean offers a counter-hermeneutic, a counter-liturgy or even a counter-theology that is rooted and grounded in its African traditional cultural heritages, music being a key example of this. The mood that is mostly invoked within these is one of lament.

This mood of lament at the heart of a Caribbean Contextual Theology, which takes the cries of the land, the sea and the people seriously, is most clearly expressed in the musical and liturgical traditions of the region. However, before parsing out this idea of lament theologically, it is important to note that beyond the Caribbean, similar conversations have been growing. Global South and Third World theologians have come to critique dominant Western theological discourses that fail to centre their reflection ecologically. Key voices in this regard include, among others, Ivone Gebara, a Latin American ecofeminist theologian from Brazil, who helps us see the deep connections between poverty and injustice and the destruction of the land, and Jione Havea, a Pacifika theologian from Tonga, who centres his reflection on the importance of the sea in articulating theologies of justice in his context.[32] A recent publication that pays attention to the need for theologies of liberation and justice to centre such concerns theologically is by A. M. Ranawana.[33] Taking the papal encyclical *Laudato Si'* into account, she surveys the range of theological and activist voices to suggest that one finds in them a kind of rage. This 'Theology of Rage', according to Ranawana, is comprised of many different emotions, including ecological grief, which is further comprised of fear and worry. Of rage she states:

> the justice narrative is key to our moral and spiritual awakening. We must look at the history and present of the world and feel prophetic rage. The climate crisis is not a new crisis, and we must come together in rage to overturn systems of enslavement, expropriation, colonization and indigenous genocide. Without feeling rage or acknowledging and centring the rage of those who have been oppressed and exploited, we cannot move forward. This rage, poured out, can be mobilizing. Our theological and pastoral space must not be afraid of rage.[34]

This parsing of the concept of rage can similarly be done when considering how lament functions theologically within the deepest of Caribbean anthropological and ecological experiences.

Lament is embedded within African Caribbean theological reflection that is most notably articulated in the musical, poetic and liturgical traditions. But this kind of lament must be understood in the light of the African Caribbean experience of isolation, dislocation and an insistence on home amid natural and political tempests. Perhaps a good place to go for further analysis would be Carolyn Cooper's reflection on Bob Marley's music and how it functions lyrically and aesthetically. She notes that Marley uses 'biblical allusion, Rastafarian symbolism, proverbs, riddle, aphorism and metaphor' in his artistry.[35] He employs a range of melodic, liturgical, poetic and literary devices, all steeped within his African Jamaican cultural heritages. He is prolific with his use of the Psalms and other parts of the Hebrew Bible, his allusions to 'Babylon' or the deep desire for 'redemption', across his music. For Cooper, 'Bob Marley's chant against Babylon is both medium and message'; Babylon is described as 'the oppressive State, the formal social and political institutions of Anglo/American imperialism'.[36] Concerning 'redemption', the theme in iconic songs such as 'Exodus', and 'Redemption Song', Cooper states:

> The religious and commercial resonances of 'redemption' suggest both divine grace and the practical justice of freeing a slave by the payment of ransom money. Liberation becomes much more than the freeing from physical chains, for true freedom cannot be given; it has to be appropriated. Authenticity comes with the slave's reassertion of the right to self-determination. Emancipation from 'mental slavery' thus means liberation from passivity – the instinctive posture of automatic subservience that continues to cripple the neo-colonized.[37]

What becomes clear is that Marley's music functions prophetically and apocalyptically. The range of biblical symbolism alluding to the event of the Exodus, the return from the Babylonian exile or the vision of divine justice, are ways of expressing the many ways in which African Caribbean people have had to come to terms with a long history of trauma and oppression both natural and ecological, as well as political. To borrow the terminology from Walter Brueggemann, Marley ignites a 'prophetic imagination', one that functions in multiple ways.[38] First, the music and lyrics are simultaneously ways of facing the pain of the trauma. In this regard, lament has the quality of making the pain of the past accessible. It becomes the place in which the past can be recalled and faced in all its painfulness. Second, and according to Brueggemann, it is also a place for energizing. Lament, certainly through Caribbean music and art, is meant to create synergy and action. It is the 'Get up, Stand up' of one of Marley's iconic songs. Lament is the space in which critical reflection takes place, or 'reasoning' according to Rastafari, and future action is decided. Finally, Lament is never divorced from hope. The apocalyptic vision in songs such as 'Time Will Tell' and 'Redemption Song' are the same kinds of hopeful longing expressed in the pan-Caribbean Calypso hit 'Rivers of Babylon', mentioned earlier in this chapter. Cooper states again, 'Marley's vision, like that of John the Revelator, is for a new heaven and a new earth from which the former evil has passed away.'[39] Michael Jagessar also reminds us that while the imagery of the sea has been traumatic for peoples and nations of the Caribbean, it is also key to a hopeful imagination. He states:

> It is not insignificant that we are described by that sea (Caribbeans). Yet for Africans and Indians, the river and water imagery stirred up an alternative beyond: that of crossing over, home, promised land, and a physical space of comfort and hope.[40]

As stated in the Introduction, Jagessar uses Derek Walcott's 'The Sea is History' to substantiate this insight. Walcott's poem is packed with biblical imagery and, in his inimitable way, invites the reader into the deeply overwhelming and rageful trauma of Caribbean life. He also offers a chance to encounter the God of the deep in whom possibilities of newness continually arise. The sea is both death and resurrection.[41] For Brueggemann, everything that a prophetic consciousness utters is precisely because of a deep hope in God's revelation that is usually imperceptible to empires and systems of oppression. Babylon does not know that it has already fallen! The prophet sings of what already exists despite suggestions otherwise, and that which is already always at hand, which is redemption and emancipation of body, mind and spirit. Ultimately, lament within the musical, hymnic, poetic and liturgical traditions of the African Caribbean is more than a mood based on a painful history. It is also a form of theological reflection and praxis towards a new world.

Conclusion

It becomes clear that doing theology in the African Caribbean context, whether acknowledged or not, has an ecological dimension. Historically, the sea and landscapes have constituted a traumatic space and place for the exercise of international politics, economics, and especially for theology and church praxis. There is a deeply embedded lament within African Caribbean musical traditions and hymnody that does not ignore this observation. In song and dance, references are made to the fact that the people, as well as the land and all its inhabitants, have all suffered significantly. People, land and sea reflect each other. They all struggle with a general sense of alienation. While on the surface, it seems the happiest place on earth, at a much deeper level much has been endured. Yet in the face of such shifting situations, the region, its lands and its people have remained strong and resilient, determined and creative. The argument of this book is that much of this is down to a deep and embodied theology that extends far beyond the Christian imagination that Missionary Christianity brought. Through African Caribbean lament, the God of the Bible, the God of the people, is encountered anew.

For deeper reflection, an eco-theology arising from the Caribbean region reminds the broader discipline of theology to think beyond the anthropocentric to include the full expanse of landscapes, seascapes and all its inhabitants. The region and its diaspora know well that anthropocentric thinking, especially in the form of theologies and philosophical assumptions that have prioritized colonial expansion, commerce and wealth extraction, must be abandoned for a deeper, embodied, ecological kind of thinking or theology. This kind of theology dares to think from multiple perspectives and to engage the imagination and creativity of the region towards a more sustainable future.

Notes

1 'Roll Jordan Roll' – versions of this popular African American Spiritual were recorded in *Slave Songs of the United States* (1867) and *Four Years of Fighting* (1866).

2 For a deeper exploration of this, see, Dwight N. Hopkins, *Down, Up, and Over: Slave Religion and Black Theology*, Minneapolis, MN: Fortress Press, 2000.

3 See George Mulrain, *Caribbean Theological Insights: Exploring Theological Themes Within the Context of the Caribbean Region*, London: Blessed Hope Publishing, 2014.

4 See, for example: George Mulrain, 'The Music of the African Caribbean', *Black Theology: An International Journal* 1, no. 1, 1998; George Mulrain, 'Is There a Calypso Exegesis?', in *Voices from the Margin: Interpreting the Bible in the Third World*, ed. R. S. Sugirtharajah, Maryknoll, NY: Orbis Books, 1995, pp. 37–47.

5 See Buju Banton, 'Boom Bye Bye', *The Early Years: 1990–1995*, 2001; '23rd Psalm', *Unchained Spirit*, 2000; 'Our Father in Zion', *Inner Heights*, 1997; *'Til Shiloh*, 1995.

6 See Beenie Man, 'Girls Dem Sugar', *Maestro*, 1996; 'Murderer', *The Magnificent Studio Album*, 2000; 'Gospel Time', *The Doctor*, 1999; 'Blessings Pon Blessings', *Blessings Pon Blessings*, 2022; 'Who God Bless', *Who God Bless*, 2019.

7 Carolyn Cooper, 'Sweet & Sour Sauce: Sexual Politics in Jamaican Dancehall Culture', The Sixth Jagan Lecture, October 2005, York University, York, ON: CERLAC, November 2007, p. 1.

8 Cooper, 'Short Sweet & Sour Sauce', p. 3.

9 Mikie Anthony Roberts, 'Hymnody and Identity: Congregational Singing as a Construct of Christian Communty Identity', PhD thesis, University of Birmingham, 2014.

10 *Sing a New Song No. 3*, ed. Patrick Prescod, Bridgetown, Barbados: The Cedar Press, 1981.

11 Noel Dexter, 'The Right Hand of God', in *Sing a New Song No. 3*, ed. Prescod.

12 Roberts, 'Hymnody and Identity', pp. 174–5.

13 Roberts, 'Hymnody and Identity', pp. 173–4.

14 Michael Jagessar, 'Chanting Down the Shitstem: Resistance with Anansi and Rastafari Optics', in *Religion and Power: Theology in the Age of Empire*, ed. Jione Havea, London: Lexington/Fortress Academic, 2019, p. 94.

15 Office for the Coordination of Humanitarian Affairs (OCHA), *Natural Disasters in Latin America and the Caribbean: 2000–2019*, The United Nations (OCHA), 2020, https://reliefweb.int/report/world/natural-disasters-latin-america-and-caribbean-2000-2019 (accessed 20.7.23).

16 OCHA, *Natural Disasters in Latin America and the Caribbean*, p. 5.

17 OCHA, *Natural Disasters in Latin America and the Caribbean*, p. 6.

18 Matthew Louis Bishop and Anthony Payne, 'Climate Change and the Future of Caribbean Development', *The Journal of Development Studies* 48, no. 10, 2012, p. 1536.

19 Kortright Davis, *Emancipation Still Comin': Explorations in Caribbean Emancipatory Theology*, Maryknoll, NY: Orbis Books, 1990, p. 15.

20 Davis, *Emancipation Still Comin'*, p. 17.

21 Davis, *Emancipation Still Comin'*, p. 17.

22 Bois Caïman was the site for the meeting and legendary Vodou ceremony that began the Haitian Revolution and the slave insurrection across the island nation.

23 Elizabeth McAlister, 'From Slave Revolt to a Blood Pact with Satan: The Evangelical Rewriting of Haitian History', *Studies in Religion* 41, no. 2, 2012, p. 188.

24 Pat Robertson, *The 700 Club*, 13 January 2010. See https://abcnews.go.com/Politics/pat-robertsons-haiti-comments-spark-controversy-discussion-countrys/story?id=9563274 (accessed 20.7.23)

25 Malcolm Ferdinand, *Decolonial Ecology: Thinking from the Caribbean World*, trans. Anthony Paul Smith, Cambridge: Polity Press, 2022.

26 Ferdinand, *Decolonial Ecology*, p. 12.

27 Marcus Torchon, 'A Methodist Perspective on Aid-Dependency in Haitian Protestantism', PhD thesis, University of Manchester, 2019.

28 Torchon, 'A Methodist Perspective', p. 45.

29 Torchon, 'A Methodist Perspective', p. 79.

30 Torchon, 'A Methodist Perspective', p. 213.

31 Torchon, 'A Methodist Perspective', pp. 215–16.

32 Ivone Gebara, *Longing for Running Water: Ecofeminism and Liberation*, Minneapolis, MN: Fortress Press, 1999. Jione Havea, *Theologies from the Pacific: Postcolonialism and Religions*, Cham, Switzerland: Palgrave Macmillan, 2021.

33 A. M. Ranawana, *A Liberation for the Earth: Climate, Race and Cross*, London: SCM Press, 2022.

34 Ranawana, *A Liberation for the Earth*, p. 122. For further reading on the need for an ecological conversion in the discipline of theology, see Samuel Ewell, *Faith Seekijng Conviviality: Reflections on Ivan Illich, Christian Mission, and the Promise of Life Together*, Eugene, OR: Cascade Books, 2020.

35 Carolyn Cooper, *Noises in the Blood: Orality, Gender, and the 'Vulgar' Body of Jamaican Popular Culture*, 1st US edn, Durham, NC: Duke University Press, 1995, p. 118.

36 Cooper, *Noises in the Blood*, p. 121.

37 Cooper, *Noises in the Blood*, p. 124.

38 Walter Brueggemann, *The Prophetic Imagination*, 2nd edn, Minneapolis, MN: Fortress Press, 2001.

39 Cooper, *Noises in the Blood*, p. 134.

40 Jagessar, 'Chanting Down the Shitstem', p. 94.

41 See Derek Walcott, 'The See is History', in Derek Walcott and Glyn Maxwell, *The Poetry of Derek Walcott 1948–2013*, Faber & Faber, 2014.

9

Conclusion:
Contours of a Caribbean
Contextual Theology

Exposing the Devil

In Chapter 1, I explained that the popular idiom 'between the devil and the deep blue sea' seeks to describe the pervasive dilemma of the African Caribbean region. I echoed the insights of Michael Jagessar and Derek Walcott, who use the image of the sea to speak about the precarious nature of Caribbean life and history.[1] I explored the sea, and particularly how it is a metaphor for a region whose history is untold, unfinished, but which also exists within a trans-historical trauma that is over-whelming, unfathomable and ineffable – like the deep blue sea. People who live in the eye of the hurricane do not 'think' God! Our very existence is predicated upon the God who holds us in the eye of that storm, and who holds us in the depths of the sea. After surveying the contents of this book, an argument can be made as to why Christianity should never have taken root in the region at all. Caribbean theologians have noted this, but have also noted how, despite the pervasive experience of alien-ation, violence and trauma, attempts have always been made to reform the Christianity that the Europeans brought.

But what about the devil? Of course, I'm not talking about a literal 'devil' here, nor am I digging into Christian history and tradition to excavate images of the 'Evil One'. But this book has been exposing the 'devil' for African Caribbean life, care-fully and chapter by chapter. I would define it as the pervasive experience of empire and colonialism, affecting all levels of

African Caribbean life and experience, including the Church. It is an experience of control, impoverishment, degradation and, at various times in the region's history, inordinate violence. One rendering of the word for 'devil' (*diabolos*) in the biblical tradition refers to that which 'tears apart', that which seeks to 'destroy'.[2] There is no better example of this than the inhumane, capitalistic, Afrophobic, patriarchal, misogynistic and hetero-sexist processes that have shaped the region and continue to do so. These are all interconnected. On the one hand, the region is continually faced with ecological threats to life and com-munity. On the other hand, the destructive reaches of empire continue to operate from without and within Caribbean soci-eties, psychologically, politically, economically, culturally and theologically. In the region, Caribbean Contextual Theology is done 'between the devil and the deep blue sea', always!

Chapter 1 framed the approach of the book, being clear that doing theology in the African Caribbean is no easy task. The region defies description. It is also a unique history that, unbeknownst to many, is at the centre of the development of the modern world. Historical events such as the arrival of Columbus, Britain's landfall on St Kitts, the Haitian Revolu-tion, apprenticeship and emancipation, the conscious movement of Marcus Garvey, the invasion of Grenada, the earthquake in Haiti and the creation of the Republic of Barbados are testament to important moments when the Caribbean has significantly influenced global history. Doing Contextual Theology in the Caribbean requires this complicated view of history, but also interdisciplinarity. The region is too politically, sociologically and economically shaped by transnational movements for it to be narrow in its theological approach. I also make the point that an insistence on 'context' continues to be a precondition for doing theology in the region for the purpose of limiting colonial and imperial oppression. Theology itself, if not quali-fied, has led to lethal consequences for the people of the region.

Chapter 2 more deeply explored the Caribbean, arguing that the concept of God has been germane to the very formation of the region. It is a region of radical paradox and liminality, difficult to systematize. Nonetheless, the legacies of plantation slavery and colonialism are enduring. These manifest in persistent poverty, migration, cultural alienation, political dependence, inner fragmentation and health crises, among others. It is also a region in which a variety of responses have occurred, including the survival of indigenous religions, mainly African-derived ones, rebellions against enslavement, revolutionary intellectual traditions, and diasporan perspectives. There is no shortage of contextual material for theologically reflecting on the Caribbean.

Chapter 3 looked at the formal theological conversations in the region. From the 1970s there was a growing sense of a Caribbean Theology sponsored by the Caribbean Conference of Churches (CCC) that paid attention to local and global movements, as well as the complex traumatic history of the region. For the past 50 years it has produced an array of Caribbean theologians employing different methodologies and advancing slightly different lenses in their theological work. What remains consistent is the utter fragility of the region amid larger geopolitical power structures. While being a region with sharp theological scholarship and creativity, it must address some shortcomings. First, there must be more contribution from women in the region. Second, Pentecostal scholarship, which is vital, is lacking. Third, there must be greater efforts of diasporic joint projects and networking. Finally, there has to be an investment (especially financial) in local theological capacity building. Opportunities must be made to increase the number of Caribbean theologians well placed within universities, seminaries and local churches.

Chapter 4 began a set of theological reflections in Part 2 of the book. It traced the development of the Church in the Caribbean since the coming of Columbus in 1492. Missionary Christianity was introduced into the region, which carried an embedded theology and missiology steeped in Enlightenment rationalism and European expansionist ideology. The underlying assumptions were, first, that there was a divine right to conquer lands and people for the nations of Europe. Second, non-European cultures and cosmologies were immediately deemed heathen, uncivilized, dangerous and chattel. This thinking led to the genocide of pre-Columbian people, who were used as labourers in the European wealth-extraction regime, and then the development of transatlantic slavery and the genocide of mainly West and Central African people through the Middle Passage, and their descendants on New World plantations. It is out of this theological ferment that the Church in the Caribbean developed and, according to Noel Erskine and Kortright Davis, it has yet to become a church that has processed its missionary history properly and become a truly enculturated church.[3]

Chapter 5 shifted focus to ATRs in the region and what they might offer a Caribbean Contextual Theology. The issue of enculturation, or the degree to which the gospel has become rooted in the various religiocultural heritages and cosmologies in the region remains a challenge. To begin with, non-European religious and cultural heritages, such as the pre-Columbian peoples and then the African ancestors of the contemporary African Caribbean, were othered by colonial and imperial Christianity that shaped Caribbean societies. In the chapter I further explored the multiple ways in which such cosmologies and religious heritages were assaulted – legally, philosophically, culturally, politically and theologically. Nonetheless, and as I have theorized, ATRs remain potent means of doing theology contextually in the African Caribbean.

Chapter 6 then moved to consider an underutilized dynamic within African Caribbean societies. It considered the wealth of decolonial and anti-colonial hermeneutical examples in the region. From Reggae to Calypso, to the works of Frantz Fanon, to the insights of Sylvia Wynter, the region has always maintained an intellectual tradition deeply critical of the hermeneutics of empire. Some of the most insightful, inspiring and penetrating critiques of the imperial project come from the lyrics of Bob Marley, the poems of Derek Walcott or the revolutionary intellect of Walter Rodney and Marcus Garvey. Many Caribbean theologians have followed in this tradition, adding their voices to Third World and other non-Western theological approaches that have maintained a hermeneutic of suspicion against Western theological discourses. It is my contention that for Caribbean Contextual Theology to flourish it must engage this tradition within the region.

Chapter 7 is the longest chapter, and for good reason. I tried, as far as possible, to highlight the work of women in the region as they discuss gender, sex and the body. The effects of Missionary Christianity and its hermeneutics around sin and the body, particularly the non-white and non-male body, cannot be overstated in the region. The trauma inflicted by the institution of enslavement has impacted every aspect of African Caribbean sexuality – gender relations, mating practices and intergenerational dynamics, for example. Also, there is an ongoing struggle for survival that continually contests European ideals around how life, particularly sexuality, should be ordered within the region. A Nannyish (Caribbean Womanist) tradition is growing that seeks deeply to interrogate these complex issues, and articulate a holistic, inclusive and liberative approach to addressing them for all within Caribbean society. Significant challenges to these goals are the popular hermeneutics around sin and the body that lead to stigmatization and violence.

Finally, Chapter 8 argued that a Contextual Theology of the Caribbean is liturgically and melodically orientated and has space to bring together reflections on the ecological, environmental, political and spiritual vulnerability of the region. Musicality and hymnody consistently integrate the social and cultural realities of the people and the deep lament about, and longing for, divine justice. They also consistently employ environmental and ecological imagery to advance a truth that Caribbean people know well: the trauma of the people and the trauma of the sea and landscapes are contiguous. Ecological crises in the region are significant and are increasing. This reality insists on the need for a contextual theology that is done is different modes.

Future Prospects and Suggestions

Part 2 of this book has taken time to reflect theologically on the different areas of African Caribbean life. Chapter 4 focused on the concept of the Church and the multiple ways in which it remains entangled with the imperialist theologies of Missionary Christianity. I have written on this in other academic output and agree with Ashley Smith that the Church in the African Caribbean remains a potted plant.[4] It is this deep complicity with empire and colonialism that makes the African Caribbean a site of reflection for Christian theology generally. The idea of complicity is key to the work of Black theologians in the British and African American contexts, such as Anthony Reddie, Robert Beckford, J. Kameron Carter and Willie James Jennings. It is also central to the work of persons like Dianne Stewart, Michael Jagessar and me, who are doing the same in the African Caribbean context. It is simply the notion that the reach of empire and its violent, Afrophobic, pernicious and destructive tendencies are deeply embedded in the very nature of Christianity in the West and its theologies of domination.[5] The nature of the post-imperial Church and the possibilities of a church that is truly reflective of the complexity of the region is worth further research.

Chapter 5 looked at the area that I have been most involved in, popular religions. My work on Junkanoo in the Bahamas and my continued interest in African Caribbean religious and cultural heritages has convinced me that these potent features of African Caribbean life deserve more than anthropological and sociological attention. They deserve deep theological respect. I eventually centred my reflection on the possibility of a Caribbean Christ, which is something that several Caribbean theologians have done specifically. Significant questions still remain. The cultural and religious complexity of the region requires a dynamic view of Christ, which in turn requires a rereading of the biblical tradition in the light of this complexity. Inherent in the question of how we conceive of Christ, and hence Christ's redemptive work on the cross, is the issue of the *imago Dei*. Christ became human, but for centuries the non-European inhabitants of the region were not considered human. Again, the imperial and colonial shaping of the region requires a deep reimagination of Christ and his redemptive work.

Chapter 6 reminded us of the revolutionary spirit of the African Caribbean. It also reminded us of the revolutionary nature of the Holy Spirit. I have written on this specifically, suggesting that the people of the African Caribbean are pneumatologically orientated and engage worship and theology from a 'pneuma-tocentric' place. This is because of the African cultural heritage and world view that has survived plantation slavery and colonialism.[6] In fact, the argument that Dianne Stewart, Barry Chevannes and I make is a valid one: ATRs within the African Caribbean have been reforming Missionary Christianity from its ordered, Christocentric, militaristic emphasis to an ecstatic, liberative, pneumatocentric one steeped in ATRs.[7] Pentecostal theological research arising from the Caribbean, by those who are Pentecostal, is needed. Another reason for this is the fact that the birth of Pentecostalism in the twentieth century passed through the African Caribbean before settling in Great Britain.

Chapter 7 was very engaging as a piece of research. I personally learned much from the writings of the Caribbean women or Nannyish theologians. The truth is, women in the African Caribbean have arguably been most traumatized and vilified by plantation society. They bring a depth of reflection that is worth paying attention to. In cultural and religious life, women have maintained a semblance of a social structure in a region that was never meant for anthropological flourishing of any kind. They have also been the conduits of ecstatic spirit possession, the guardians of ancestral traditions, and architects of survival amid overwhelming traumas. They speak about the body, sin and salvation as those who have every right to rage and anger, but read within Scripture a different path, a creative one, an empathetic one, and a prophetic one that is inclusive, life-affirming, generous and generative. We must invest in more women and Nannyish theologians who know better than most how to weave multiple disciplines, experiences and traditions into one salvific pattern.

Chapter 8 considered how the region could never have afforded to be anthropocentric in its theological outlook. The history of the people is also the history of the land. Malcolm Ferdinand reminds us that the colonial project did not only happen to people, it also profoundly shaped the environment of the African Caribbean. The treatment of the region as an ecological and environmental space is concomitant with the racism, othering and devaluation of its people.[8] Furthermore, climate change due to the continued wealth and prosperity of the West increasingly leads to more severe ecological crises. As it was in colonization, it remains the case in post-independence eras that the wealth and flourishing of the West is predicated upon the impoverishment of the African Caribbean. This leads to a contemplation of the musical and hymnic traditions of the region. Theology for people of the African Caribbean can most readily be discerned in the mood of lament and praise in the people's musical traditions. Also, this is a fruitful area for further contextual theological research. Slavery was not something that 'happened' to African Caribbean people, it was rather something they 'survived'. They survived through theological devices framed through ancestral cultural productions. In short, they were forced to do theology in different ways. Their hermeneutics on God, salvation, faith, survival, freedom and so on, were hidden within their dynamic, embodied and melodic cultural practices. This process deserves further theological attention.

A Strong Plea: Wholeness *not* Rightness

I will end this book with something that has become stronger within me as I've been writing and reflecting through these chapters. In previous publications I have explored the need for healing or wholeness as primary objectives in the theological task when engaging in postcolonial and post-slavery contexts. In my research into Junkanoo in the Bahamian context I argue that ATRs such as Junkanoo and other Myalist traditions have an inherent healing purpose.[9] Traditions such as Obeah, Spiritual Baptists, Carnival, Calypso and Reggae music are simultaneously socio-political critique, theological commentary and embodied practices of soul healing. They address trauma and, more than anything else, they allow a direct engagement with the deep structures of anthropological impoverishment resulting from centuries of colonial trauma passed down through generations. These are moments of encounter with the African soul!

Throughout the book I have been alerting us to the need for

an insistence on the deeper, therapeutic work of theology. In Chapter 5 one of the insights that surfaced when considering a Caribbean Christ through George Mulrain's use of the image of the Calypsonian, is that Christ is not only a liberator but a healer.[10] In Chapter 6, I made the point that the potent pneumatology of the region is both resistant and also healing and affirming. In fact, an important part of the decolonial and anti-colonial impulse within the region is the need to bring about a kind of psychological, cultural, spiritual and theological wholeness. In Chapter 7, African Caribbean women theologians have interrogated the legacies of traumatic, disembodied and misogynistic theological hermeneutics and practices in the region. They challenge the narrow views on sex, sin and the body, and open space for a deeper, more anthropologically whole theology. They insist that the ordering of colonial imperialist theology was the problem. It did not allow for other ways of theologizing, experiencing and being. Finally, in Chapter 8 we learnt that wholeness is the subtext of ecological conversations in the region. The fragility of the region is not only environmental, but also political, economic, social and theological. This sense of fragility and despair pervades every aspect of the African Caribbean. Wholeness, then, cannot be considered in terms of healthcare, but rather must be the framework for every aspect of existence in the region. However, despite all this, theologies of domination remain pernicious, deeply entrenched and Afrophobic. Usually they are colonial and imperialistic, steeped in post-Enlightenment rationalism, and they still hold significant power over the psyches of the people within the region.

In my opinion, the exercise of theology in the West, mostly, seems to pursue the question of 'rightness'. The goal is to prove the logical consistency of a claim or to explore the philosophical contours of a doctrine. The approach is often relegated to understanding, or systematizing thought. This is important. And this is something that must be done in any context. However, in a context in which colonial trauma and genocide have shaped its very emergence, simply understanding is insufficient. Instinctively, when Caribbean people read the Bible, the approach isn't about what I understood, but how it has inspired me, how

I received a 'word' to nourish my soul, my being, something that helps me to survive. A Caribbean Contextual Theology is concerned about being right, clearer or more deeply analytical; but more primary than this, it is concerned with being 'whole', 'healed', 'integrated' and 'authentic'.

Finally, if I were to offer some idea as to how this emphasis on wholeness might look within a Caribbean Contextual Theology, it would be in these few humble suggestions. First, religious and cultural healing amid the significant historical violence and fragility within the region must be central. History must be interrogated and excavated, and there are many areas in which the voices of our ancestors remain unheard. Second, it must engage in conversations around reparations. At the time of writing this book, this is a growing conversation in Europe and North America, and the African Caribbean finds itself at the centre. It is a space in which a Caribbean Contextual Theology can make significant contributions as it engages with other disciplines. Third, it must be interdisciplinary. I cannot state enough the fact that the region is complex and has to be viewed from different angles if any sense of liberative ways forward is to be achieved. One area that I continue to argue for is an ongoing dialogue with the psychological sciences. I have written on this, arguing that the legacies of trauma in the African Caribbean necessitate a 'more than' theological assessment.[11] In fact, the African Caribbean is a site in which cross-training in theology and psychology would yield significant fruit for the discipline of theology globally. Fourth, decolonial and postcolonial perspectives are needed. While these are not perfect, and can become new forms of colonization themselves, they are important tools. Again, the African Caribbean is in a unique position to continually lend new insights into this intellectual space. Finally, we must explore the imagination.[12] Caribbean people are creative. Colonial trauma did not destroy all that we are. We remain people who have imagined our survival. It is now time to imagine a new Caribbean, and even a new world, beyond the limiting grips of empire. We have existed 'between the devil and the deep blue sea', yet we abide.

Notes

1 Michael Jagessar, 'Chanting Down the Shitstem: Resistance with Anansi and Rastafari Optics', in *Religion and Power: Theology in the Age of Empire*, ed. Jione Havea, London: Lexington/Fortress Academic, 2019. Derek Walcott, 'The Muse of History', in *What the Twilight Says: Essays*, New York: Farrar, Straus & Giroux, 1998. Derek Walcott and Glyn Maxwell, *The Poetry of Derek Walcott 1948–2013*, London: Faber & Faber, 2014.

2 There are multiple meanings of the word 'devil', one of which is 'Tear to pieces, break up, score, scratch'. See 'Devil', in *Shorter Oxford English Dictionary*, ed. Angus Stevenson, Oxford: Oxford University Press, 2007, p. 667.

3 Kortright Davis, *Emancipation Still Comin': Explorations in Caribbean Emancipatory Theology*, Maryknoll, NY: Orbis Books, 1990, p. 72; Noel L. Erskine, *Decolonizing Theology: A Caribbean Perspective*, Trenton, NJ: Africa World Press, 1998, p. 99.

4 Ashley Smith, *Real Roots and Potted Plants: Reflections on the Caribbean Church*, Mandeville, Jamaica: Eureka Press, 1984; Carlton Turner, 'Women Speak, Men Share, and Everyone Rush! Prophetic Consciousness, Junkanoo and the Church in Bahamian Society', *Rethinking Mission*, Spring 2017; Carlton Turner, 'Self-Negation within African Caribbean Christianity: Towards an Understanding of Junkanoo and its Significance for Christian Praxis within Contemporary Bahamian Society', *Black Theology: An International Journal* 11, no. 1, 2013; Carlton Turner, 'Taming the Spirit? Widening the Pneumatological Gaze within African Caribbean Theological Discourse', *Black Theology: An International Journal* 13, no. 2, 2015.

5 Anthony Reddie, *Theologising Brexit: A Liberationist and Postcolonial Critique*, Routledge New Critical Thinking in Religion, Theology and Biblical Studies, London: Routledge, 2019; Robert Beckford, *Documentary as Exorcism: Resisting the Bewitchment of Colonial Christianity*, London: Bloomsbury Academic, 2014; Willie James Jennings, *The Christian Imagination: Theology and the Origins of Race*, New Haven, CT: Yale University Press, 2010; J. Kameron Carter, *Race: A Theological Account*, Oxford Oxford University Press, 2008; Dianne M. Stewart, *Three Eyes for the Journey: African Dimensions of the Jamaican Religious Experience*, Oxford: Oxford University Press, 2004; Carlton Turner, 'Could You Be Loved? BAME Presence and the Witness of Diversity and Inclusion', in *Bearing Witness in Hope: Christian Engagement in Challenging Times*, ed. Cathy Ross and Humphrey Southern, London: SCM Press, 2020; Carlton Turner, 'Conceal to Reveal: Reflections on Sexual Violence and Theological Discourses in the African Caribbean', in *When Did We See You Naked? Jesus as a Victim of Sexual*

Abuse, ed. Jayme R. Reaves, David Tombs and Rocío Figueroa, London: SCM Press, 2021.

6 Turner, 'Taming the Spirit?'

7 Turner, 'Taming the Spirit?'; Stewart, *Three Eyes for the Journey*; Barry Chevannes, *Rastafari: Roots and Ideology*, Syracuse, NY: Syracuse University Press, 1995.

8 Malcolm Ferdinand, *Decolonial Ecology: Thinking from the Caribbean World*, trans. Anthony Paul Smith, Cambridge: Polity Press, 2022.

9 Carlton Turner, *Overcoming Self-Negation: The Church and Junkanoo in Contemporary Bahamian Society*, Eugene, OR: Pickwick Publications, 2020. For this point, see also Stewart, *Three Eyes for the Journey*.

10 George Mulrain, *Caribbean Theological Insights: Exploring Theological Themes Within the Context of the Caribbean Region*, London: Blessed Hope Publishing, 2014.

11 Carlton Turner, 'Deepening the Postcolonial Theological Gaze: Frantz Fanon and the Psychopathology of Colonial Christianity', *Modern Believing* 62, no. 4, Autumn 2021. In this article I engage the work of Frantz Fanon as an anti-colonial intellectual underutilized within Caribbean Theology. In fact, Fanon helps us explore the psychological dimensions of coloniality, an area that is becoming more and more important.

12 This is an insight that deeply influenced me in the writings of Michael Jagessar. See Michael Jagessar, 'Spinning Theology: Trickster, Texts and Theology', in *Postcolonial Black British Theology: New Textures and Themes*, ed. Michael Jagessar and Anthony Reddie, Peterborough: Epworth, 2007.

Bibliography

(OCHA), Office for the Coordination of Humanitarian Affairs, *Natural Disasters in Latin America and the Caribbean: 2000–2019*, The United Nations (OCHA), 2020, https://reliefweb.int/report/world/natural-disasters-latin-america-and-caribbean-2000-2019 (accessed 7.7.23).

'After the Flood: The Church, Slavery and Reconciliation Film Screening', news release, 5 May 2022, https://www.thersa.org/fellowship/news/after-the-flood-the-church-slavery-reconciliation-film-screening (accessed 7.7.23).

Anthony, Patrick A. B., 'A Case Study in Indigenization', in *Out of the Depths*, ed. Idris Hamid, San Fernando, Trinidad: W. I. Rahaman Printery Ltd, 1977, pp. 185–215.

Arnfred, Signe, '"African Sexuality"/Sexuality in Africa: Tales and Silences', in *Re-Thinking Sexualities in Africa*, ed. Signe Arnfred, Uppsala: Nordiska Afrikainstitutet, 2004, pp. 59–76.

Ashwood, Nicqui, 'Self-Questioning from the Caribbean', in *When Pastors Prey: Overcoming Clergy Sexual Abuse of Women*, ed. Valli Boobal Batchelor, Geneva: World Council of Churches, 2013, pp. 117–20.

Atluri, Tara L., *When the Closet is a Region: Homophobia, Heterosexism and Nationalism in the Commonwealth Caribbean*, Centre for Gender and Development Studies (CGDS), The University of the West Indies, 2001.

Augustus, Earl, 'The Spiritual Significance of Black Power in the Christian Churches', in *Troubling of the Waters*, ed. Idris Hamid, San Fernando, Trinidad: W. I. Rahaman Printery Ltd, 1973, pp. 109–24.

Beckford, Robert, *Documentary as Exorcism: Resisting the Bewitchment of Colonial Christianity*, London: Bloomsbury Academic, 2014.

Beckles, Hilary, *Britain's Black Debt: Reparations for Caribbean Slavery and Native Genocide*, Jamaica: University of the West Indies Press, 2013.

——— *How Britain Underdeveloped the Caribbean: A Reparation Response to Europe's Legacy of Plunder and Poverty*, Jamaica: University of the West Indies Press, 2021.

Beckles, Hilary McDonald and Verene A. Shepherd, *Liberties Lost: Caribbean Indigenous Societies and Slave Systems*, Cambridge: Cambridge University Press, 2004.

Bediako, Kwame, '"Whose Religion is Christianity?" Reflections on Opportunities and Challenges in Christian Theological Scholarship: The African Dimension', in *Mission in the 21st Century: Exploring the Five Marks of Global Mission*, ed. Andrew Walls and Cathy Ross, Maryknoll, NY: Orbis Books, 2008.

Bevans, Stephen B., *Models of Contextual Theology*, revised and expanded edn, Maryknoll, NY: Orbis Books, 2002.

Bevans, Stephen B. and Roger Schroeder, *Constants in Context: A Theology of Mission for Today*, American Society of Missiology Series, Maryknoll, NY: Orbis Books, 2004.

Bhaba, Homi K., *The Location of Culture*, 1st edn, New York: Routledge, 1994.

Biddle, Mark E., *Missing the Mark: Sin and its Consequences in Biblical Theology*, Nashville, TN: Abingdon Press, 2005.

Bilby, Kenneth, 'Gumbay, Myal, and the Great House: New Evidence of the Religious Background of Jonkonnu in Jamaica', *ACIJ Research Review* 4, 1999, pp. 47–69.

Bishop, Matthew Louis and Anthony Payne, 'Climate Change and the Future of Caribbean Development', *The Journal of Development Studies* 48, no. 10, 2012, pp. 1536–53.

Bisnauth, Dale, *A History of Religions in the Caribbean*, Kingston: Kingston Publishers Ltd, 1989.

Bisnauth, Dale A., 'Mission Impossible?', in *The Caribbean: Culture of Resistance, Spirit of Hope*, ed. Oscar L. Bolioli, New York: Friendship Press, 1993, ch. 13.

Boff, Clodovis, *Theology and Praxis: Epistemological Foundations*, Maryknoll, NY: Orbis Books, 1987.

Boff, Leonardo and Clodovis Boff, *Introducing Liberation Theology*, Maryknoll, NY: Orbis Books, 1987.

Bolioli, Oscar L. (ed.), 'Reclaiming Identity: The Verdun Proclamation', *The Caribbean: Culture of Resistance, Spirit of Hope*, New York: Friendship Press, 1993.

Boodoo, Gerald, 'In Response to Adolfo Ham (1)', in *Caribbean Theology: Preparing for the Challenges Ahead*, ed. Howard Gregory, Barbados: Canoe Press, 1995, ch. 2, pp. 7–11.

Bosch, David Jacobus, *Transforming Mission: Paradigm Shifts in Theology of Mission*, American Society of Missiology Series, Maryknoll, NY: Orbis Books, 1991.

Bowleg, Etienne, 'The Influence of the Oxford Movement Upon the Church of England in the Province of the West Indies,' PhD thesis, McGill University, 1986.

Bowleg, Etienne E., 'Liturgical Implications of Junkanoo', in *Junkanoo and Religion: Christianity and Cultural Identity in the Bahamas*, Nassau: Media Enterprises, 2003, pp. 89–94.

Brett, Mark G., *Political Trauma and Healing: Biblical Ethics for a Postcolonial World*, Grand Rapids, MI: Eerdmans, 2016.

Brown, Annette, 'Church and Dancehall: Challenges to Mission among Young People in the Churches in Jamaica', *Rethinking Mission*, April 2011, https://d3hgrlq6yacptf.cloudfront.net/uspg/content/pages/documents/1596109978.pdf (accessed 17.7.23).

Browning, Don S., *A Fundamental Practical Theology: Descriptive and Strategic Proposals*, Minneapolis, MN: Fortress Press, 1991.

Brueggemann, Walter, *The Prophetic Imagination*, 2nd edn, Minneapolis, MN: Fortress Press, 2001.

Burton, Richard D. E., *Afro-Creole: Power, Opposition and Play in the Caribbean*, New York: Cornell University Press, 1997.

Cardoza-Orlandi, Carlos F., 'Rediscovering Caribbean Christian Identity: Biography and Missiology at the Shore (between Dry Land and the Sea)', *Voices from the Third World* 27, no. 1, 2004, pp. 114–44.

Carter, J. Kameron, *Race: A Theological Account*, Oxford Oxford University Press, 2008.

Césaire, Aimé, *Discourse on Colonialism*, New York: Monthly Review Press, 1972.

Chambers, Donald Dean, 'The Faces of Jesus Christ in the Literary Works of Caribbean Preachers and Theologians: Towards a Constructive Christology for the Caribbean', PhD thesis, Pontificia Università Gregoriana, 2005.

Chevannes, Barry, 'Our Caribbean Reality', in *Caribbean Theology: Preparing for the Challenges Ahead*, ed. Howard Gregory, Barbados: Canoe Press, 1995, pp. 65–71.

—— *Rastafari: Roots and Ideology*, Syracuse, NY: Syracuse University Press, 1995.

—— 'Towards an Afro-Caribbean Theology: The Principles for the Indigenisation of Christianity in the Caribbean', *Caribbean Quarterly* 37, no. 1, 1991, pp. 45–54.

Clarke, Knolly, 'Liturgy and Culture in the Caribbean', in *Troubling of the Waters*, ed. Idris Hamid, San Fernando, Trinidad: W. I. Rahaman Printery Ltd, 1973, pp. 141–64.

Colijn, Brenda B., *Images of Salvation in the New Testament*, Downers Grove, IL: InterVarsity Press, 2010.

Columbus, Christopher, *The Journal of Christopher Columbus (During His First Voyage, 1492–93) and Documents Relating the Voyages of John Cabot and Gaspar Corte Real*, ed. and trans. Clements R. Markham, Cambridge: Cambridge University Press, 2010, doi:http://dx.doi.org/10.1017/CBO9780511708411, Cambridge Library Collection – Hakluyt First Series, 1893.

Cone, James H., *A Black Theology of Liberation*, 40th Anniversary edn, Maryknoll, NY: Orbis Books, 2010.

—— *God of the Oppressed*, New York: Seabury Press, 1975.

Cooper, Carolyn, *Noises in the Blood: Orality, Gender, and the 'Vulgar' Body of Jamaican Popular Culture*. 1st US edn, Durham, NC: Duke University Press, 1995.

—— 'Sweet & Sour Sauce: Sexual Politics in Jamaican Dancehall Culture', The Sixth Jagan Lecture, October 2005, York University, York, ON: CERLAC, November 2007.

Cotman, John Walton, 'Coming in from the Cold: Grenada and Cuba since 1983', *The Round Table: The Commonwealth Journal of International Affairs* 102, no. 2, 2013, pp. 155–65.

Davis, Edmund, *Roots and Blossoms*, Bridgetown, Barbados: Cedar Press, 1977.

Davis, Kortright, *Cross and Crown in Barbados: Caribbean Political Religion in the Late 19th Century*, Eugene, OR: Wipf & Stock, 1983.

—— *Emancipation Still Comin': Explorations in Caribbean Emancipatory Theology*, Maryknoll, NY: Orbis Books, 1990.

—— 'Theological Education for Mission', in *Out of the Depths*, ed. Idris Hamid, San Fernando, Trinidad: W. I. Rahaman Printery Ltd, 1977, pp. 217–30.

Dayfoot, Arthur C., 'The Shaping of the West Indian Church: Historical Factors in the Formation of the Pattern of Church Life in the English-speaking Caribbean 1492–1870', ThD thesis, Emmanuel College, Victoria University, 1982.

—— *The Shaping of West Indian Church 1492 to 1962*, Kingston, Jamaica: University of the West Indies Press, 1999.

Dexter, Noel, 'The Right Hand of God', in *Sing a New Song No. 3*, ed. Patrick Prescod, Bridgetown, Barbados: The Cedar Press, 1981.

Douglas, Kelly Brown, *Sexuality and the Black Church: A Womanist Perspective*, Maryknoll, NY: Orbis Books, 1999.

—— *Stand Your Ground: Black Bodies and the Justice of God*, Maryknoll, NY: Orbis Books, 2015.

Du Bois, W. E. B., *The Souls of Black Folk*, Signet Classics, New York: New American Library, 1969.

Durant, Karen Elizabeth, 'Imitation of God as a Principle for Ethics Today: A Study of Selected Psalms', PhD thesis, University of Birmingham, 2010.

Edmonds, Ennis B. and Michelle A. Gonzalez, *Caribbean Religious History: An Introduction*, New York: New York University Press, 2010.

Erskine, Noel L., *Decolonizing Theology: A Caribbean Perspective*, Trenton, NJ: Africa World Press, 1998.

—— *From Garvey to Marley: Rastafari Theology*, Gainesville, FL: University of Florida Press, 2005.

——— *Plantation Church: How African American Religion was born in Caribbean Slavery*, Oxford: Oxford University Press, 2014.

Ewell, Samuel, *Faith Seekijng Conviviality: Reflections on Ivan Illich, Christian Mission, and the Promise of Life Together*, Eugene, OR: Cascade Books, 2020.

'Exhibition Shows Church of England's Links to Slave Trade', Movement for Justice and Reconciliation, 2023, https://www.mjr-uk.com/news/exhibition-shows-church-of-englands-links-to-slave-trade (accessed 3.5.23).

Fabella, Virginia and R. S. Sugirtharajah (eds), *Dictionary of Third World Theologies*, Maryknoll, NY: Orbis Books, 2000.

Fanon, Frantz, *Black Skin, White Masks*, New York: Grove Press, 1967.

——— *The Wretched of the Earth*, Harmondsworth: Penguin, 1967.

Ferdinand, Malcolm, *Decolonial Ecology: Thinking from the Caribbean World*, trans. Anthony Paul Smith, Cambridge: Polity Press, 2022.

Garvey, Marcus and Amy Jacques Garvey, *The Philosophy and Opinions of Marcus Garvey*, Dover, MA: Majority Press, 1986.

Gebara, Ivone, *Longing for Running Water: Ecofeminism and Liberation*, Minneapolis, MN: Fortress Press, 1999.

Goodridge, Sehon S., *Facing the Challenge of Emancipation: A Study of the Ministry of William Hart Coleridge, First Bishop of Barbados, 1824–1842*, Barbados: Cedar Press, 1981.

Gordon, Charles Jason, 'Theology, Hermeneutics and Liberation: Grounding Theology in a Caribbean Context', PhD thesis, University of London, 2003.

Graham, Elaine L., Heather Walton and Frances Ward, *Theological Reflection: Methods*, London: SCM Press, 2005.

——— *Theological Reflection: Sources*, London: SCM Press, 2007.

Gregory, Howard (ed.), *Caribbean Theology: Preparing for the Challenges Ahead*, Barbados: Canoe Press, 1995.

Gutiérrez, Gustavo, *A Theology of Liberation: History, Politics, and Salvation*, Maryknoll, NY: Orbis Books, 1981.

Ham, Adolfo, 'Caribbean Theology: The Challenge of the Twenty-First Century', in *Caribbean Theology: Preparing for the Challenges Ahead*, ed. Howard Gregory, Barbados: Canoe Press, 1995, pp. 1–6.

Hamid, Idris, 'In Search of New Perspectives', Caribbean Ecumenical Consultation for Development, Bridgetown, Barbados, 1971.

——— (ed.), *Out of the Depths*, San Fernando, Trinidad: W. I. Rahaman Printery Ltd, 1977.

——— (ed.), *Troubling of the Waters*, San Fernando, Trinidad: W. I. Rahaman Printery Ltd, 1973.

Handler, Jerome S. and Kenneth M. Bilby, *Enacting Power: The Criminalization of Obeah in the Anglophone Caribbean 1760–2011*, Jamaica: University of the West Indies Press, 2012.

Havea, Jione (ed.), *Religion and Power: Theology in the Age of Empire*, Lanham, MD: Lexington Books/Fortress Academic, 2018.

—— *Theologies from the Pacific: Postcolonialism and Religions*, Cham, Switzerland: Palgrave Macmillan, 2021.

Hewitt, Roderick R., Hopeton S. Dunn and Jane Dodman, *Caribbean Prophet: The Public Theology of Ashley Smith*, Kingston, Jamaica: Ian Randall Publishers, 2022.

Holder, John, *Codrington College: A Brief History*, Bridgetown, Barbados: Codrington College, 1988.

Hood, Robert, *Must God Remain Greek? Afro Cultures and God-Talk*, Minneapolis, MN: Fortress Press, 1990.

Hopkins, Dwight N., *Down, Up, and Over: Slave Religion and Black Theology*, Minneapolis, MN: Fortress Press, 2000.

Hull, John, *Towards the Prophetic Church: A Study of Christian Mission*, London: SCM Press, 2014.

Jagessar, Michael, 'Chanting Down the Shitstem: Resistance with Anansi and Rastafari Optics', in *Religion and Power: Theology in the Age of Empire*, ed. Jione Havea, London: Lexington/Fortress Academic, 2019, ch. 7, pp. 87–104.

—— 'Pan Recipe: Philip Potter and Theology in the Caribbean', *Black Theology: An International Journal* 3.1, no. 5, November 2000, pp. 68–89.

—— 'Spinning Theology: Trickster, Texts and Theology', in *Postcolonial Black British Theology: New Textures and Themes*, ed. Michael Jagessar and Anthony Reddie, Peterborough: Epworth, 2007.

Jagessar, Michael and Anthony Reddie (eds), *Postcolonial Black British Theology: New Textures and Themes*, Peterborough: Epworth, 2007.

James, C. L. R., *Beyond a Boundary*, Durham, NC: Duke University Press, 1993.

—— *The Black Jacobins: Toussaint L'Ouverture and the San Domingo Revolution*, 2nd edn, New York: Vintage Books, 1963.

Jennings, Stephen, 'Caribbean Theology or Theologies of the Caribbean', *Caribbean Journal of Religious Studies* 8, no. 2, 1987, pp. 1–9.

Jennings, Willie James, *The Christian Imagination: Theology and the Origins of Race*, New Haven, CT: Yale University Press, 2010.

Josiah, Novelle, 'The Develoment of Calypso in Antigua and its Continuity with Old Testament Traditions', unpublished MPhil thesis, University of the West Indies, 2003.

Julien, Terry, 'Christian Mission, Cultural Traditions and Environment', in *Out of the Depths*, ed. Idris Hamid, San Fernando, Trinidad: W. I. Rahaman Printery Ltd, 1977, pp. 9–28.

Kirton-Roberts, Winelle J., *Created in their Image: Evangelical Protestantism in Antigua and Barbados, 1834–1914*, Bloomington, IN: AuthorHouse, 2015.

Lewis, Marjorie, 'Diaspora Dialogue: Womanist Theology in Engagement with Aspects of the Black British and Jamaican Experience', *Black Theology: An International Journal* 2, no. 1, 2004, pp. 85–109.

—— 'Towards a Systematic Spirituality of Black British Women', PhD thesis, University of Birmingham, 2007.

Lumpkin, Joseph B., *The Negro Bible – the Slave Bible: Select Parts of the Holy Bible, Selected for the Use of the Negro Slaves, in the British West-India Islands*, Blountsville, AL: Fifth Estate, 2019.

Malzaire, Gabriel, *Christ & Caribbean Culture(s): A Collection of Essays on Caribbean Christology and its Pastoral Implications*, Philadelphia, PA: Parchment Global Publishing, 2019.

Marshall, Sheila (dir.), *After the Flood: The Church, Slavery and Reconciliation*, documentary, Movement for Justice and Reconciliation, 2022.

Mbiti, John S., *African Religions and Philosophy*, 2nd edn, Oxford: Heinemann Educational Publishers, 1969.

McAlister, Elizabeth, 'From Slave Revolt to a Blood Pact with Satan: The Evangelical Rewriting of Haitian History', *Studies in Religion* 41, no. 2, 2012, pp. 187–215.

McCartney, Timothy, *Ten, Ten, the Bible Ten: Obeah in the Bahamas*, Nassau, Bahamas: Tinpaul Publishing Company, 1976.

McGrath, Alister E., *Christian Theology: An Introduction*, 5th edn, Oxford: Wiley-Blackwell, 2011.

McKenzie, Dulcie A. Dixon, 'Black British Theology in Gospel Music', in *Postcolonial Black British Theology: New Textures and Themes*, ed. Michael Jagessar and Anthony Reddie, Peterborough: Epworth, 2007, ch. 3, pp. 25–9.

McKittrick, Katherine (ed.), *Sylvia Wynter: On Being Human as Praxis*, Durham, NC: Duke University Press, 2015.

Miller, Michael St A., 'He Said I was Out of Pocket: On Being a Caribbean Contextual Theologian in a Non-Caribbean Context', *Black Theology: An International Journal* 9, no. 2, 2011, pp. 223–45.

—— *Reshaping the Contextual Vision in Caribbean Theology: Theoretical Foundations for Theology which is Contextual, Pluralistic, and Dialectical*, Lanham, MD and Plymouth: University Press of America, 2007.

Minshall, Peter, *Dear Promoter (Official Short Film)*, 2020.

Mitchell, David (ed.), *With Eyes Wide Open*, Barbados: CADEC, 1973.

Moltmann, Jürgen, *The Spirit of Life: A Universal Affirmation*, Minneapolis, MN: Fortress Press, 1992.

Moore, Robert, 'The Historical Basis of Theological Reflection', in *Troubling of the Waters*, ed. Idris Hamid, San Fernando, Trinidad: W. I. Rahaman Printery Ltd, 1973, ch. 3, pp. 37–45.

Mosala, Itumeleng J., *Biblical Hermeneutics and Black Theology in South Africa*, Grand Rapids, MI: Eerdmans, 1990.

Mulrain, George, *Caribbean Theological Insights: Exploring Theological Themes within the Context of the Caribbean Region*, London: Blessed Hope Publishing, 2014.

—— 'Hermeneutics within a Caribbean Context', in *Vernacular Hermeneutics*, ed. R. S. Sugirtharajah, Sheffield: Sheffield Academic Press, 1999, pp. 116–32.

—— 'Is There a Calypso Exegesis?', in *Voices from the Margin: Interpreting the Bible in the Third World*, ed. R. S. Sugirtharajah, Maryknoll, NY: Orbis Books, 1995, ch. 2, pp. 37–47.

—— 'The Music of the African Caribbean', *Black Theology: An International Journal* 1, no. 1, 1998, pp. 35–45.

—— *Theology in Folk Culture: The Theological Significance of Haitian Folk Religion*, Frankfurt: Peter Lang, 1984.

Murphy, Joseph, *Working the Spirit: Ceremonies of the African Diaspora*, Boston, MA: Beacon Press, 1994.

Murrell, Nathaniel Samuel, *Afro-Caribbean Religions: An Introduction to their Historical, Cultural, and Sacred Traditions*, Philadelphia, PA: Temple University Press, 2010.

Murrell, Nathaniel Samuel, William David Spencer and Adrian Anthony McFarlane (eds), *Chanting Down Babylon: The Rastafari Reader*, Philadelphia, PA: Temple University Press, 1998.

Nathan, Ronald, 'Caribbean Youth Identity in the United Kingdom: A Call for a Pan-African Theology', *Black Theology in Britain: A Journal of Contextual Praxis* 1, October 1998, pp. 19–34.

Osborne, Francis J. and Geoffrey Johnston, *Coast Lands and Islands: First Thoughts on Caribbean Church History*, Jamaica: UTCWI, 1972.

Owens, Joseph, 'The Rastafarians of Jamaica', in *Troubling of the Waters*, ed. Idris Hamid, San Fernando, Trinidad: W. I. Rahaman Printery Ltd, 1973, pp. 165–70.

Paton, Diana, 'A Legacy of Emancipation in the Diaspora', *StabroekNews.com*, 18 March 2013, http://www.stabroeknews.com/2013/features/in-the-diaspora/03/18/a-legacy-of-emancipation/ (accessed 5.9.13).

Paton, Diana and Maarit Forde, *Obeah and Other Powers: The Politics of Caribbean Religion and Healing*, Durham, NC: Duke University Press, 2012.

Patterson, Orlando, *The Sociology of Slavery: An Analysis of the Origins, Development and Structure of Negro Slave Society in Jamaica*, Studies in Society, London: MacGibbon & Kee, 1967.

Perkins, Ana Kasafi and Carlton Turner, '"Monotonous Rhythm on the Heart of God?" Drumming, Theological Aesthetics and Christianity in the Caribbean', in *The T&T Clarke Companion to Theology and the Arts*, ed. Imogen Adkins and Stephen Garrett, London: Bloomsbury, 2024.

Perkins, Anna Kasafi, 'Christian Norms and Intimate Male Partner Violence: Lessons from a Jamaica Women's Health Survey', in *The*

Holy Spirit and Social Justice: Interdisciplinary Global Perspectives – History, Race and Culture, ed. Antipas L. Harris and Michael D. Palmer, Lanham, MD: Seymour Press, 2019.

—— '"Tasting Tears and [Not] Admitting Defeat": Promoting Values and Attitudes through the Music of Tanya Stephens?', Inaugural Lecture of the Centre for Social Ethics, St Michael's Theological College, Academia.edu, 12 January 2008.

—— 'The Wages of (Sin) is Babylon: Rastafari Versus Christian Religious Perspectives of Sin', in *Rastafari in the New Millennium: A Rastafari Reader*, ed. Michael Barnett, Syracuse, NY: Syracuse University Press, 2012, ch. 12, pp. 239–52.

Pinn, Anthony B., *Embodiment and the New Shape of Black Theological Thought*, New York: New York University Press, 2010.

Prior, Michael, *The Bible and Colonialism: A Moral Critique*, Sheffield: Sheffield Academic Press, 1997.

Ranawana, A. M., *A Liberation for the Earth: Climate, Race and Cross*, London: SCM Press, 2022.

Rawlins, Clifford, *A Theology of Carnival and Other Provocations: Realigning Christian Thought for a Post-Modern World*, San Fernando, Trinidad and Tobago: Trinity Hill Publishing, 2021.

Reddie, Anthony, 'An Interactive Methodology for Doing Black Theology', in *Postcolonial Black British Theology: New Textures and Themes*, ed. Michael Jagessar and Anthony Reddie, Peterborough: Epworth, 2007, ch. 1, pp. 1–14.

—— 'Dramatic Improvisation: A Jazz Inspired Approach to Undertaking Theology with the Marginalized', in *Reading Spiritualities: Constructing and Representing the Sacred*, ed. Dawn Llewellyn and Deborah F. Sawyer, Aldershot: Ashgate, 2008.

—— *Theologising Brexit: A Liberationist and Postcolonial Critique*, Routledge New Critical Thinking in Religion, Theology and Biblical Studies, London: Routledge, 2019.

Reid-Salmon, Delroy, *Home Away from Home: The Caribbean Diasporan Church in the Black Atlantic Tradition*, London: Equinox, 2008.

Roberts, Mikie Anthony, 'Hymnody and Identity: Congregational Singing as a Construct of Christian Community Identity', PhD thesis, University of Birmingham, 2014.

Rodney, Walter, *A History of the Guyanese Working People: 1881–1905*, Baltimore, MD: Johns Hopkins University Press, 1981.

—— *How Europe Underdeveloped Africa*, London: Bogle-L'Ouverture Publications, 1972.

—— *The Groundings with My Brothers*, London: Bogle-L'Ouverture Publications, 1969.

Rogers, John Augustine, 'Siege-Mentality and the Book of Deuteronomy', PhD thesis, University of Birmingham, 2019.

Rohlehr, Gordon, 'Man's Spiritual Search in the Caribbean through Literature', in *Troubling of the Waters*, ed. Idris Hamid, San Fernando, Trinidad: W. I. Rahaman Printery Ltd, 1973, pp. 187–205.

Russell, Horace, 'The Challenge of Theological Reflection in the Caribbean', in *Troubling of the Waters*, ed. Idris Hamid, San Fernando, Trinidad: W. I. Rahaman Printery Ltd, 1973, ch. 2, pp. 25–36.

Said, Edward W., *Orientalism*, 1st edn, New York: Pantheon Books, 1978.

Saliers, Don, Joyce Burkhalter Flueckiger, Dianne Stewart Diakité and Don E. Seeman, 'Ethnography and Theology: A Critical Roundtable Discussion', *Practical Matters*, 3, Spring 2010, pp. 1–14.

Sands, Kirkley C., *Early Bahamian Slave Spirituality: The Genesis of Bahamian Cultural Identity*, Nassau, Bahamas: The Nassau Guardian Ltd, 2008.

—— 'Junkanoo in Historical Perspective', in *Junkanoo and Religion: Christianity and Cultural Identity in the Bahamas*, Nassau, Bahamas: Media Enterprises, 2003, pp. 10–19.

—— 'Missionary Bishops and Education in the British Caribbean 1824–1841: Christopher Libscomb and William Hart Coleridge', *Vox Collegii Codringtoniensis*, 22 October 2015.

Sankeralli, Burton (ed.), *At the Crossroads: African Caribbean Religion and Christianity*, St James, Trinidad and Tobago: Caribbean Conference of Churches, 1995.

Schreiter, Robert J., *Constructing Local Theologies*, Maryknoll, NY: Orbis Books, 1985.

—— *The New Catholicity: Theology between the Global and the Local*, Faith and Cultures Series, Maryknoll, NY: Orbis Books, 1997.

Select Parts of the Holy Bible for the Use of the Negro Slaves in the British West-India Islands, vol. derived from the King James Version 1611, London: Law & Gilbert, 1807.

Sertima, Ivan van, *They Came before Columbus: The African Presence in Ancient America*, New York: Random House, 1976.

Sheerattan-Bisnauth, Patricia, 'Editorial', in *Righting Her-Story: Caribbean Women Encounter the Bible*, ed. Patricia Sheerattan-Bisnauth, Geneva: World Communion of Reformed Churches (WCRC), 2011.

—— (ed.), *Righting Her-Story: Caribbean Women Encounter the Bible*, Geneva: World Communion of Reformed Churches (WCRC), 2011.

Sheerattan-Bisnauth, Patricia and Doreen Wynter, 'Bible Study Training Guide', in *Righting Her-Story: Caribbean Women Encounter the Bible*, ed. Patricia Sheerattan-Bisnauth, Geneva: World Communion of Reformed Churches (WCRC), 2011.

Shorter Oxford English Dictionary, 6th edn, Oxford: Oxford University Press, 2007.

Sing a New Song No. 3, ed. Patrick Prescod, Bridgetown, Barbados: The Cedar Press, 1981.

Smith, Ashley, *Real Roots and Potted Plants: Reflections on the Carib-bean Church*, Mandeville, Jamaica: Eureka Press, 1984.

—— 'The Religious Significance of Black Power in the Caribbean', in *Troubling of the Waters*, ed. Idris Hamid, San Fernando, Trinidad: W. I. Rahaman Printery Ltd, 1973, pp. 83–108.

Soares, Judith, 'Gender Justice and the Christian Mission', *Journal of Religious Thought* 57, no. 2, 2001, pp. 67–82.

Sobrino, Jon, Paul Burns and Francis McDonagh, *Jesus the Liberator: A Historical-Theological Reading of Jesus of Nazareth*, Alexandria, VA: Alexander Street Press, 2014.

Spencer, Stephen, *SCM Studyguide to Christian Mission: Historic Types and Contemporary Expressions*, London: SCM Press, 2007.

Spivak, Gayatri Chakravorty, 'Can the Subaltern Speak?', in *Marxism and the Interpretation of Cultures*, ed. Cary Nelson and Lawrence Grossberg, Urbana, IL: University of Illinois Press, 1988.

Stewart, Dianne, *Three Eyes for the Journey: African Dimensions of the Jamaican Religious Experience*, Oxford: Oxford University Press, 2004.

—— 'Womanist Theology in the Caribbean Context: Critiquing Cul-ture, Rethinking Doctrine, and Expounding Boundaries', *Journal of Feminist Studies in Religion* 20, no. 1, 2004, pp. 61–82.

Stewart-Diakité, Dianne M. and Tracey E. Hucks, 'Africana Religious Studies: Towards a Transdisciplinary Agenda in an Emerging Field', *Journal of Africana Studies* 1, no. 1, 2013, pp. 28–77.

Strachan, Ian G., *Paradise and Plantation: Tourism and Culture in the Anglophone Caribbean*, New World Studies, Charlottesville, VA: University of Virginia Press, 2002, https://www.loc.gov/catdir/toc/fy036/2002010190.html (accessed 24.7.23).

Sugirtharajah, R. S., *Postcolonial Criticism and Biblical Interpretation*, Oxford: Oxford University Press, 2002.

Sugirtharajah, R. S., *The Bible and the Third World: Precolonial, Colo-nial, and Postcolonial Encounters*, Cambridge: Cambridge University Press, 2001.

Swinton, John and Harriet Mowat, *Practical Theology and Qualitative Research*, London: SCM Press, 2006.

Thomas, Oral, *Biblical Resistance Hermeneutics within a Caribbean Context*, London: Equinox, 2010.

Titus, Noel, *The Amelioration and Abolition of Slavery in Trinidad, 1812–1834: Experiments and Protests in a New Slave Colony*, Bloom-ington, IN: AuthorHouse, 2009.

—— *Mission in a Volatile Society: Reflections on Christian Churches in Caribbean Slave Societies*, London: Blessed Hope Publishing, 2017.

—— 'Our Caribbean Reality', in *Caribbean Theology: Preparing for the Challenges Ahead*, ed. Howard Gregory, Barbados: Canoe Press, 1995, ch. 8, pp. 57–64.

Torchon, Marcus, 'A Methodist Perspective on Aid-Dependency in Haitian Protestantism', PhD thesis, University of Manchester, 2019.

Tracy, David, 'The Foundations of Practical Theology', in *Practical Theology: The Emerging Field in Theology, Church, and World*, ed. Don. S. Browning, San Francisco, CA: Harper & Row, 1983, pp. 61–82.

Turner, Carlton, 'Conceal to Reveal: Reflections on Sexual Violence and Theological Discourses in the African Caribbean', in *When Did We See You Naked? Jesus as a Victim of Sexual Abuse*, ed. Jayme R. Reaves, David Tombs and Rocío Figueroa, London: SCM Press, 2021, pp. 149–64.

—— 'Could You Be Loved? Bame Presence and the Witness of Diversity and Inclusion', in *Bearing Witness in Hope: Christian Engagement in Challenging Times*, ed. Cathy Ross and Humphrey Southern, London: SCM Press, 2020.

—— 'Deepening the Postcolonial Theological Gaze: Frantz Fanon and the Psychopathology of Colonial Christianity', *Modern Believing* 62, no. 4, Autumn 2021, pp. 340–8.

—— *Overcoming Self-Negation: The Church and Junkanoo in Contemporary Bahamian Society*, Eugene, OR: Pickwick Publications, 2020.

—— 'Self-Negation within African Caribbean Christianity: Towards an Understanding of Junkanoo and its Significance for Christian Praxis within Contemporary Bahamian Society', *Black Theology: An International Journal* 11, no. 1, 2013, pp. 5–30.

—— 'Taming the Spirit? Widening the Pneumatological Gaze within African Caribbean Theological Discourse', *Black Theology: An International Journal* 13, no. 2, 2015, pp. 126–46.

—— 'Women Speak, Men Share, and Everyone Rush! Prophetic Consciousness, Junkanoo and the Church in Bahamian Society', *Rethinking Mission*, Spring 2017.

Walcott, Derek. 'The Muse of History', in *What the Twilight Says: Essays*, New York: Farrar, Straus and Giroux, 1998, pp. 36–64.

Walcott, Derek and Glyn Maxwell, *The Poetry of Derek Walcott 1948–2013*, London: Faber & Faber, 2014.

Walls, Andrew and Cathy Ross, *Mission in the 21st Century: Exploring the Five Marks of Global Mission*, Maryknoll, NY: Orbis Books, 2008.

Watty, William, 'The De-Colonization of Theology', in *Troubling of the Waters*, ed. Idris Hamid, San Fernando, Trinidad: W. I. Rahaman Printery Ltd, 1973, pp. 49–82.

—— *From Shore to Shore: Soundings in Caribbean Theology*, Kingston, Jamaica: Cedar Press, 1981.

Webster, Carol Marie, 'Body as Temple: Jamaican Catholic Women and the Liturgy of the Eucharist', *Black Theology: An International Journal*, 15, no. 1, 2017, pp. 21–40.

West, Gerald O., *Biblical Hermeneutics of Liberation: Modes of Reading the Bible in the South African Context*, The Bible and Liberation Series, Maryknoll, NY: Orbis Books, 1995.

—— *Reading Other-Wise: Socially Engaged Biblical Scholars Reading with their Local Communities*, Society of Biblical Literature Semeia Studies, Atlanta, GA: Society of Biblical Literature, 2007.

Williams, Eric, *Capitalism and Slavery*, Chapel Hill, NC: University of North Carolina Press, 1961.

Williams, Geoffrey B., 'Classicism and the Caribbean Church', in *Out of the Depths*, ed. Idris Hamid, San Fernando, Trinidad: W. I. Rahaman Printery Ltd, 1977, pp. 49–90.

Williams, Lewin L., *Caribbean Theology*, New York: Peter Lang, 1994.

—— *The Caribbean: Enculturation, Acculturation, and the Role of the Churches*, Gospel and Cultures, Geneva: WCC Publications, 1996.

Wynter, Sylvia, *The Hills of Hebron*, London: Jonathan Cape, 1962.

Index of Bible References

Index of Names and Subjects